D0371412

what YOU SHOULD

KNOW about

POLITICS

★ ★ ★ BUT DON'T

A NONPARTISAN GUIDE TO THE ISSUES

what YOU SHOULD

KNOW about

POLITICS

... BUT DON'T

JESSAMYN CONRAD

 ARCADE PUBLISHING • NEW YORK

Copyright © 2008 by Jessamyn Conrad

All rights reserved. No part of this book may be reproduced in any form or by any electronic or mechanical means, including information storage and retrieval systems, without permission in writing from the publisher, except by a reviewer who may quote brief passages in a review.

FIRST EDITION

Library of Congress Cataloging-in-Publication Data
Conrad, Jessamyn
  What you should know about politics...but don't : a nonpartisan guide to the issues / Jessamyn Conrad. —1st ed.
      p. cm.
  Includes bibliographical references.
  ISBN 978-1-55970-883-8 (alk. paper)
  1. United States—Politics and government—Handbooks, manuals, etc.
I. Title.

  JK275.C66 2008
  320.60973—dc22   2008021599

Published in the United States by Arcade Publishing, Inc., New York
Distributed by Hachette Book Group USA

Visit our Web site at www.arcadepub.com

10 9 8 7 6 5 4 3 2

Designed by API

EB

PRINTED IN THE UNITED STATES OF AMERICA

For my parents

Contents

Preface / xiii
An Introduction to Political Affiliations / xvii

1: Elections / 1

Background to Current Debates / 2
Electoral College 3 • *Bush v. Gore* 5 • Help America Vote Act 6

Mechanics of Voting / 7
Voter Registration, Voter Fraud, Voter Suppression 7 • Congressional Redistricting 10 • Gerrymandering 10 • Voting Machines 14 • Campaign Finance 16

Presidential Elections / 20
Party Conventions 20 • Primaries and Caucuses 22 • Electoral College 26 • Popular Vote Reform 28

2: The Economy / 29

Background to Current Debates / 30
Economic Pie 31 • Fiscal vs. Monetary Policy 31 • Federal Reserve 31 • Great Depression 31 • GDP Growth 32 • Stagnation, Recession, Depression, Stagflation 33

Current Debates: The Subprime Mortgage Crisis and the 2001 Tax Cuts / 33
Subprime Mortgage Crisis 33 • Interest Rates 36 • Alan Greenspan 36 • Inflation 37 • 2001 Tax Cuts 37 • Alternative Minimum Tax 38 • Capital Gains and Dividend Taxes 39 • Estate Tax vs. Death Tax 39 • Pay-Go 39 • Flat Tax 42 • Regressive vs. Progressive Taxation 42 • Reaganomics: Supply-Side and Trickle-Down Economics 42 • Compassionate Conservatism 44 • Federal Deficit 44 • National Debt 44 • Discretionary vs.

Mandatory Spending 45 • Social Security 46 • Deficits Don't Matter 47 • Value of the Dollar 49 • Oil Denominated in Dollars 50

3: Foreign Policy / 52

Background to Current Debates / 53
From Isolationism to Intervention 54 • Appeasing Hitler 57 • Postwar Consensus: Soviet Containment 57 • Vietnam 58

The Ideological Groups / 59
Isolationists 60 • Paleoconservatives 60 • Liberal Internationalists 61 • Realists 62 • Neoconservatives 62 • Liberal Hawks 63

Background to the Iraq War / 64
US and Iran 64 • First Gulf War 65 • Operation Desert Fox 68 • Afghanistan and Al-Qaeda 72

The Case for War / 73
Preemption 73 • Weapons Inspection 74 • Media Support for War 76 • Use of Force Measure in Congress 76

Planning the Invasion of Iraq / 78
Liberation 78 • Iraqi National Congress 79 • Troop Numbers 79 • De-Baathification 80 • Disbanding the Iraqi Military 80 • Al-Qaeda-in-Mesopotamia 81 • The Surge 81

What's Ahead: Beyond Iraq / 82
Iran 82 • Pakistan 83 • Russia 83 • China 83 • India 84 • North Korea 84

4: The Military / 85

Background to Current Debates / 86
The Draft 87 • GI Bill 88

Current Debates / 88
Post-Traumatic Stress Disorder 88 • Homeless Veterans 89 • Walter Reed Scandal 90 • Recruiting Difficulties 92 • Lower Standards 92 • Military Contractors 94 • Order 17 and Contractors' Accountability 97 • Black-water and the Fallujah Attack 98 • Overextension of Supply Lines 99 •

No-Bid Contracts 101 • Dick Cheney and Halliburton 102 • Blackwater and Its Political Ties 102

5: Health Care / 104

Background to Current Debates / 105
Health Insurance 107 • HMOs 108 • Medicare 109 • Medicaid 110 • S-CHIP 110 • Universal Access and Universal Coverage 111

Current Debates / 113
Universal Health Care 113 • Rising Costs 114 • Tort Reform 116 • Liability Laws 117 • Big Pharma 117 • Medicare Part D 119 • Emergency Care 120 • Single Payer, One Risk Pool, Socialized Medicine 122 • Health Care Rationing 123

6: Energy / 125

Background to Current Debates / 126
Growing Energy Use 127 • Shrinking Energy Supply 128

Current Debates / 128
Nuclear Power 129 • Coal 133 • Electricity Deregulation and the California Energy Crisis 135 • Peak Oil Production 136 • Recessions 137 • OPEC 138 • Oil and the First Gulf War 139 • CAFE or Fuel Standards 140 • ANWR 141 • Natural Gas 145

7: The Environment / 146

Background to Current Debates / 147
Rachel Carson's *Silent Spring* 148 • Nixon and the EPA 148 • Clean Air Act 148 • Superfund Toxic Waste Cleanup 149 • Acid Rain 149 • Ozone Hole 150 • Environmental Groups 151

Current Debates / 153
Climate Change 153 • Global Warming 153 • Greenhouse Effect 153 • Effects of Global Warming 154 • Kyoto Accords 154 • Cap-and-Trade 155 • Carbon Offset 155 • Carbon Market 156 • Carbon Tax 156 • Conservation 156 • *An Inconvenient Truth* 158 • Resource Wars 158 • Regional Greenhouse Gas Initiative 158 • Massachusetts Sues the EPA 158 •

CONTENTS

Arsenic and Lead in Drinking Water 159 • Healthy Forests Act 160 • ANWR 160 • Wind Power 161 • Ethanol 162 • Biodiesel 163 • Hydrogen Fuel 164 • Solar Power 165

8: Civil Liberties / 167

Background to Current Debates / 168

Second Amendment / 171
Gun Control vs. Gun Rights 171

Fourth Amendment / 175
Warrantless Wiretapping 175 • FISA 177 • USA PATRIOT Act 179

Fifth Amendment / 180
Eminent Domain vs. Private Property Rights 180

Sixth Amendment / 183
Habeas Corpus 183 • Extraordinary Rendition 183 • Black Sites 184 • Guantánamo Bay 186 • Military Tribunals 187

Eighth Amendment / 188
Torture 188 • Abu Ghraib 191 • Waterboarding 194 • Signing Statements and the McCain Amendment 195 • Capital Punishment 196

9: Culture Wars / 199

Background to Current Debates / 200
Counterculture 201 • Family Values 201 • Wedge Issues 201

Current Debates / 202
Legal Abortion 202 • Partial-Birth Abortion / D&X 206 • Right to Die 207 • Living Will 209 • Physician-Assisted Suicide 209 • Stem Cell Research 210 • Same-Sex Marriage 213 • Civil Unions 213 • Defense of Marriage Act 215 • School Prayer 218 • Pledge of Allegiance 218 • Public Display of the Ten Commandments 218

10: Socioeconomic Policy / 220

Background to Current Debates / 221

Immigration / 222
Undocumented Workers 222 • Texas Fence 223 • Deportation 223 • Illegal Immigration and Wages 225 • English as Official Language 225 • Amnesty Programs 225 • Eliot Spitzer and Driver's Licenses 226

Labor and Social Security / 226
Unions 227 • Minimum Wage 228 • Living Wage 229 • Unemployment Insurance 229 • COBRA 229 • Family Medical Leave Act 229 • Pensions 230 • ERISA 230 • Social Security 232 • Privatization 233 • Lockbox 234 • Salary Cap 234

Agriculture Subsidies / 235
Michael Pollan's *The Omnivore's Dilemma* 235 • Crop Insurance 237 • International Competition 237

Food Aid and Welfare / 238
Food Stamps 238 • Head Start 240 • Welfare Reform 241 • Working Poor 242

11: Homeland Security / 244

Background to Current Debates / 245
Pork 246 • Bridge to Nowhere 247 • Earmarks 247 • Recission 248

Current Debates / 248
Department of Homeland Security 248 • Highway Privatization 250 • Amtrak 252 • Airline Bankruptcy 252 • Transportation Security Administration 253 • Minnesota Bridge Collapse 254 • Disaster Preparedness 255 • Hurricane Katrina 255 • FEMA and Michael Brown 258 • California Fires 260

12: Education / 262

Background to Current Debates / 263
Universal Education 263 • *Brown v. Board of Education* 265 • Desegregation and School Busing 265

Current Debates / 266
Affirmative Action 266 • 2003 Supreme Court Rulings on Affirmative Action 269 • School Vouchers 271 • Campus Military Recruitment 275 • No Child Left Behind 276 • Student Loans 278

13: Trade / 280

Introduction / 281

Basic Terms / 282
Trade Liberalization 282 • Free Market 282 • Protectionism 282 • Tariffs 283

Background to Current Debates / 283
Smoot-Hawley Tariff 284 • Reciprocal Trade Agreement Act 284 • World War II 285 • World Bank 285 • International Monetary Fund 285 • World Trade Organization 286 • Seattle Protests 287

Current Debates / 288
Milton Friedman and Friedrich Hayek 288 • Classical Economics 289 • Comparative Advantage 289 • Globalization 290 • Free Trade Agreements 291 • NAFTA 291 • John Edwards's "Two Americas" 291 • Lou Dobbs 291 • Outsourcing 291 • Tax Loopholes 293 • Labor Standards 293 • Pollution 294 • Race to the Bottom 294 • Trade Deficit 294 • CAFTA, GAFTA, AFTA 295 • Banana War 295 • Steel Tariffs 296 • Development Economics: Joseph Stiglitz, Amartya Sen, Jeffrey Sachs 297

Acknowledgments / 301
Notes / 303

Preface

I'm surprised that nobody has written this book before. You'd think that in the United States, one of the largest functioning democracies on earth, someone already would have produced an issue-based, non-partisan guide to the often mucky world of contemporary American politics. But nobody has — until now.

I wrote this book to fill a void, the existence of which has been made all the more apparent by myriad mudslinging volumes in the Ann Coulter / Michael Moore mold, books that are more about theater than ideas, that have more to do with misplaced hate than thoughtful contemplation of the issues ahead. In a world of sound bites and deliberate misinformation, a political scene that has become literally colored by what's probably a false divide — blue vs. red — how is anybody supposed to get unadulterated facts? Now that TV news is increasingly partisan, newspapers decreasingly relevant, bloggers, YouTube newscasters, and PACs like MoveOn more potent, where can the average educated American find reliable sources? Well, hopefully, you can come here.

Like many Americans, and like most Americans my age, I wasn't active in politics or even very interested until a few years ago, even though I grew up in an intensely political environment. I have to fess up now: My dad's been in the United States Senate since 1987. My uncle, my mother's brother, was a two-term governor in our home state of North Dakota and became secretary of agriculture in 2008. My dad is a somewhat conservative Democrat; my uncle is a Republican. I myself was once a write-in candidate for soil conservation officer (Alice, I appreciate your vote). Yes, I know, it's weird, but as my mom always used to say, we're from North Dakota. Everybody gets to be something for a while. As long as you bring a hot dish.

I've been privileged to see not only the insides of our political system but to experience many different political environments. North Dakotans are an unusual blend of conservative and liberal. In a state where George W. Bush got a bigger percentage of votes than in his own home county in Texas, our entire congressional delegation is Democratic. North Dakotans are middle-class, rural, and largely religious. I now live in New York, one of the richest, most urban, and least religious places on the planet. I grew up in Minnesota as well, a place with a perplexing mix of liberalism and conservatism that is still the only state where people think that a career in professional wrestling might plausibly qualify you to be governor. New England was home for several years, and I spend time in California. I've also lived in Italy, England, Morocco, and India, so I've been exposed to how a diverse array of people approach political issues.

I became interested in politics when we invaded Iraq. I had studied Islamic art, Middle Eastern history, and Arabic in college, and I was shocked by how little even the media knew about the issues they were covering. I realized that they probably didn't know much more about monetary policy than they did about mosques, and so I got more involved. As a historian by training and nature, though, my instinct is to do a lot of research and try to figure out who wants what and why — then write about it. It's a way of working that has led to this book, which is essentially a political primer with a dash of anthropology and cultural history, rather than a diatribe by someone who decided long ago who she hated and what she loved. I'm still trying to figure that out.

Personally, I'm not much of an ideologue. Because North Dakota does not require me to register to vote, I have no party affiliation. If I had one, I'd be a disappointed Democrat with a strong libertarian streak. In another era, I probably would have been a Rockefeller Republican. I loathe the entrenched political machines of both parties, which I think are dangerous and far too often misleading, manipulative, and fundamentally dishonest. So in that sense, you might say I'm a populist. My most politically informed friend calls me a pragmatist, and that's about right. I get my undies in a bunch when people lie. I want things to work well. I think we probably should be nice to other people as much as possible, but I believe there's such a thing as evil in the world, too. Mostly, I'm glad I don't have to make these decisions. I don't know what I would do about gun control, or the death penalty, or trade agreements, if it were up to me. Like most Americans, I'm conflicted on many issues. Writing this book gave me a lot to think about. My hope is that it will help you learn more about the issues, decide who you think you should vote for, and why.

The most common response I got while writing this book was also probably the most telling. "A nonpartisan guide?" people asked. "How can you even do that?" I was always a bit baffled by that question. I don't think it's very hard to give people all sides of the story. Even if I have a personal position, it doesn't mean I don't see the other side's point. I'm pro-choice, for example, but I understand the pro-life argument. I'm more than happy to present both viewpoints.

After all, it's up to you to make your own decisions. I'm just going to put all the pertinent information in one place, and I'll describe who argues over what and why. I'm going to explain how systems can affect outcomes, and I'll give you an insider's secrets to decode political spin. While most chapters have a background section to orient you on how the various debates are framed, some chapters, such as the one on socioeconomic policy, are a grab-bag of issues that don't share one common historical or ideological background. Some, like the chapter on trade, necessitate defining some basic terms, because you simply need to know a little lingo to talk about it.

The chapters are arranged to reflect how Americans prioritize the issues. However, I begin with elections because they are necessary for everything that follows: it takes officials to enact policy, after all. Each chapter, however, stands alone. You may read the book from cover to cover, or you may use it as a reference and look up an issue or policy area if you want to learn more about something you've seen on TV or read in the paper.

So if you read this and find yourself a little less confused when someone brings up wiretapping at a dinner party, or Iran over drinks, I figure I've done my job. If this gets you a little more involved, a little more interested, and a little more informed, I'm happy — because one of the things we can probably all agree on is that an engaged electorate is ultimately in everyone's best interests.

An Introduction to Political Affiliations

When it comes to definitions in politics, nothing is written in stone. A label like "conservative" has meant different things at different times — and a conservative's definition of "conservative" will be very different from a liberal's. The definition problem is even greater for parties, which are made up of numerous smaller factions with various interests. It's hardest to make generalizations about the two major parties, Democrats and Republicans, since they comprise the greatest number of interest groups.

One way to distinguish between the two is by their attitudes toward government and the market. Republicans believe that the free market should be left alone and that government should get out of the way. Democrats believe that the market can be unfair and that government is needed to help people and to make the system work better. Another way to distinguish them is to look at what they believe government ought to govern: generally speaking, Democrats want to regulate economic life but stay out of individuals' personal lives, while Republicans want as little economic regulation as possible but often support laws regulating moral behavior.

Republicans are typically described as **conservatives** or **right-wingers**. There are various kinds of conservative: economic or fiscal conservatives concerned with reducing taxes and deregulating businesses; national security conservatives who promote a hawkish foreign policy; and social conservatives, who are chiefly concerned with **values issues** such as abortion and gay marriage. The Republican platform thus tends to focus on tax cuts, smaller government, "traditional" social values, and a strong national defense.

Democrats are often called **liberals** or **left-wingers**. Liberals are also diverse in their viewpoints but broadly agree that government should be used to promote equal opportunity, through policies such as universal health care and an increase in the minimum wage. The Democratic coalition includes labor unions, the environmental movement, civil rights organizations, and the pro-choice movement. On foreign policy, liberals tend to be more internationalist, supporting strong diplomatic efforts before using military force.

At least a third of Americans are **independents**, who are unaffiliated with either major party. Some of them are **moderates** or **centrists**, with a mix of liberal and conservative views, depending on the issue. Most independents think they should vote for a candidate rather than for a party. Many end up being **swing voters**, up for grabs in a close race and courted by both Republicans and Democrats. Meanwhile, some moderates identify with one of the major parties, voting that way most of the time, but occasionally switching sides to support an appealing candidate.

Libertarians basically want to be left alone. Their mantra is "Live and let live." They favor a minimal government — often one that only provides for national defense — and very little taxation. Almost all oppose government interference in private life; for example, many support the legalization of drugs. Some libertarians wish to eliminate government's role in the economy, aligning them with Republicans for the past few decades. Those libertarians who are especially opposed to legislation of morality have been voting Democratic in increasing numbers.

Progressives are an emerging group on the left who seek to remake the Democratic Party, which they think has drifted too far to the right. Their numbers have grown through the Internet, blogs, and online organizing — often referred to as the **netroots**. They're especially concerned with ending the war in Iraq, achieving energy independence, and promoting civil liberties and open, transparent government. The distinction between progressives and liberals can be blurry: many left-leaning Democrats, especially younger ones, debate what label to use and what it should stand for.

Populist is often used to describe any philosophy or rhetorical style that pits the common good against special interests, the little guy against the establishment, and rural interests against urban ones. Populism is currently associated with certain issues, specifically trade protectionism and opposition to illegal immigration.

what **YOU SHOULD**

KNOW about

POLITICS

★ ★ ★ **BUT DON'T**

1

Elections

➢ Both national and state elections are run by state governments; there is enormous variability in voting mechanisms among states.

➢ Voter registration is thought to disproportionately affect minority, disadvantaged, and younger voters by making it less likely that they will vote.

➢ Supporters of increased voter requirements worry about fraud; others contend that voter fraud is minimal.

➢ Concerns have been raised over the security of DREs, or Direct Record Electronic voting machines, such as touch-screen machines.

➢ McCain-Feingold was a major campaign finance reform bill passed in 2002 that targeted soft money contributions. Its effects are still being debated.

➢ Gerrymandering is the practice of drawing congressional districts to influence the outcome of elections based on demographic information. Used by both parties, it can render some voters' interests almost irrelevant and tends to help incumbents.

➢ The Republicans' Texas redistricting plan drew fire in 2003.

➢ Democratic presidential nominations rely on primaries. New Hampshire's early primary and the Iowa caucuses are especially important.

➤ Republican presidential nominations are more centralized. The South Carolina primary is important, as are early nonbinding straw polls.

➤ Many states have moved their primaries forward in order to gain more influence over the presidential nomination process, leading to an earlier Super Tuesday.

➤ There have been calls to reform the Electoral College, which elects the president and vice president. Many would prefer direct election via the popular vote.

Background to Current Debates

Most Americans know that we use a simple majority system to elect senators and representatives, and many have heard of the Electoral College, but few of us understand how a candidate gets his or her name on the ballot, or even how ballots are counted and tallied. We know even less about the groups that maintain a continuing interest in how we choose our leaders on the local, state, and national levels. But almost every aspect of voting can be contentious. After all, *how* an election is held can strongly influence *who* is elected.

Electoral processes are at the heart of democratic government, but they aren't usually political issues because they are complex, are local rather than national, and vary by state, county, and even precinct. For some critics, this fact is in itself problematic; they feel a uniform national mechanism would be inherently fairer. Few of us are ever aware of any problems that may exist — except when a race is so close that irregularities could affect its outcome. That's all the more reason to pay attention to elections *before* they go wrong.

Every current debate about elections is somehow informed by the **2000 presidential race** between then Republican Texas governor **George W. Bush** and Democratic vice president **Albert "Al"**

Gore. Though the election was the most closely contested in decades, it was less anomalous than we might think. In fact, several elections in the 1800s were just as close and heavily debated, and had similarly vast repercussions on American history.

An issue during the 2000 election that also caused difficulties in other elections was a conflict between the outcome of the popular vote and that of the **Electoral College**, one of America's least loved and probably least understood institutions. The Electoral College consists of 538 **electors**, and *they* are the ones who actually elect the president and vice president, not the millions who cast their votes on election day. There is one elector for every US representative and senator, plus three for Washington, DC. So California has fifty-four electors, and Delaware has three. The way electors are nominated varies by state, but *we* elect electors loyal to a particular candidate by voting for them on election day. If you read your ballot carefully, you may see that it actually says "the electors for" the various candidates for president and vice president. Since their position is never disputed and there's no contest for the position on the ballot, many of us simply never notice that we vote for electors, we just check the box next to their name. Electors meet forty-one days after the general election in their state capitol and (with rare exceptions) cast all their state's votes for whichever candidate won a plurality of the popular vote in their state. A **plurality** just means the biggest percentage of votes; a **majority** means more than 50 percent.

The Electoral College was created by the founding fathers as a last-ditch compromise on how to choose the president, one of the most hotly debated questions faced by the **Constitutional Congress** in 1787. Some wanted Congress to choose the president, thinking that they would be best informed and would choose the most qualified candidate; others argued for direct election by the citizens as a more democratic and egalitarian method. The solution was to have state legislatures elect representatives to the Electoral College, whose members would subsequently choose the president. Soon enough there was a problem: in 1800 Thomas Jefferson and Aaron Burr each received seventy-three electoral votes, so the decision passed to the House of Representatives, as dictated by the Constitution in case of a tie in the College. Jefferson won, while Burr went on to kill Alexander Hamilton in a duel. And you think *today's* politics are cutthroat? The 1824 and 1876 elections were also decided by the House, both times electing someone who had *not* won the popular vote.

In 2000 Al Gore won the popular vote by 600,000 but lost Florida and its twenty-one electors by only 937 votes. He lost the Electoral College 271–267. Early on election night, Gore appeared to be winning Florida comfortably, and major networks called the state in his favor. Experts often "call" an election based on projections: knowing *some* of the results, they use exit polls and statistical analyses to guess the remainder. But later that night, Florida was called for Bush, giving him a projected majority in the Electoral College, and he was declared the winner. The following morning, however, Florida was deemed "too close to call" and the entire election was thrown into limbo. The margin was so close that an automatic recount was ordered to determine the winner. Democrats were concerned that the recount effort was effectively fixed in advance because the official in charge was Republican secretary of state **Katherine Harris**, the co-chair of the Bush campaign in Florida. Harris's boss was George Bush's brother, Florida's Republican governor **Jeb Bush**. Republicans responded that any recount would present opportunities for fraud — and insisted that the election was over and that Democrats were trying to steal it.

Allegations of unfair voting practices flew thick and fast, and both sides filed lawsuits, but some of the problems weren't necessarily partisan. **Ballot design** was an issue: one county used the now infamous **butterfly ballot** that made it quite easy to vote for a different candidate than intended. Some people realized their mistakes and ended up voting *twice* — voiding their ballot. Other conflicts erupted over how to count ballots marked by punch-card voting machines, which rely on voters using a metal stylus to punch holes into cardboard ballots; this is what created the notorious **hanging chads**, produced when the small piece of cardboard meant to be punched out did not detach completely. Some counties counted hanging chads as votes, while others did not.

These mechanical issues led to political fistfights. Democrats said that voters' intentions were what mattered, so all the ballots should be recounted. Plus, they proposed that disputed districts hold runoff elections, which they expected Gore to win. Republicans wanted to avoid this and countered that Bush's victory should be deemed final. They also argued that a runoff would be unfair because it would alter the circumstances of the vote, and give runoff voters extra influence. Some accounts of the recount allege flagrant fraud, including the theft and destruction of ballots and the intimidation of election officials by angry mobs allegedly bused in by the Republican Party. Meanwhile, news reports followed the rising and falling vote totals like the stock market, and Bush's margin of victory slowly shrank.

It was unclear how the debate would be resolved: Would it be thrown to the House? In that case, Bush would surely prevail, as the House was Republican-controlled. There was no precedent for a national recount or reelection: the Constitution and federal statutes are both silent on this. Florida, meanwhile, had a self-imposed deadline for reporting its result. While the recount continued, so did the lawsuits. One reached the Florida Supreme Court, which ordered that the recount continue, and Bush appealed to the US Supreme Court.

The Supreme Court's 5–4 ruling in **Bush v. Gore** stopped the recount, judging it to be unconstitutional, and stated that no alternative method of deciding the vote could be found before Florida's self-imposed reporting deadline.[1] To Democrats, this was insane — how could determining the intentions of voters be unconstitutional? The Court's opinion stated that since there was no uniform statewide standard for determining whether or not a vote was valid, the recount violated the Fourteenth Amendment's equal protection clause. The real nail in the coffin, however, was the Court's conclusion that there simply wasn't enough time to come up with a new result. The Court split along conservative/liberal lines, leading most Democrats and some Republicans to say that the decision was partisan.

There were several post-election analyses, and the consensus is that under the rules the Bush camp proposed to resolve the dispute before it went to the courts, Gore would have won, while under the rules the Gore campaign proposed, Bush would have won. Major press organizations asked the University of Chicago National Opinion Research Council (NORC) to conduct an investigation to determine what the outcome of a recount would have been. The NORC concluded that either Gore or Bush would have won, depending on how ballots were counted.[2] Independent recounts by *USA Today* and the *Miami Herald* both showed that Bush would have won a hand recount of the disputed ballots, but that a recount over the entire state would have given Gore a narrow victory.[3] Basically, more Floridians *intended* to vote for Gore than there were votes counted for him, indicating that had there been a runoff in various counties, the outcome probably would have favored Gore.[4]

Many Democrats remain convinced that the election was effectively stolen. Democrats in government had one chance to challenge the Supreme Court decision by objecting to Florida's electoral votes when they met — as they always must — to certify the election. Twenty representatives formally lodged objections, but these must be presented by both a representative and a senator to take effect, and no senators rose to register a complaint. This enraged many progressive Democrats, who found the official party response to the Florida debacle craven. Republicans, on the other hand, felt that justice had been served by leaving the original electoral results alone. In any case, Gore submitted to the Supreme Court's decision, and George W. Bush became America's forty-third president. After the problems during the 2000 election, in 2002 Congress passed the **Help America Vote Act**, or **HAVA**, which helped precincts replace punch-card voting systems and attempted to establish voting standards. The entire Bush-Gore experience led to more public scrutiny of voting mechanisms, and the extra attention has meant more partisan debates. Indeed, many voting issues, from registration to counting, are highly partisan. Some, like gerrymandering, aren't partisan, but involve politically independent advocacy groups. But first let's see *how* candidates become elected officials.

Mechanics of Voting

In most states, you have to **register to vote**, usually thirty to sixty days prior to election day. The rationale for registration is to **prevent voter fraud** by allowing state governments to keep track of who has voted, but it has had the effect of **making voting harder**, and therefore less likely, for many. Studies have shown that popular interest in a campaign peaks in the final two to three weeks before an election — but by then it's too late to register in most states. Plus, registration laws disproportionately impact people who change addresses more often, especially the poor and less educated, as well as younger voters. Several states have same-day voter registration; a few have none at all. Calls for states to adopt same-day registration, which balances fraud prevention with accessibility, have grown in recent years.

Both Republicans and Democrats make a point of helping likely supporters register, but many registration groups are nonpartisan and operate out of a sense of civic duty and political engagement. Many **get out the vote programs** provide transportation and/or child care to encourage voting among lower-income individuals, for whom it may be hard to get to the polls because they work several jobs, don't have a car, or can't find a babysitter. Ironically, voter registration itself is sometimes a conduit for voter fraud: voter registration services can selectively destroy or file applications. In 2004 such allegations in Oregon received national attention.[5]

Voter suppression and **voter intimidation** are variations on voter fraud. Voter suppression often entails **misinformation**: people are told polls are closed, or that there are requirements for voting that don't actually exist — like showing a Social Security card or a government-issued photo ID. Sometimes the intimidation is physical: a heavy, though fake, security presence may be displayed at polling locations, and sometimes voters are aggressively questioned outside the polls. Typically, voter suppression and intimidation **target low-income, socially marginalized populations**. There were reports that voter intimidation and suppression in Florida in the 2000 presidential election affected mostly poor African Americans, who were expected to vote for Al Gore. People for the American Way, a nonpartisan (though left of center) watchdog organization, asserts that voter intimidation occurs nationwide and "is not the province of a single political party, although patterns of intimidation have changed as the party allegiances of minority communities have changed over the years."[6]

Some of these actions are illegal under the Voting Rights Act of 1965, passed under Democratic president Lyndon Baines Johnson (LBJ) to extend the **franchise**, or the **right to vote**, especially to African Americans in the South. The Voting Rights Act reflects what we *perceive* as the right to vote; however, no blanket right to vote is guaranteed by the Constitution. Subsequent amendments removed restrictions on the right for certain groups: African Americans (theoretically) in 1870's Fifteenth Amendment; women in 1920's Nineteenth Amendment. The Voting Rights Act permanently and nationally abolished **literacy tests** and **poll taxes** (payments) required in order to vote; these had been especially prevalent in the South as part of **Jim Crow** laws, which included forced segregation and numerous restrictions on African Americans. The Voting Rights Act forced some states, counties, and towns to pre-clear all changes in voting practices with the Department of Justice (DOJ). It also had a partisan impact, as African Americans shifted their allegiance to the Democrats, while formerly Democratic white Southerners began trending Republican.

The **Voting Section** of the **DOJ** has faced scrutiny for its implementation of the Voting Rights Act. In 2005 the DOJ approved a program in Georgia that would require all voters to show certain kinds of ID at polling places. People who could not provide appropriate ID were to buy a twenty-dollar digital ID card. Republicans argued that it was a necessary measure against voter fraud, while Democrats feared it would make minorities less likely to vote. Low-income African Americans in Georgia are mostly Democrats, so Democrats saw this move by the Republican-controlled legislature as an underhanded political swipe. Under the Voting Rights Act, Georgia had to submit its changes in electoral practice to the DOJ. An initial internal report by the DOJ suggested that the Georgia ID requirement would dilute minority votes because significant numbers did not have the necessary documentation. However, section head John Tanner allowed the ID program to move forward. The Georgia law was overturned by an injunction; that decision was reversed. Then in 2008 the Supreme Court upheld an Indiana law requiring voter ID.

The DOJ has also been accused of selectively implementing the 1993 **National Voter Registration Act**. The **NVRA** requires states to help welfare recipients register to vote; it also contains directives on who cannot vote. Some groups, most of them liberal, have argued that the DOJ has focused on **purging voter rolls** rather than registering voters; they contend that this is a partisan political effort because those people who are not registered and cannot vote are more likely to vote Democratic.

Lately, allegations of voting irregularity have tended to fall on Republicans. But in many big cities from the mid-1800s to the mid-1900s, Democrats were often implicated. The **political machines** that ran urban areas were mostly (but not always) Democratic, providing jobs and other social services to recent immigrants in exchange for their votes and support. This was easier to monitor before our system of **secret ballots** was instituted: in those days, most votes were cast in public, without a booth. Reformers criticized the most infamous machines, such as New York's **Tammany Hall**, for paying for votes or encouraging people to cast multiple ballots. As a result, the first voter registration laws were passed around 1900. In 1960, Chicago's Democratic mayor **Richard M. Daley** was accused of running up votes for Democratic senator John F. Kennedy's presidential bid. That election was very close, and many believe that Kennedy won Illinois, and ultimately the presidency, because of Daley. A number of investigations concluded that while there were some voting irregularities, they were minor and did not affect the statewide outcome; but the belief that Daley fixed the election was widespread. Kennedy's vice president, LBJ, was accused of similar dealings in Texas, which was then predominantly Democratic.

So we see two basic patterns to electoral disputes. The party alleging irregularities is always the party who just lost: the winners, of course, are content with the results. And since Democrats have tended to rely more on the votes of working-class and African American voters, they've had a stronger incentive to make voting more accessible; conversely, Republicans have been more likely to allege voter fraud and to support tighter restrictions on voting.

Controversy has dogged many elections for the House of Representatives, as well. The number of representatives in Congress is currently fixed at 435; each state has at least one. The more populous the state, the more representatives it has: Wyoming gets a single **at-large** representative, whereas California has fifty-two. In states with more than one congressman or congresswoman, each represents a physical area of the state. Creating these districts is often a matter of extreme political debate because how districts are drawn affects who is elected.

Congressional redistricting occurs every ten years, after the national census. The purpose is to ensure that each congressman or congresswoman represents the right number of constituents, and that each state has the appropriate number of representatives. Redistricting also occurs on the state level to determine districts that elect representatives to the state legislature. **Gerrymandering** is a much-maligned form of drawing congressional districts to influence the outcome of elections based on demographic information and past election returns, which can be used to predict the level of partisan support in a given area. It derives its name from a bizarre sala**mander**-shaped Massachusetts district reluctantly signed into law by Governor Elbridge **Gerry** in 1812. Gerrymandering is often used to cluster together people with similar identities or interests, called **vote packing**, but it can also serve to dilute the interests of certain groups, known as **vote cracking**. The ultimate result is that the same state can yield two very different sets of House representatives — it all depends on who's drawing the lines.

Let's say there are two political parties, the Urbans and the Rurals, in a state with one city, Electopolis. The state has five House districts, of which Electopolis has two. Everyone in Electopolis votes Urban, while the countryside goes Rural. One way to pack votes would be to draw districts almost entirely within the city. These areas would vote Urban, and any Urban incumbent in good standing would have an easy time winning reelection. The Rurals may be content to leave Electopolis to the Urbans because then they still have a 3–2 edge. This arrangement is stable but not competitive, since all five districts would be safe for their incumbents.

If the Urbans win a majority in the state legislature, they may try to redistrict. They might divide Electopolis among three or four districts by redrawing districts that would spread out their votes. So instead of having two districts that vote 90 percent Urban, they may be able to create four that vote 55–45 in favor of the Urbans. The remaining district would be packed with as many Rural voters as possible. The three original Rural representatives now would be forced to compete among themselves for the same district. So the Urbans could make a deal: by drawing the boundaries of the safe Rural seat to include one of the incumbent Rural representatives, the Urbans could effectively co-opt her. She might get to keep her seat, but the Urbans would expect some favorable votes from her. They may even get her to support their redistricting plan by guaranteeing her seat and shutting out her party-member rivals. The Rurals could implement a similar redistricting plan given the chance, dividing Electopolis five ways, thus diluting, or cracking, the Urban vote, allowing them to take over the state's entire House delegation. Or they could leave a packed Urban district, again with a co-opted representative.

Vote dilution and vote packing are extremely common. Packing tends to **polarize the political field**; the increasingly partisan politics in Washington have been blamed in part on computerized redistricting, which allows for more effective use of socioeconomic data to create fewer politically mixed districts. Redistricting is also accused of **increasing rates of incumbency** over time: House members who run for reelection win around 98 percent of the time. This is why **open seats**, left when an incumbent retires or dies, are so prized: they're usually the only chance for a seat to change parties.

Both dilution and packing effectively **waste votes**: those of the extra voters in a packed district, and those of the minority contingent in a diluted district. Vote dilution is probably a bigger problem, because it means that a representative can ignore significant numbers of constituents from the opposing party. In fact, the more you look at Gerrymandering and partisan redistricting, the more egregious it is: it enables representatives to choose their constituents, instead of the other way around.

There are many organizations that advocate for either a different kind of voting or a different kind of districting that would be more democratic and fair. One group, **Range Voting**, designed a totally objective system that draws districts using a mathematical formula, the state's physical boundaries, and the population.[7] Another idea that is ofen proposed is **ranked voting**, in which everyone ranks candidates first, second, third, etc.; the candidates below the top two are then eliminated, and their votes are redistributed based on the second and third choices. This allows for more moderate and broadly popular winners to emerge because many voters would get their second, if not first, choice. For example, in 2000 nearly all of Ralph Nader's supporters would have picked Gore as their second choice; a ranked voting system would have given those Nader votes to Gore, allowing him a clear victory. In 1992 a ranked voting system might have helped George H. W. Bush defeat Bill Clinton, since it was estimated that the majority of independent candidate Ross Perot's voters would have picked Bush as their second choice.

There is less popular support for voting reform than one might expect, probably because most of us don't know that politicians design districts so that some of our votes just don't count — and because issues of process (like elections) tend to draw less attention than issues of outcome (like taxes). And since it would take politicians to change the law, it's unlikely to happen, because they are the ones who benefit.

Sometimes, though, fights over redistricting make front-page news. In 2001 the Texas state legislature was controlled by Democrats, who could not reach an agreement with the state Republicans on redistricting due after the 2000 census. The Republican minority asked an independent panel of judges to arbitrate, but the resulting map still favored Democrats. When the Republicans won a majority in the state legislature in 2002, redistricting became their top priority. Republican Representative **Tom DeLay**, who was then the House majority leader and the head of Texas's Republican delegation in Congress, was closely involved in the effort. The plan was criticized, in part because it occurred **mid-census**; redistrictings normally take place only after the census.

Unwilling to vote on the Republicans' redistricting bill in 2003, Democratic state legislators fled Texas so that there would be too few representatives to form a **quorum** (the minimum number of lawmakers required for a vote). In 2006 the plan reached the Supreme Court, which rejected one district because it found that it was drawn on racial lines in order to dilute, or even discount, minority votes. Other districts split along racial lines were allowed because the Court decided that the purpose of that districting was political rather than racial — and therefore legal. Some legal activists have argued that under the *Bush v. Gore* ruling, political gerrymandering violates the equal protection clause by making some voters' ballots effectively count less than others. But the Supreme Court has repeatedly held that political gerrymandering is constitutional — at least so far.

How we cast our votes is essential to free and fair elections, but it varies quite a bit from state to state and even from county to county. Though controversial during the 2000 presidential election,

punch card ballots have the advantage of leaving a paper trail. Yet as with any physical means of voting, they can be destroyed or hidden by someone determined to commit voter fraud. Punch cards have other problems: there's no way to correct a mistake, and if the chad doesn't detach completely, the vote might not be counted. **Optical scanning systems** work just like standardized tests: voters pencil in a bubble or complete an arrow, and the ballot is read by machines that quickly and reliably tally the results. They leave a paper trail, but can be altered by anyone with a pencil and, like punch cards, are easily destroyed. **Direct recording machines**, commonly called **lever machines**, use wheel-driven mechanisms to record votes internally. There is no check on or paper trail from these systems, which rely entirely on accurate recording and reporting by election staff.

New **direct recording electronic voting machines**, called **DREs**, drew a lot of press after concerned scientists raised questions about their security. DREs, also known as touch-screen machines, work a lot like ATMs — minus the cash. They are easy to use, may be programmed in multiple languages, and can ask voters for confirmation before finalizing their votes. They can leave a paper trail by producing a receipt, which could then be manually audited if necessary, although most DREs currently aren't built and/or programmed to do so. Some studies suggest that DREs increase the likelihood that minorities' votes are recorded.[8]

Though criticizing DREs was originally a pet cause of politically active technophiles, concerns have increased and reached many in government. Servers crash. Software freezes. Printers jam. And there's often no sure way to check that backup systems, which can produce a copy of the votes, are working. In late 2007, Ohio's secretary of state required one county to return to paper ballots before the state's 2008 presidential primaries after a series of server crashes disrupted a previous election. Worried about their potentially problematic effects, Senate Democrats **Bill Nelson** of Florida and **Sheldon Whitehouse** of Rhode Island proposed a bill to ban the machines outright.

A test-case scenario may already have been played out in the political hotbed that is Florida. In 2006, Democrat Christine Jennings lost a congressional race by 369 votes. Or did she? According to the DREs that recorded the votes, 18,000 people, or 13 percent of those who voted, voted in other elections but not in Ms. Jennings's congressional race. Considering that the normal rate for this — called **undervoting** — is 3 percent, there was rampant speculation that the machines had screwed up the vote. Indeed, Jennings's staff received numerous complaints from voters that the voting machines they used did not work.[9] Those complaints have been echoed in other races nationwide. Though disputed votes represent a small portion of the total votes cast, when machines do malfunction, they can throw an entire race.

One potential problem with DREs is that they run on **proprietary**, or **private**, **software**, leaving no way for election officials, oversight committees, or courts to check the vote count. A panel from Johns Hopkins University found several security flaws in machines made by **Diebold**, the largest manufacturer of DREs. Votes were recorded on a removable "smart card," raising worries that someone could replace the smart card with one that contained a virus to miscount votes.[10] DREs could also be **vulnerable to hacking** while transmitting votes — someone could intercept the signal the machine sends to tally the vote at a central server.[11] Diebold has provoked controversy: in 2004 the chairman of the company circulated a fundraising letter in which he wrote he was "committed to helping Ohio deliver its electoral votes to the President."[12] Ohio ultimately gave President Bush his margin of victory over John Kerry; some have questioned what they believe were voting irregularities in the state.

It's possible that advances in DRE technology will right some problems. To allow officials to check or recount votes, DREs could run on **open source code** like Linux, accessible to all, or DRE manufacturers could allow election officials access to their software. By early 2008, Diebold was considering running new machines on open platforms. More DREs also could employ a **voter-verified paper trail**, printing a ballot in a secure chamber that the voter would have to approve. Those that do this still have problems, though. Printers are notoriously unreliable. Allowing voters to keep a copy of their ballot would create another check, but currently machines don't provide voters with a receipt.

However, there are reputable groups that oppose such changes, including the League of Women Voters. They argue that DREs are just as functional as other methods, all of which are susceptible to some malfunction, and that DREs are generally reliable, cost-effective, and less prone to fraud than paper-based systems. They are vastly outnumbered, though, by those who oppose DREs altogether.

Campaign finance is another murky area that is increasingly in the political spotlight. Nowadays candidates need a lot of money — millions of dollars for even a statewide race — to run a viable campaign. TV airtime for commercials is the most expensive item; pollsters and consultants cost a pretty penny, too. Politicians of both parties are frequently accused of taking donations from certain industries, corporations, or other **special interests** and then supporting positions accordingly, in what is sometimes called a **quid pro quo** arrangement. While political scientists stress that candidates generally receive money from interests with which they are already aligned, most of us believe that when people make large donations, they at least tacitly expect something in return. If nothing else, political donations often provide access to officeholders.

Campaign finance reform has a long history. In 1907 the first major federal reform, the **Tillman Act**, attempted — though largely failed — to prohibit corporations from making political donations. Senate and House campaigns were subjected to spending limits and disclosure requirements soon thereafter, and in 1925 the fabulously named **Federal Corrupt Practices Act** set donation limits. In 1971 the **Federal Election Campaign Act** (**FECA**) was passed, which obliged campaigns to **disclose donations** and how they are spent. In 1974 the **Federal Election Commission** (**FEC**) was established, along with new donation and spending caps. Spending caps were overturned by the Supreme Court in 1976; the Court equated a political campaign's money with speech, ruling that any restriction on a candidate's spending was a violation of First Amendment rights. Conservatives hailed the decision as a victory for free speech, while many progressive legal scholars believe it was one of the Court's worst mistakes. As it is, no spending caps are allowed, though donation limits remain.[13]

In **2002** Congress passed the **McCain-Feingold Act** — named for its sponsors, Republican senator John McCain of Arizona and Democratic senator Russ Feingold of Wisconsin — to clean up soft money contributions. Before 2002 the amount of **soft money**, or donations to organizations such as the Democratic or Republican National Committees (DNC or RNC), was *unlimited*. **Hard money**, or direct contributions to candidates, was capped. Therefore, a rich individual or organization could donate, say, $3 million to the DNC, which the DNC could then give to a specific campaign, thus bypassing hard money limits to individual candidates. McCain-Feingold placed caps on soft money and doubled limits on hard money; soft money is harder to trace back to its sources. For the 2008 cycle, an individual or Political Action Committee could give a candidate up to $2,300 for the general election and another $2,300 for the primary season, and this amount will rise over time. Before McCain-Feingold, the limit was $1,000.

Political Action Committees, or **PACs**, are funded by corporations, organizations, and individuals. Regulated by the FEC, PACs can contribute money to campaigns and engage in issue advocacy. A PAC's **spending is limited**, as is its ability to use advertising: PACs cannot run ads that directly support or attack a candidate within sixty days of the general election or thirty days of a nominating convention. Almost every large organization or corporation has at least one PAC, including the Sierra Club, Trial Lawyers' Association, League of Conservative Voters, GOPAC (Republican leadership PAC), and Wal-Mart. Many state parties and individual politicians also run PACs.

McCain-Feingold's restriction on soft money has made other avenues for fundraising more popular. **Issue-advocacy groups**, often called **527s** after a section of the tax code, technically cannot advocate for the election or defeat of any specific political candidate but may engage in political activity. They are tax-exempt and not regulated by the FEC. 527s have proven controversial: both the **Swift Boat Veterans for Truth**, which Democrats accused of coordinating with the Bush campaign to smear presidential candidate John Kerry in 2004, and **America Coming Together**, or **ACT**, which Republicans accused of vilifying President George W. Bush in 2004, are 527s. Such coordination is prohibited. 527s are supposed to be independent groups that care about certain issues, rather than groups affiliated with a campaign that were created to circumvent the FEC and its donation limits. ACT ultimately paid a multimillion-dollar settlement to the FEC to avoid going to court; the Swift Boat Veterans were fined, but only a fraction of that amount.

Most people in Washington will tell you that **McCain-Feingold didn't really clean up campaign financing**. If you really want to cheat the system, they argue, you'll find a way to do it. McCain-Feingold also put more emphasis on certain kinds of financing. Since single donors can give less money to parties and hard money limits were increased, McCain-Feingold made **bundlers** — fundraisers who can get a bunch of other people to donate — more important. A good example is George W. Bush's **Pioneers**, individuals who raised $100,000 or more during the 2000 presidential election. But McCain-Feingold responded to a *perception* that money had gotten dirtier in DC — one shared by some leftist progressives and conservatives. Al Gore got into trouble for making donor calls from his office in the Old Executive Office Building during his first vice-presidential term. His 1996 fundraiser at a Buddhist temple proved an unholy mess when it was revealed that monks and nuns had illegally served as conduits for other people's contributions. Meanwhile, Bill Clinton raised moderate eyebrows and conservative ire for inviting big donors to stay in the White House's Lincoln bedroom.

But just three years after McCain-Feingold, the biggest money scandal in decades rocked DC from K Street to the Capitol. In 2005, Republican Tom DeLay had to step down as House majority leader when he was indicted on allegations of campaign finance misconduct centering on the 2002 race. Bush Pioneer **Jack Abramoff** was found guilty on charges of fraud, tax evasion, and corruption in 2006. Abramoff defrauded several Native American tribes that had hired him to help with casino proposals. The corruption charges focused on favors Abramoff dealt to politicians and their families and staff. Handouts included meals in a restaurant he owned, free sports and concert tickets, and swanky Scottish golf trips (one of which was for Tom DeLay).

Reformers have declared McCain-Feingold a mixed blessing. On the upside, because the law limited soft money, the major parties increased emphasis on individual hard money contributions. With the rise of online fundraising, this has led to an explosion of small-dollar donations. And that's important for upstart nonestablishment candidates. The 2004 campaign featured the completely unexpected rise of Democratic former Vermont governor **Howard Dean**, fueled by a not-so-small army of supporters making online donations. In 2007 the presidential campaign of libertarian Republican congressman **Ron Paul** of Texas broke a Republican record by raising more than $5 million in a single day, nearly all of it online. In January 2008 insurgent Democratic presidential candidate Senator **Barack Obama** of Illinois raised $32 million largely through hundreds of thousands of small online contributions. Many, especially progressives and libertarians, applaud this development, saying it levels the playing field by giving candidates independence from corporations and wealthy donors. On the downside, 527s — another result of McCain-Feingold — have been criticized as being too opaque. Without FEC regulation, it's difficult to know where their money comes from.

Some continue to advocate for **full public financing of elections**. A limited system of public matching funds already exists, providing public financing in exchange for a spending cap, but major candidates in both parties have **opted out** of the system. If *all* of a campaign's financing were public, reformers argue, politicians wouldn't need donations at all. Politicians are ambivalent about public financing: On the one hand, they wouldn't have to spend so much time and effort fundraising. On the other, there would be hard limits on what they could spend. So far, they've stuck to raising money.

Presidential Elections

Now that we know how candidates raise their money, let's talk about what they're spending it on — trying to win votes to send them to the White House. Presidential candidates are officially chosen at a political party's **national convention**, held the summer before the election. Republicans and Democrats choose their candidates differently: the Republicans' process is more centralized, while the Democrats' system is more diffuse and depends heavily on state primary elections. This also means that the parties can have two very different selection processes in the same state.

At Democratic primaries and caucuses, voters express their preferences for the party's nominee — but choosing the nominee is an indirect process that is filtered through the delegates to the national convention, who actually pick the nominee. In 2008, 4,049 delegates were slated to attend the Democratic convention (this number varies by year), and a candidate needs only a simple majority to win the nomination — 2,025 delegates. The number of delegates from each state, plus the US Virgin Islands, Guam, American Samoa, Puerto Rico, and Washington, DC, is determined by the state's share of the total Democratic popular vote in the last presidential election and its proportion of the electoral vote. The party also selects delegates to represent its state leadership.

How do you become a delegate? It varies. At a primary or caucus, voters pick delegates who go to the county party convention. County conventions choose delegates for the state convention, and the state convention chooses delegates for the national convention. Usually. In some states it's not that complicated. This process allocates most — but not all — of a state's delegates to the national convention, who are called **pledged delegates** because they are loosely tied to a candidate by the results of their state's primary or caucus process.

Pledged delegates are apportioned by a complex formula that varies by state. All states now apply a **proportional system**, wherein delegates are awarded according to the percentage of votes each candidate received in the state primary or caucuses by district or county. An extra number of delegates is often awarded by the state primary or caucus popular vote. Legally, delegates don't have to support whichever candidate they are pledged to support — and candidates can reject a delegate if they think he or she might not be loyal — so while a major insurrection among delegates is possible under the current system, it's not terribly likely.

A number of unpledged or uncommitted **superdelegates** are chosen by the national party leadership. Usually, all Democratic members of Congress and Democratic governors are superdelegates, as are high DNC and state party officials. In 2008, 796 superdelegates were chosen. Superdelegates can be **kingmakers** — those who ultimately decide the party nominee — or sheep — those who reflect the popular vote. Understanding how superdelegates think is important to grasping the practical process of elections. Superdelegates are party insiders. One factor they consider is a candidate's national viability — they are more likely to pick a candidate with broad appeal. However, they may also judge a candidate's "coattails" — his or her ability to lift up other party candidates to victory — and this can actually make them choose a candidate with local, rather than national, appeal. Put another way, superdelegates will support candidates who appeal to their state's voters, because it makes it easier for their party's politicians to get elected if they are running on the same ballot. Superdelegates also look long and hard at a candidate's supply of money, particularly their **cash on hand**, the money that's actually in the campaign's bank account. In most years, the superdelegates can't swing a nomination by their actual votes at the convention; but by endorsing, campaigning, and fundraising for a presidential candidate, they always have a lot of sway.

Republicans, on the other hand, elect about half as many delegates as Democrats to their national convention: in 2008 there were 2,380. Some delegates are chosen at state conventions, others by the state party leadership — it depends entirely on the state. Each state is entitled to six delegates, while the US Virgin Islands, Guam, and American Samoa are given four each, and Puerto Rico and Washington, DC, have a whopping fourteen each. This reflects the federal aspect of the delegation. Each state gets an additional three delegates for every member of Congress (a total of 435), which preserves proportional representation. States can also earn **bonus delegates** for their level of local Republican support: for instance, if a majority of the state voted for a Republican in the last presidential election.

There are two big differences between Republican and Democratic nomination procedures. First, a majority of the Republican primaries and caucuses have a **winner-take-all** system, awarding *all* of the state's pledged delegates to the statewide winner; this makes it far more likely for a candidate who wins a number of early states, even by narrow margins, to pull away from the pack. Second, many more Republican delegates than Democratic delegates are unpledged. Again, it varies by state: in some states, all Republican delegates are unpledged; in others, most are pledged. The upshot is that the Republican process tends to be more **top-down,** while the Democratic process is more **bottom-up**. Republicans are more likely to have their candidate chosen by kingmakers in the national party; the Republicans' method is generally less divisive and more orderly than the Democrats'. Many think this allows Republicans to field stronger candidates in the general election.

Not only are there differences between the Democratic and Republican procedures, but there are also differences among the various types of primaries and caucuses. Primaries are run by each party, administered on the state level, and overseen by state governments. In an **open primary**, anyone can vote regardless of party affiliation — a Republican could vote for Democratic candidates and vice versa. Open primaries are rare, though, and what's more common is a **semi-open system** in which independent voters can vote in either the Democratic or Republican primary. In a **closed primary**, only registered party members are allowed to vote, and independents are left out in the cold.

Many contenders drop out of the presidential race as primaries are conducted, because primaries are increasingly considered indicators of potential success. Whoever wins early primaries receives a lot of media attention and more donations. Thus, states with early contests such as **New Hampshire** and **Iowa** are often said to enjoy **disproportionate influence** in presidential elections. The national party committees allow them to hold early primaries in order to ensure that small states have some influence in the process and to force candidates to campaign there in person — feasible in small states, while large ones rely more heavily on TV ads. However, the committees sometimes reschedule states' primaries to give more weight and influence to various groups. In 2008, for example, Nevada's primary was moved up in order to give Hispanics more visibility in the election process. Republican presidential hopefuls are more reliant on **straw polls**, nonbinding votes that help measure how much popular support each candidate enjoys. One key poll, the **Ames Straw Poll** in Ames, Iowa, has been held since 1979 in the August before an election year when there is no incumbent Republican presidential nominee.

Iowa employs a caucus system instead of a primary; the Republican and Democratic versions are significantly different. The **Iowa caucuses** became nationally important for Democrats in 1976, when Democratic Georgia governor Jimmy Carter used his second-place win (most who voted were in fact undecided) as a sign of success. The Democratic caucus is a sort of **community debate**. Participants vote in their precinct, where they gather in a room divided into areas by candidate. There's also a section for undecided voters. Then everybody tries to persuade everyone else to support their chosen candidate. The competing groups bring signs and T-shirts, start chants and songs, and serve food. While monetary bribery is frowned upon, luring your rivals' supporters with cupcakes is fair game. After a half hour, the mini-election is stopped and officials determine which candidates are "viable," namely, those who receive at least 15 percent of the initial vote. This whittles down the choices, and people who were support-ing an "unviable" candidate have another half hour to choose some-one else. The **realignment process** is perhaps the biggest difference between Democratic primaries and caucuses, because it means that being some people's second favorite candidate can really help a cam-paign. Republican caucuses are usually a secret poll, and there is no realignment.

New Hampshire, unlike Iowa, has some claim as an important national indicator because there is a plurality of independent voters in the state — around 37 percent. A little over one-third are registered Republicans, and about one-quarter are registered Democrats, but the state is trending increasingly Democratic. Like New Hampshire, Iowa is a small state, and its caucus voters do not reflect the nation's demographic makeup. Iowa caucusgoers are almost all white, slightly wealthier than the average American, much more likely to be in-volved in agriculture, and older — nearly half are over fifty-five. But in 2008, Democratic senator Barack Obama led a huge get-out-the-vote effort among young Iowans, who helped carry him to a large and unexpected victory.

New Hampshire and Iowa are extremely important for **Democrats**. For **Republicans, New Hampshire** has traditionally been a key primary, but attention has shifted to **South Carolina** be-cause New Hampshire hasn't predicted the eventual Republican nominee lately, since it isn't a mainstream Republican state. New Hampshire residents display a libertarian streak; they like maverick, outsider candidates. For instance, in 2000 they chose John McCain over George W. Bush; they even chose Pat Buchanan over George H. W. Bush (then the sitting president) in 1992. South Carolina, on the other hand, seems to mirror the national Republican Party more closely.

People in New Hampshire and Iowa wind up having a lot of in-fluence on the national race, and they also experience more personal contact with presidential hopefuls because of the huge amount of effort put into early primary campaigning. The fact that low-population states have so much clout has angered larger states, spurring several to move the dates of their 2008 primaries forward: **California** started the rush when it moved its primary from June to February 5; Michigan and Florida then moved theirs to January. The major primary day, on which many states vote, is called **Super Tuesday**. The original Super Tuesday took place in March, and involved a bloc of Southern states that wanted to create a regional primary to exercise more influence over the nominating process. In 2008, February 5 became the new Super Tuesday, with more than twenty states voting. The effects of the compressed primary schedule — and whether to change it — is sure to be debated for years to come.

The **Democratic National Committee** decided to **boycott** Florida's and Michigan's 2008 primaries as retribution for the states' decisions to move their primaries forward, which the DNC thought went against the party's best interests. In theory, this meant the two states' convention votes were forfeit, but exactly what would happen to the states' delegates remained up in the air well into the nominating process. Florida's Democratic senator Bill Nelson and Democratic representative Alcee Hastings sued the DNC for disenfranchising their state, but the case was thrown out. As the Democratic nominating process wore on and proved close, what to do became a big problem. Some proposed a do-over election, but nobody could agree on who should pay for it. Others wanted to seat the existing delegates. The problem was that in Michigan, only Hillary Clinton's name was actually on the ballot, so it seemed that seating those delegates would be unfair to the other candidates. In Florida, technically, candidates weren't allowed to campaign (though many visited and held fundraisers), so how that affected the outcome was uncertain.

Many argue that early primaries merely grease the wheels for **establishment candidates** because underdog or independent candidates need more time to catch voters' attention. Some worry that the early schedule exacerbates a presidential hopeful's need for money because it is **financially demanding** to run ground operations — let alone to buy airtime — in several states all at once and early on.

If primaries aren't conclusive, a **brokered convention** can result, meaning that a candidate is actually chosen at the national convention by insider wheeling and dealing. This was the norm before the 1970s; the chaos and violence surrounding the 1968 Democratic National Convention, much of it captured on live TV, persuaded both parties to turn their conventions into scripted media events with defacto nominees.

Once the parties have decided on their presidential nominees, campaigning shifts into high gear for the election in November. The Constitution mandates that the presidential elections be held every four years on the first Tuesday after the first Monday in November. Many think that we should move the election to a weekend or make election day a national holiday to encourage voter turnout, which is what most developed nations do.

This brings us back to the **Electoral College**, which has come under increased criticism. The 538 electors are relatively obscure individuals ultimately selected by the state parties, but in some states they also appear on the ballot. Electors are pledged, but not bound, to cast their votes according to the dictates of the popular vote in their state, but every once in a while someone doesn't. In 2000 one of the DC electors cast a blank ballot to protest Washington, DC's lack of congressional representation — a rare example of a **faithless elector**. Twenty-four states have laws to punish faithless electors, though none have ever been prosecuted. Many advocates for voter reform think that we should **"dehumanize" electors**. They propose that whoever wins the popular vote in any given state should *automatically* be allocated the state's electoral votes. Thus, a serious rebellion among electors would be impossible.

Advocates of the Electoral College insist that it captures the federalist nature of American government by preserving the importance of states. They also argue that the system forces candidates to pay attention to minority interests. Since the state winner gets all the electoral votes, the stakes in gaining a plurality are magnified — a single vote could in theory be the difference between all fifty-four of California's electoral votes and none at all. Others believe the Electoral College is in dire need of reform. The strongest criticism is that it **dilutes the votes of the political minority** in each state. If your state is 51 percent or 99 percent Republican, the Republican candidate wins all the electoral votes. Votes in the minority would count more if we used a system that more closely reflected the outcome of the popular vote. Many contend that the Electoral College encourages candidates to campaign almost exclusively in **swing states** — states that can go either Democrat or Republican and which tend to do so by a small margin.

Republican or Democratic strongholds receive no real attention from either party; instead, contestants focus on states where support is nearly evenly split: lately, Florida, Ohio, Michigan, Pennsylvania, Iowa, New Mexico, and New Hampshire. Critics also point out that **small states lose out** because they have few electoral votes. Recent elections, however, have been so close that even small states' electoral votes count: in 2000, New Hampshire, with its four electoral votes, would have given Gore the victory. Finally, the Electoral College makes it almost impossible for third parties to emerge because it allocates votes based on plurality not on proportion. Thus, a new party would have a very difficult time ever getting any electoral votes. Some see this as an advantage because they think that the two-party system we have is much more stable than a multi-party system.

The most basic and decisive reform would be to abolish the Electoral College altogether and move to a **direct popular vote**. This would require a **constitutional amendment**, which demands **ratification by three-fourths** (thirty-eight) **of the states**. There is a precedent: while senators were originally appointed by state legislatures, the Seventeenth Amendment, added in 1913, mandated their direct popular election. **Proportional allocation** of electoral votes would not require a constitutional amendment. Instead of the winner of the state's popular vote taking *all* of the state's electoral votes, electoral votes would be divided according to the percentage of the popular vote received by each candidate. Maine actually uses a modified version of this system. In Maine, the statewide vote determines two electors, with each congressional district's results dictating the vote of that elector. In 2007 proportional allocation was debated in California and North Carolina; Democrats worried that such a move in California could hand twenty electoral votes to Republicans, and that if only *some* states adopted the reform, the result could be skewed. An alternative proposal would trigger the reform only if a number of other states approved it as well.

One plan that has begun to receive support is the **National Popular Vote Interstate Compact**, or **NPV**, which would effectively shift the election of the president to the popular vote *through* the Electoral College and by the authority of the states. Here's how it would work: The Constitution allows each state to determine independently how it will apportion its electors. Any state that passes the compact agrees to give *all* its electoral votes to whichever candidate wins the *national* popular vote. The agreement would be activated only when states accounting for half of the Electoral College passed it — a form of ratification. With half of the Electoral College accounted for, though, the popular vote winner would be guaranteed to win the election. The plan radically reduces the number of states needed to enact reform when compared to that required to ratify a constitutional amendment.

Electoral issues are so fundamental to our system of government, and affect us all so profoundly, that it's a good thing so many of them have been brought to public attention recently. Though the status quo usually serves the interests of incumbent politicians, calls for various kinds of electoral reform are mounting. The beauty of our system is, after all, its responsiveness to public demand — even if change takes time.

2

The Economy

> The government's goal is to grow the economy at a moderate pace in order to prevent recessions and depressions.

> Fiscal policy refers to the federal government's taxing and spending and is controlled by both Congress and the president.

> Monetary policy controls the supply of money and is set by the Federal Reserve Bank ("the Fed") and the Treasury Department; both are governed by officials appointed by the president.

> Many blame the mortgage meltdown on deregulation of the lending industry.

> The Fed cannot set, but can only target, interest rates. It does so by selling or buying government securities.

> Interest is rent paid on money. Banks' interest rates are based on federal rates.

> Low interest rates are good for exports and bad for imports, can decrease the value of the dollar, and can make lenders less likely to lend money to the United States.

> Tax cuts or hikes have different effects depending on who gets them. Their short-term and long-term effects can vary.

> Many worry about our national deficit; others think deficits don't matter.

> Mandatory spending accounts for two-thirds of all government outlays and includes entitlement payments for Medicaid, Medicare, and Social Security.

> Discretionary spending accounts for one-third of all government outlays and pays for things like roads, national parks, and funding for scientific research.

> The fact that oil is denominated in dollars is key to our economy; Russia and Iran are threatening to redenominate oil in euros and rubles.

Background to Current Debates

The economy is perennially one of voters' top issues, but very few of us fully grasp how specific economic indicators — such as the value of the dollar or the amount of the national debt — affect our everyday lives. Few of us know how a politician's views on such indicators are relevant to us, even though the decisions that politicians and officials make about interest rates, taxes, and government spending are critical to our personal economic reality — not to mention the nation's future.

The economy is so big, complicated, and variable that it's often hard to see the big picture. We tend to focus on specific issues such as tax cuts or the subprime mortgage crisis. But it's important to recognize that the economy is a complex system in which one policy can have multiple, even contradictory effects and that there aren't necessarily fixes for economic problems. Pundits often liken the economy to a patient: some maladies can be cured, but for others, all you can do is address the symptoms and wait it out. Either way, there's always the possibility that the medicine's side effects will do more damage than the initial complaint.

Since there's no way to test specific economic policies except to enact them, even published PhDs with expensive computers and pro-prietary statistical software don't fully understand what effects various policies really have. So keep in mind that any economic debate is always somewhat theoretical. Plus, economists themselves are politicized, and a lot of economic talk is really just ideology veneered by analysis.

The economy creates strange political bedfellows and reflects major ideological shifts. For one thing, policies such as deficit spend-ing and economic intervention advocated by Democrats and strongly opposed by Republicans in the early twentieth century eventually caught on so that by the 1960s Republicans supported some formerly liberal economic ideas. However, conservative views about managing the deficit and debt that were touted by Republicans during the '80s are now more commonly held by Democrats.

The American economy is often compared to a **pie**. We want to make a bigger pie, or we want a bigger slice of the pie. (President George W. Bush once memorably asserted that we need to make the pie *higher*.) But in banking as in baking, there's such a thing as a **per-fect temperature**.

The government manages the economy to shield it from major fluctuations. An economy that's too hot, or growing too fast, is a problem — but so is one that's cooling. To keep the economy hum-ming along at moderate warmth, the government taxes, spends, bor-rows, prints money, and helps determine interest rates. How we tax and spend is called **fiscal policy**; how we control the supply of money by targeting interest rates and printing money is called **mon-etary policy**. Fiscal policy is set by Congress, but the president has some control, too. Monetary policy is run almost entirely by govern-ment officials at the **Treasury Department** and the **Federal Re-serve Bank** who are appointed by the president.

Any discussion of the American economy is inherently set against the backdrop of America's biggest bust, the **Great Depres-sion** of 1930–39. The causes of the Depression were many, and schol-ars still argue about them, but the Depression was precipitated by the **stock market crash** of 1929. **Government borrowing and**

spending on World War I made it harder for the economy to recover. Some, including current Federal Reserve chair **Ben Bernanke**, think that **consumer debt** was partly to blame, too. In the 1920s, Americans borrowed heavily to buy houses and cars, and when the economy slowed down, they had to radically decrease their spending in order to meet their interest payments — leading to a major contraction in the economy. A **drought** and subsequent agricultural crises beginning in 1930 only made matters worse.

The boom and bust cycle, of which the Depression was the ultimate bust, was common a century ago. In 1907, for example, the stock market fell 50 percent, and serious financial crisis was averted by a cash injection from the Treasury and by the swift action of private banker J. P. Morgan, who helped organize an effective national response. Known as the **Panic of 1907**, this crisis led to the creation of the **Federal Reserve System** in 1913, which, through the Federal Reserve Bank, devises and implements most American monetary policy.

The Federal Treasury Department and the Federal Reserve share an overarching goal: **grow the economy, but not too quickly**. We want more money, but we don't want to make too much too fast because that can lead to bubbles, and those eventually pop, creating recessions, depressions, and panics. To grow the economy is to increase our national **Gross Domestic Product**, or **GDP**, an estimation of how much value the country produces in a year. In 2007 America's GDP was estimated to be around $14 trillion, the largest of any single nation in the world — although the European Union has a collective GDP that is now slightly higher. To provide some scale, a **trillion dollars** is a thousand billion, a million million, or $1,000,000,000,000. GDP can be measured in several different ways, so you might see slightly different numbers from different sources.

Even more important may be **GDP growth**, measured every fiscal quarter (a period of three months) and expressed as a percentage of the GDP. For most developed countries, anything over **3 percent** growth per year is considered healthy. US annual growth was around 4 or 5 percent during the late 1990s — which was considered a **boom**, or a period of high growth — and under 2 percent in 2007–8. By contrast, China has achieved growth of 8 to 10 percent a year for the last *fifteen years.* If GDP levels off, we say there's **stagnation**. If GDP shrinks for two consecutive quarters, there is officially a **recession**. A **depression** is a severe or long recession; during the Great Depression, the United States lost over one-fourth of its GDP. **Stagflation** — stagnation combined with high inflation (a measure of how much the value of money depreciates over time) — is a government economist's worst nightmare because measures taken to reduce inflation are usually the opposite of those used to stimulate the economy.

Boom and bust cycles still happen, and always will: the trick is to make sure the economy never swings too far out of equilibrium. Billionaire financier and Democrat George Soros explains that these phases "usually revolve around credit and always involve a bias or misconception. This is usually a failure to recognise a reflexive, circular connection between the willingness to lend and the value of the collateral."[1] There's a feedback loop that inflates bubbles: Money is easy to come by (interest rates are low, there's lots of cash in the economy), so people overvalue investments. Then interest rates go up, money is harder to come by, and the value of investments is reassessed — downward. This is why stock market slumps are sometimes called **reevaluations** or **readjustments**.

Current Debates: The Subprime Mortgage Crisis and the 2001 Tax Cuts

In 2007 a slowdown in the once-fiery housing market turned talking heads, and the words "subprime mortgage crisis" fell from pundits' lips like so many economic pie crumbs. **Mortgages** are loans for real estate that take the property itself for collateral (the asset used to guarantee the loan). **Subprime loans** cost more than normal loans because they are particularly risky, or more likely to go into foreclosure. **Foreclosures** happen when people cannot pay their mortgage and the property they have bought with the loan is taken by the lending agency. Banks lost billions on bad loans as families across the country fell into foreclosure. Though the media generally blamed a cooling housing market for the troubles, the mortgage crisis had complex — and instructive — roots. In fact, understanding just what happened gets you to the heart of America's monetary policy.

It all started when the government decided to deregulate the banking industry. **Deregulation** occurred over a period of fifteen years, beginning in 1980. Before then, strict laws controlled how banks could market mortgages, what interest rates they could charge, and even under what criteria people could take out a loan. People who couldn't afford mortgages weren't given them; this led to a basic understanding that when you applied for a mortgage, a lender would give you only an amount you were likely able to repay. That expectation proved disastrous for many Americans.

To entice people into taking out mortgages, many lenders offered **teaser rates**, very low interest rate mortgages that required either **no down payment** or a very small one, usually attached to a variable rate mortgage. **Variable rate mortgages** are loans whose interest rate can change, while normal mortgages are **fixed rate loans** whose rate doesn't change. Variable rate mortgages seem attractive when interest rates are low, but they are risky because if interest rates go up, loan payments can rise significantly overnight. If you have no financial cushion, that can be devastating — and people who bought these loans were by definition subprime borrowers, people with less than sterling credit ratings who didn't have extra money.

Variable rate mortgages were popular when the real estate market was very hot and people were buying property to make a quick buck by **flipping**, meaning that they only held the variable rate mortgage for a short time, thus minimizing their financial risk. But if there's a downturn in the housing market and your house doesn't sell and you have a variable rate mortgage with an increasing rate, you could have a big problem. In addition to dealing with higher payments from rising interest rates, if you put down no or only a little money, you aren't actually paying down the debt on the house; you're mostly paying interest. If you put down $100,000 on a $500,000 house, you already own 20 percent of it. If you put down nothing, you don't own anything, and your mortgage payments will mostly be interest on the loan — you'll be buying the house at a very slow rate.

Other kinds of deregulation also spurred the growth in subprime mortgages. Key laws passed in 1986 and 1999 allowed for what's called **increased securitization**. This is pretty complicated, but the upshot is that the new laws created incentives for the finance industry to invest in mortgages by betting on the risk of the loans. These new financial tools were so complex, however, that investors couldn't accurately assess the risks of the investments they were buying.

Unfortunately, they were ultimately betting on people's ability to pay back questionable loans. When increasing numbers of Americans couldn't make their payments, the value of these securities dropped precipitously, sending many large and imprudent banks into a tailspin. A more serious crisis was averted when a big Main Street bank, Bank of America, bought a big Wall Street mortgage lender, Countrywide, bailing it out from near ruin. So there were really two pieces to the mortgage crisis: one, there were the people who took out loans they couldn't afford and the lenders who pushed and sold those loans; and two, there were banks investing in those loans in new and risky ways. Both were products of deregulation.

Many Democrats feel that the lending industry hoodwinked gullible consumers into taking out mortgages they couldn't afford. Pro-business Republicans and some Democrats stress personal responsibility and point out that if people make bad financial decisions, it's their own fault. They weren't *forced* to take out risky loans; they did it of their own free will. Most Democrats respond that it's only natural that low-income people wanted to buy a house — a staple American dream — the second it looked feasible. They argue that many just assumed a bank would not extend a risky mortgage. Before deregulation, that was a reasonable assumption.

Both Democrats and Republicans are right. Of course people

want to buy a house, of course many are ignorant when it comes to money, and of course it's fundamentally our own responsibility to read the fine print. The real question is who should assume responsibility now that the housing market has failed on the weakness of bad loans. Should we force the lending agencies to be less harsh? Should we freeze interest rates so fewer people lose property? Are the other effects of freezing interest rates too detrimental to the economy? Should we let banks operate independently?

To mitigate the crisis and to attempt to thwart a recession, the Fed slashed *two* key interest rates by 1.25 points in late 2007 and early 2008, hoping to keep more people out of foreclosure and stimulate the economy by encouraging people to borrow — and spend — money. Though many say that the Fed sets interest rates, it only has the power to directly dictate the **discount rate**, which is what the Fed charges a member bank (very stable banks that are chartered with the Fed) for a short-term loan backed by government securities. The **benchmark rate**, against which other rates are set by banks and lending agencies, is called the **federal funds rate**, and the Fed can only **target** that number by selling or buying government securities called **Treasury bills**. This is **open market operations**, the way the Fed influences the money supply by either taking some out or putting more into circulation. The Fed can also print money to accomplish the same goal.

Some blame the Fed for the mortgage meltdown. In the 1990s, chair **Alan Greenspan** kept interest rates low to make borrowing easy and thereby encourage investment. Those low interest rates were thought to inflate and then explode the Internet bubble — to overvalue the stock market and then cause it to contract quickly. Many stockholders lost lots of money in 2000–1 from this economic turnaround. But the overall economy stayed afloat, partly because the housing market soared. What people lost in stock, they made up in the rising value of their homes. And houses gained value partly because money was *still* easy to come by — deregulated banks let most anyone take out a mortgage, and low interest rates made buying a house relatively cheap. The increased demand, however, inflated prices.

A common by-product of low interest rates is **inflation**, a measure of how much the value of money depreciates due to higher prices. Economists determine inflation by measuring the prices of various goods and services in the **consumer price index**. High levels of inflation are bad for business because mounting prices make predicting future costs difficult and because dropping values of money inherently decrease one's purchasing power. US inflation averaged around 2 percent a year in the 1990s and the first decade of the new century. So, say you left a dollar in a pair of jeans buried in your closet in 2005. A year later, you find the dollar. Technically, that dollar is worth only about ninety-eight cents, because everything in 2006 was, on average, about 2 percent more expensive than in 2005.

Interest rates and inflation bring up other issues, too, that spill beyond our domestic shores. But to explain this, we need to get into fiscal policy, or how the government taxes and spends. **Major tax reform** occurred under Republican president **George W. Bush**, who cut several different taxes in 2001. Though they were popular, politicians and economists debated the tax cuts' effects. Some were convinced that the cuts were reckless; others were certain they stimulated the economy. Part of the debate stems from the fact that all tax cuts are not created equal: tax cuts for the middle class have different effects from those for the wealthy, and the short-term and long-term effects of tax cuts — or tax hikes — can vary greatly. First, let's examine what the tax cuts were, and then look at their results.

The tax cuts that helped low- and middle-income citizens included the establishment of a 10 percent bracket, an increase in the child care tax credit, the elimination of the so-called marriage penalty, and a mitigation of the alternative minimum tax. Cuts on dividend taxes, capital gains, and the estate tax mostly benefited the wealthy, but also upper-middle-class and some middle-class citizens.

Congressional Democrats supported the first group of cuts, while most opposed the second. Republicans generally favored all the cuts. Though Republicans would have liked to make the cuts "permanent," they couldn't because congressional rules force them to offset at least part of any loss in revenue caused by a tax cut. Congressional Republicans therefore had to squeeze tax cuts under a certain monetary cap and within a given time frame, so they set most of the 2001 tax cuts to expire in 2010 or 2011. Plus, there's no such thing as a truly permanent tax cut because Congress can always pass a new law nullifying or changing old ones. Making tax cuts "permanent" really means making them into standing law that won't automatically expire at a given time.

The lowest income tax rate before the tax cuts appropriated 15 percent of a family's income. The cut lowered the rate to 10 percent for low-income families, called the **10 percent bracket**. The child care credit was raised from $400 to $1,000, but only for middle-income families. The **marriage penalty**, which varies by year, can affect a surprising number of Americans; in up to 43 percent of married couples, each individual pays more income tax once married than they would have if they were single and filed their income tax returns separately. The problem occurs when two people who make about the same amount of money start filing joint tax returns — it doesn't affect couples with disparate incomes. The average extra cost for the marriage penalty was about $1,400 in 2000. The 2001 tax cuts mitigated its effect for lower-income couples, while the 2003 tax cuts and subsequent extensions eliminated the marriage penalty through 2010. The marriage penalty is heartily opposed by both Democrats and Republicans since it's clearly unfair.

The **alternative minimum tax** was created in the 1980s when it was revealed that many people didn't pay any income tax even though they were making significant amounts of money — for example, those with high deductions from medical expenses or real estate losses. The law stated that people who made over $200,000 but who wouldn't pay any income tax under existing regulations would instead pay the alternative minimum tax. The law, however, wasn't pegged to inflation, so it's begun affecting millions of people that it was never meant to tax.

Capital gains taxes take a percentage of the money made from selling assets, including real estate, stocks, and bonds. Capital gains taxes are a disincentive to sell these assets and make money, so they have always been serious bugaboos for the wealthy. Now that **over half** of all Americans own stocks and bonds, more of us are concerned about capital gains and **dividend taxes**, applied to the periodic profit-based payments from stocks and bonds. The common liberal argument that capital gains and dividend taxes affect the wealthy is less true than it used to be: they now touch many middle-class households. However, they affect the wealthy *more*, and they don't involve low-income individuals.

The tax that most disparately affects the wealthy is what liberals call the **estate tax** and conservatives call the **death tax**. Among conservatives and libertarians, this tax is downright detested, but there is a group of Democrats who are very committed to maintaining it. The death/estate tax allows the government to appropriate significant portions of **estates**, or the net worth of a deceased individual. The tax may be unpopular, but it brings in a fair amount of money, so it's hard for even politicians most opposed to it to eliminate it entirely. Most years, the tax only applies to estates worth more than a certain amount, but this benchmark has been extremely variable because of a congressional rule called **pay-go**, which requires any reduction in tax revenue to be offset by reductions in spending or increases in other revenue. In 2009 the exemption was set at $3.5 million, in 2010 there's no estate tax, and in 2011 we're back to the low $1 million cap. By eradicating the death tax in 2010, Republicans were able to say they eliminated the death tax; but because they had to pay for it, the numbers changed by the year.

The underlying ideologies of the estate/death tax divide are pretty interesting and illustrate one of the few really neat rifts in the worldview between conservatives and liberals. Conservatives and libertarians have made the death tax one of their pet issues because they feel that it's an absolute, unmitigated violation of property rights that flies in the face of the American dream. Their reasoning goes something like this: If you work hard, you can do well financially, and a main reason to do that is to provide for your family and friends. The government, therefore, should not take your property when you die. Further, they say the tax is a violation of individual liberty because it allows the government to usurp an individual's own wishes as to the disbursement of his or her property. Many contend that the death tax is a *disincentive* to work hard, earn money, and get ahead. What's the point if you don't get to pass on the fruit of your labor?

Fascinatingly, liberals make exactly the opposite argument about incentives. They feel that eliminating the estate tax is a disincentive to achievement because it encourages heirs not to work hard, since they stand to inherit lots of money from their wealthy families. This is a classic difference between conservatives and liberals: conservatives often focus on the interests of the individual, while liberals tend to want to further the interests of society in general.

Another argument against the estate tax that particularly rankles many Democrats is the claim that it taxes money twice, or is a form of **double taxation**. Double taxation, estate tax advocates point out, happens all the time. For instance, income is taxed on both a federal and a state level (except in a few states like Texas), plus we pay sales tax, yet another form of double taxation. Furthermore, many of the wealthiest Americans, who have inherited stakes in family companies, have never paid taxes on large portions of their wealth because it has never been converted into capital gains or income.

Finally, because the estate tax brings in significant revenue, most proposals to end it include a provision to change the basis of taxation from a stepped-up basis, what we currently have, to a **carryover basis** — which few supporters of eliminating the death tax know. Here's how it would work: You inherit a house from your grandmother. Grandma bought it in 1940 before the area developed, and she paid $25,000. When she passed away in 1995 the house was valued at $800,000, but because of a housing boom, it's now worth

$1,000,000. You're never going to go live there, so you decide to sell the house. Under a stepped-up basis, you'd owe capital gains tax on $200,000 — the amount the house gained in value while you owned it — if you sold the house now. Under a carryover basis, you would pay capital gains not on what the house was worth when you inherited it, but on what it was worth when your grandmother acquired it. So you wouldn't pay capital gains on $200,000, but on $975,000! And that would only work if you knew how much Grandma paid in the first place. What if there were no records? How would you value the house in 1940? Are there historical real estate agents? The impracticality of carryover is one reason these plans have never made it very far in Congress.

All that explains what some of the tax cuts were — but what did they *do*? For one thing, the tax cuts did not affect all Americans equally. By many measures, the prime beneficiaries of the cuts were the wealthy: the somewhat left-leaning Brookings Institution estimated that the top 10 percent of earners received 81.8 percent of the benefit from the cuts on investment taxes such as capital gains.[2] While the tax cuts increased everyone's available income, the greatest percentage change by 2005 was seen in the income of those in the top 1 percent, earning over $1.2 million a year. This group's income went up 7.6 percent; the lowest income group had an income increase of only 1.6 percent from the tax cuts. Democrats think this is unfair and counterproductive; Republicans believe it's just and ultimately best for the economy.

To lift the economy, money from tax cuts has to be spent. Low-income families usually spend the money they get back from tax cuts. The wealthy tend to save that money: they have enough to buy what they want and need anyway. Since half of the dollars given back by Bush's tax cuts went to the wealthiest 1 percent of Americans, a significant portion of the cuts would not be expected to stimulate the economy in the short term. They would have encouraged savings. And since the wealthy usually invest their savings in stocks, bonds, and other financial funds, the tax cuts probably stimulated the finance industry.

Many Republicans would argue that's fundamentally good for the economy.

Republicans reasoned that cutting taxes on the wealthy helped the economy so much that the Bush cuts paid for themselves. However, even conservative institutions like the *Wall Street Journal* disagreed, indicating that their benefit to the economy was less than their cost in lost federal revenue.[3]

Most Republicans think that taxes in general are bad. Small-government Republicans believe taxes only encourage a bloated bureaucracy; they think that more socialized governments are less free and are concerned with the political — not just economic — implications of taxation. A different strand of conservative thought shuns taxes as a fetter to the free market, which will do best and produce most with the least regulation. They are sometimes derisively called **market fundamentalists**, since they believe in the power of the market to right all wrongs.

Two important conservative groups that focus on taxation are the **Club for Growth** and **Americans for Tax Reform**, the latter headed by staunch small-government Republican **Grover Norquist**. There is a group of moderate Democrats that also support limiting taxation, especially on corporations. They were powerful under President Bill Clinton and have ties to the **Democratic Leadership Council**, or **DLC**. Libertarians also oppose almost all taxes, and the Libertarian Party has supported the **flat tax**, a single tax rate that would apply to all Americans equally. The flat tax was the center of publishing heir **Steve Forbes**'s presidential bids in 1996 and 2000. Democrats counter that the flat tax is **regressive**: the effective rate *decreases* as the amount of money to which the tax is applied increases. Income taxes, by contrast, are **progressive**: the rate *increases* as the amount of money to which the tax applies increases. The idea behind progressive tax rates is that the more disposable income you have, the more you can afford to give to the government.

Conservative economics had its heyday under Republican president **Ronald Reagan**, when **supply-side economics** came to the fore. Supply-side and trickle-down economics are different, but both are usually conflated into the term **Reaganomics**. Supply-side economics focuses on cutting **marginal tax rates** — the tax rate per dollar of extra income earned — in order to create incentives for people to work efficiently and effectively. The argument is that marginal tax rates that increase as people earn more deter people from working harder, and instead encourage them to do things that will reduce their tax burden, such as taking paper losses on depreciating investments. Supply-siders think this is counterproductive because such taxes effectively discourage people from adding value to the economy. They assume that reducing taxes encourages economic activity, spurring growth, thus increasing tax revenues. Supply-side economics had some support from economists, but its real champions were politicians, pundits, and conservative commentators.

Trickle-down economics posits that money at the top of the fiscal food chain drips down to the lower levels: the rich spend, creating a livelihood for others. Trickle-down economics supporters therefore think that taxes on corporations and wealthy individuals should be lowered because the wealthy spend more and invest more in new enterprises that grow the economy. Trickle-down economics, however, is basically a pejorative term.

Some of the Republican skepticism toward taxes stems from a sense that **taxes are unfair** because the rich pay more than the poor. In absolute terms that's true. By some assessments, the top 1 percent of earners pay almost 40 percent of all federal income tax revenues.[4] But in relative terms — measured by percentage of income — the rich don't pay more. Democrats counter that those who make more and have more should contribute more: they focus on the relative figures rather than on absolute numbers. Furthermore, Democrats aren't ideologically opposed to taxation in the same way that most Republicans are.

Liberals think **taxes are justifiable** for three main reasons: One, taxes pay for the infrastructure, legal system, educational resources, and economic opportunities that allow people to make a lot of money in the first place. Second, providing for social programs and safety nets raises the overall standard of living, allowing for more productive employees, a larger number of active consumers, greater entrepreneurship, and a more dynamic economy overall. Finally, many really do believe in giving back through their taxes — having done well in life, they feel that it is their moral obligation to help others. Underlying this is a belief that the **government can fix problems**. Many Republicans believe in giving back, too; they just think we should do so privately. Perhaps the most influential such Republican is **Marvin Olaskey**, who coined the term **compassionate conservatism**. His view is that it's important to take care of the socially disadvantaged, but that private, preferably faith-based organizations should do this rather than the government.

The last piece of this taxing puzzle is debt and deficits, because cutting taxes can affect how much revenue the country brings in. A **federal deficit** occurs when the government spends more than it brings in. When federal income is greater than spending, there is a **surplus**. The **national debt** is an aggregate measure of all the government's accumulated debt, including the interest owed on borrowed money. In 1998–2001 there was a surplus — one of the reasons the Bush administration thought the nation could afford to cut taxes. In 2007 the deficit totaled $163 billion, the lowest deficit since 2002. However, if you factor in what we borrowed from Social Security (which the White House did not), that figure was more like $350 billion. Republicans credited the 2001 tax cuts with the improvement, since corporate taxes brought in significantly more money in 2007 than 2006 and spending didn't increase much that year. Democrats countered that the tax cuts in 2001 were what brought back the deficit in the first place. In 2007 the gross national debt was over $9 trillion.

Deficit spending began during the Great Depression under Democratic president **Franklin Delano Roosevelt**, who involved the government in financial matters to an unprecedented degree. Roosevelt's **New Deal economics** was essentially **Keynesian**, based on the theories of British economist John Maynard Keynes. Keynes believed that during times of economic downturn the government should take an activist position and pump money into the economy, for example, by funding public works. If cash wasn't available, Keynes advocated borrowing money to spend, known as **deficit spending**. At the time, deficit spending was considered extremely liberal and was a major break from prevailing economic theories. Because America's first deficit spending began during the New Deal, both government economic intervention and deficit spending came to be associated with Democrats. Now, however, Republicans support deficit spending more than do Democrats, though everyone accepts the basic Keynesian position.

Today, deficits exist because we aren't willing to tax at the rate we spend. And our spending is a little unintuitive. It isn't discretionary items like the Iraq War that are the biggest spending culprit — though they contribute — but the government's rising fixed costs for entitlement programs like Social Security and Medicare. **Discretionary spending** accounts for about one-third of the federal government's overall outlay and includes money for defense, parks, schools, highways, and other national priorities. **Mandatory** spending pays for Medicare, Medicaid, S-Chip, and Social Security. These programs are called **entitlements** because all Americans are entitled to them if they qualify. Two-thirds of the federal budget used to go toward discretionary spending and one-third to mandatory spending, but over time that **pattern reversed** and now almost two-thirds of federal dollars are spent on mandatory programs.

One reason we're spending more is the **higher number of benefit recipients**, a demographic issue about which the government has been remarkably shortsighted, though various experts have been worrying about it for years. **Baby boomers**, the huge generation of Americans born from 1946 to 1964, helped buoy the economy by creating a large, able workforce when they were young, but now that they are retiring, around 80 million of them will be eligible for benefits from Social Security and Medicare over the next twenty years, creating a drain on the nation's coffers.

Social Security is funded by **payroll taxes**, those deducted automatically from one's paycheck. The catch with Social Security is that the funds paid in by each person don't sit there waiting to be redeemed at the time of an individual's retirement — they pay for current retirees' benefits. The system doesn't correct for demographic shifts. If the number of workers stays the same or declines relative to the number who reach retirement, as is the case now, Social Security is in a pinch. When the program started, there were around fifteen workers for every retiree; by 2025 or so, that number will have dropped to something like two workers for every retiree. What's troubling is that everyone in government *knows* about this (or they should) — they just haven't *done* anything about it.

Because Social Security has money coming in all the time, it's like a rich uncle in a poor family — everyone's always asking it for loans. Here's how it works: The Treasury's general fund borrows from the Social Security trust fund. They then physically deposit certificates that record the amount the general fund owes Social Security in a bank vault. These certificates are backed by the **full faith and credit** of the United States, but at the end of the day, they are nothing more than certificates. They are a promise, but one that is unsecured, and therefore easily broken. This is exactly what many fiscal conservatives fear: that Social Security is effectively being robbed to pay for other expenditures.

Borrowing from Social Security accounts for the difference between radically different deficit numbers cited by various sources. People who want to downplay the deficit tend not to include the amount we owe Social Security. However, unless they don't plan on paying back that money, and instead aim to renege on already paid-for benefits, then citing the lower figure is pretty misleading. Always be suspicious of deficit numbers quoted by any politician who has an interest in making the economy look good.

Medicare is the eight-hundred-pound gorilla in the budget, because the cost of Medicare has gone through the roof. While the baby boom generation requires big payouts because of their sheer numbers, Medicare's larger problem is the ballooning **cost of health care**. Driven by many factors, including marketing, research, and increased use of expensive technology, health care costs have risen precipitously over the past few decades. Controlling health care costs is going to be key to dealing with the country's finances.

Given demographic pressures, increasing costs, and inadequate revenue, the federal deficit rose to unprecedented levels in the first decade of the twenty-first century. There has been a big debate over deficits, with many Republicans claiming **deficits don't matter** and many Democrats concerned that not only do they matter, **deficits are too high**.

There are two camps of Republicans who regard deficits with nonchalance. Supply-siders reason that deficits resulting from tax cuts don't matter because tax cuts will spur economic growth, ultimately paying for themselves. Others, mostly political strategists, think deficits are a good thing because they force the government to cut services in order to lower the debt — thus enforcing a smaller government. These positions are actually in opposition. If tax cuts pay for themselves, there's enough money for services; if spending has to be cut, tax cuts aren't raking in money. The only way around this ideological stalemate would be the following scenario: You cut taxes, expecting the economy to run up a big deficit in a few years but then rebound and make all that money back soon thereafter. In the intervening time, you cut services, thus lowering expectations about what government will provide.

Those who don't worry about deficits always mention **Reagan's 1981 tax cuts**, which drove deficits to then record highs. The economy subsequently did very well, and both Republicans and Democrats use this as evidence that deficit spending can help kick-start growth. Others say this assessment is overly simplistic. For one, Reagan's tax cuts were followed by tax *hikes* in the late 1980s and early

'90s. Though supply-siders were convinced this would hurt the economy, it didn't — a period of high growth followed. In addition, at the time, Social Security was running a big surplus that we weren't borrowing from.

The argument that deficits are acceptable rests on the notion that the money borrowed is invested in order to grow the economy. It's the same idea as taking a loan for business school. Sure, it's expensive, but you'll be able to repay the loan in a year or two of employment — and you probably wouldn't be able to make as much money without the business degree. However, many worry that our deficit spending isn't going toward good investments. As long as we keep making more money, modest deficits don't matter. It makes sense: it's okay if you charge an extra $200 on your credit card every month if your salary rises by at least that amount. The problem is that the economy doesn't always grow, and if it takes a turn for the worse, deficits and accumulated debt can prove to be a very big problem. This is why deficits tend to be related to GDP: If the debt doesn't grow faster than GDP, we're okay, because the country is producing more and eventually can be expected to pay everything back. If debt outpaces GDP, however, most agree there's cause for worry. Be aware, however, that some argue that even extremely high deficits aren't necessarily a problem.

One of the main arguments against high deficits and debt is that they **crowd out** other forms of investment. In other words, government borrowing makes it difficult for others to invest because it raises interest rates. You can keep this from happening by printing more money so more cash is available for more people to invest, but this lowers the value of the dollar and feeds inflation. President Clinton's secretary of the treasury **Robert Rubin** is one of the nation's biggest **deficit hawks** — those who want to minimize deficits and debt — and he often invokes crowding out as a serious danger. In the 1980s deficit hawks were usually Republicans, but now most are Democrats. That may really have to do with who is in power at any given time: it's in the majority party's interest to spend money, and it's in the minority's to criticize them for it.

To make up the deficits in our national budget, we borrow money from other countries. **Japan** is the biggest holder of American debt. We owe the Japanese about $600 billion. **China** is second with about $300 billion, followed by the **United Kingdom** at $200 billion. The fact that we are debtors to these nations can be a decisive factor in foreign and monetary policy. By holding American debt, lender countries inherently have some control over our economy. Which gets us right back to where we started — interest rates.

Lowering interest rates is not good for our relationships with all the countries we borrow from. Why? Lowering interest rates makes the debt we owe worth less. It also lowers the **value of the dollar** relative to other currencies. Interest, after all, is a kind of rent. You want to park your money in a high-rent neighborhood because you want to make as much off it as possible, right? Lowering interest rates also injects more cash into the system — and increased supply lowers the value of the dollar.

If dollars aren't worth much, then you might not want to have any at all. You would rather hold a high-value currency than a low-value one. Let's say you are a banker at the government bank in China. If the dollar is low against the euro, and the pound is high against the euro, and you have a million yuan in cash to invest, you probably would prefer to take that money in pounds, because pounds are worth more than anything else. They can buy more goods, and the rent on them is higher — you can make more money loaning out a pound than you can loaning out a dollar. But you're a *Chinese* central banker. You hold lots and lots of dollars already because your government has loaned hundreds of billions of dollars to the United States. We aren't going to pay you back in euros or pounds. If our currency is weak, or if interest rates are low, it's not an attractive investment. Thus, lowering interest rates devalues the price of debt — making others less likely to want to hold it.

Being a debtor nation makes it harder for us to make monetary policies independently. Lower the interest rate to inject cash into the economy? Sure, but you also lower the value of your debt, which will annoy Japan, China, and Britain. And if you push them too far, they just might call in their loans. That would be a real disaster because we'd owe them a lot of money, fast. Plus, when people get rid of dollars, they increase the supply of dollars on the world market, which drives down the price even further. All this sounds dire simply because we haven't looked at the upside of a weak dollar, and there is one: **exports**. When the dollar is low, other countries are more likely to buy our products because they're cheap. A low dollar can also stimulate the domestic economy because it makes imports more expensive. In an economic downturn, you might not buy as many Italian olives and eat Virginia peanuts instead. And that's good for American peanut farmers.

The lurking beast in this discussion is oil, as it is in many American political discussions, but oil is a particularly dangerous beast around monetary policy. Here's the key: **oil is denominated in US dollars**. No matter where you are in the world, oil is tied to the greenback. Americans have been lucky: we have to deal with the fluctuating cost of oil, but not with any *currency* fluctuations in oil. A weak dollar, though, also means that oil is relatively cheap for others — and when it's cheaper, other countries buy more, decreasing supply and driving up prices. Many economists and oil industry executives think this is exactly what happened in the first decade of the twenty-first century. Concerned by the weak dollar, oil-producing nations have been selling our currency right and left, holding reserves in euros and pounds instead.

If oil were suddenly denominated in euros — and this is a real possibility — we would be paying not just for oil, but for the value of the euro, too. Those consequences could be huge. In 2001, for example, a euro was worth only about 84 cents. By 2007 it was worth around $1.45. If oil were priced in euros, its cost would have doubled for

Americans in seven years *just in currency costs*. The real price of oil has already doubled, so that means the overall price would have quadrupled.

Russia and Iran have both been trying to denominate oil differently. That wouldn't be a problem except that Russia and Iran have huge oil and gas reserves, so they have the power to influence this kind of policy. Russia began denominating contracts in rubles in 2007, while since 2005, Iran has planned to open an oil market, the **Iranian Oil Bourse**, or **IOB**, denominated in euros. Some speculate that this move is what really spurred recent standoffs between America and Iran, not arguments over nuclear weapons or sanctions.

In sum, every monetary action has complex, even unpredictable, results. Democrats and Republicans, as well as economists, frequently disagree about the consequences of measures like tax cuts and interest rate changes. They disagree on deficits and debt, too. Most agree, however, that the nation faces some serious economic challenges. It's possible that the most important questions we could ask our politicians are economic: How do they plan to keep oil denominated in dollars? What should we do about inflation? How do we deal with China when we owe them $300 billion? Who should chair the Fed? Basically, we should ask our politicians at what temperature we should set our economic oven — and if they can't stand the heat, they definitely shouldn't be in the nation's kitchen.

3

Foreign Policy

➤ Though the United States was originally isolationist, there has been a steady trend toward international intervention. Isolationism is no longer thought practical by politicians and scholars, but there is some support for it among the general public.

➤ Liberal internationalism and realism are two important schools of foreign policy that developed after World War II, as America's global influence increased.

➤ Many Americans' views on war and foreign policy are shaped by World War II and/or the Vietnam War, which is now widely considered to have been a political and military failure.

➤ The first President Bush waged the first Gulf War against Iraq in 1991, but did not depose Saddam Hussein in the interest of maintaining regional security.

➤ The United States successfully ousted the Taliban regime in Afghanistan in 2001, but a more recent Taliban resurgence has eroded that victory.

➤ President George W. Bush cited three reasons for invading Iraq in 2003: to stop Saddam Hussein from using weapons of mass destruction (WMDs), to prevent him from supporting international terrorism, and to liberate oppressed Iraqis.

➤ There were no WMDs in Iraq nor any substantial links to international terrorism.

➤ Why we invaded Iraq is hotly debated; most agree intelligence failures are partly to blame.

➤ Some of the general public, most of the international community, and many top military and intelligence officials objected to plans to invade Iraq.

➤ Congress and the media helped convince the public that we should invade Iraq.

➤ Neoconservatives believe the United States should proactively support democracy abroad, by force if necessary; they were the core supporters of the 2003 Iraq War.

➤ The situation in Iraq deteriorated into a violent internal conflict, which some call a civil war.

➤ The Israeli/Palestinian conflict is perhaps the world's most intractable dilemma; its persistence has damaged and complicated the US position in the Middle East.

➤ There is a growing debate over how much of a threat Iran poses to US security.

➤ Some think that our relationships with Russia, India, Pakistan, China, and North Korea are ultimately more important to US interests than the conflict in the Middle East.

Background to Current Debates

Foreign policy is hugely contentious and exceptionally complicated: America deals with many multilayered international issues, for which there is a rich theoretical and ethical literature, and we have a long history of international engagement all over the world. A true history of American foreign policy would make this book a thirty-volume tome; merely unraveling the different missions of the State Department, CIA, and NSA would fill a thousand pages.

Instead, I'm going to present enough information to help you untangle the basic current politics behind American foreign policy. It's important to understand the interest groups involved in foreign policy and their often powerful ideological foundations. It's vital to know something about the specific issues most debated in the Iraq War: the justifications for the invasion, why there was an insurgency, and what America's future course should be. Though I'm not going to go very far into the issues we face concerning other nations such as Israel, Iran, Russia, Pakistan, India, China, and North Korea, it's also important to be aware of the status of American foreign policy — or lack thereof — toward these countries.

Isolationism and **interventionism** are the two extremes on the continuum of international engagement. While early American foreign policy was very isolationist, there has been a discontinuous but clear trend toward intervention throughout our history. The United States began as an international endeavor. Without French military support and Dutch loans, American revolutionaries might never have been able to fight a viable insurrection against England. George Washington himself, however, cautioned against **entangling alliances** in his farewell address in 1796. He thought the young republic should stay out of foreign affairs.

Washington's admonition set the tone of American foreign policy for the next century. The United States stayed out of Europe's Napoleonic wars and only reluctantly went to war with England again in 1812 — and even then, all the fighting was in North America. Throughout the 1800s the United States focused on expanding westward. War with Mexico in 1848 won California and the Southwest; a series of increasingly brutal Indian wars decimated, removed, and eventually isolated Native American populations throughout US territory, allowing European American populations to settle from sea to shining sea. And those seas cannot be underestimated: it was America's *geographic* isolation from Europe and Asia that allowed the policy of isolationism to exist.

From 1823 the **Monroe Doctrine** shaped American foreign policy, and its ideological power was profound — and lasting. Issued by the administration of President James Monroe, the doctrine followed Washington's vision of a neutral national stance, free from major involvement in other nations' foreign or domestic policy. But it also warned Europe not to interfere in New World affairs. In 1898 the United States invoked the doctrine against Spain, which was accused of oppressing Cuba, one of Spain's last remaining colonies. American expansionist zeal and an alleged Spanish attack on the USS *Maine* in Havana harbor led to the Spanish-American War. Winning a swift victory, the United States gained some of its first overseas possessions: Cuba, Puerto Rico, and the Philippines. This sudden change in America's global position — combined with an emerging naval power and what was already one of the world's largest economies — necessitated a new approach to foreign policy.

In 1901 Theodore "Teddy" Roosevelt, the first president to envision the United States as an active world power, became president. His **Roosevelt Corollary** to the Monroe Doctrine set the stage for greater American intervention in foreign affairs — not the colonial European brand, but a uniquely American form that would focus on propping up friendly governments, and if necessary "liberating" allied nations. Roosevelt asserted American authority in Latin America and the Caribbean, threatening military action against any outside intrusion into the Western Hemisphere.

Roosevelt also developed a strong dislike of colonial administration and what we would call "nation building" today. Like many of his era, Roosevelt embraced a central tenet of imperialism — that Western rule would somehow uplift less developed countries. Yet he and many Americans came to believe that such efforts were not worth the costs in American lives and resources. He engineered a speedy end to the occupation of Cuba, handing off the country to a sovereign (but friendly) regime. In the Philippines a violent insurgency erupted; Roosevelt advocated withdrawal, but was criticized for the excesses of the US counterinsurgency, which included charges that American soldiers committed torture and killed civilians. Remarkably, a century ago, America was debating problems very similar to those we discuss today.

Roosevelt's maxim "Speak softly and carry a big stick," referring to diplomacy coupled with strong defense, summed up an extremely successful strategy. During his tenure, Roosevelt deftly avoided war with Germany, helped negotiate an end to the Russo-Japanese War, and set the tone for contemporary American foreign policy. His successor President William Howard Taft's **dollar diplomacy** attempted to promote stability abroad as a means to economic development at home — another crucial precedent, as much contemporary American foreign policy focuses on either creating or protecting economic opportunities for both domestic and foreign economies.

American foreign policy underwent another major reformulation under President **Woodrow Wilson** (1913–21). Wilson initially took an isolationist stance toward World War I, but after a series of German threats to ships in the North Atlantic, he urged the nation to war. This was a watershed moment in US foreign policy: after 130 years of refusing to get involved in Europe's wars, Yanks were crossing the pond. Authoritarian Germans and Austrians were fighting democratic Britain and France. Wilson said we had "to make the world safe for democracy," and helped galvanize the American will to side with democratic governments.

At the close of the war, Wilson went to France to negotiate the Treaty of Versailles. His Fourteen Points plan attempted to bring America into the **League of Nations**, a new international diplomatic and peacekeeping organization that was the precursor to the **United Nations (UN)**. Wilson stressed the right of **self-determination** — that people should be able to determine their own nationhood. The **Wilsonian school** of foreign policy focused on active intervention to support democracy abroad, along with support (if not intervention) on behalf of ethnic groups seeking nationhood. This philosophy would later strongly influence liberal internationalism and neoconservatism.

While Wilson laid the foundation for contemporary American foreign policy, he faced strong opposition from isolationists during his presidency. Resurgent isolationism triumphed over a nascent internationalism when isolationists torpedoed the Treaty of Versailles in the Senate because many lawmakers erroneously assumed that the treaty stipulated that American troops would be committed automatically to any breach of the agreement. But two decades later, Adolf Hitler's rampant expansionism would force America's interventionist hand.

World War II may have been the only morally clear international engagement in American history — and whether it could have been prevented is still fiercely debated in foreign policy circles. Faced with Hitler's rabid appetite for territory, British prime minister Neville Chamberlain negotiated the **Munich Agreement**, allowing Hitler to hold part of Czechoslovakia if he agreed to halt further expansion. It didn't work — and the agreement is always offered as Exhibit A in any argument against **appeasement**. Many think the Allies should have gone to war with Hitler *before* he attacked Poland, which might have prevented the Holocaust. President Franklin Delano Roosevelt would be similarly criticized for appeasing Soviet premier Josef Stalin's Eastern European expansionism at the **Yalta Conference** in 1945. Current scholarly debates are about much more than history and hindsight: they're also about how to handle expansionist dictators today.

The near collapse of Western Europe and the ruination of Eastern Europe following the end of hostilities created an economic and political vacuum. The United States emerged as the world's leading economic power. We also became a political superpower, uncomfortably sharing that status with the communist Soviet Union. During the **postwar consensus**, conservatives, realists, and liberal internationalists all agreed that aggressive communism had to be opposed but that all-out war with the Soviets would spell nuclear cataclysm. Countering expansionist Soviets became the object of decades of

American foreign policy, drawing us into the long **Cold War**. What divided left and right then was competition over who could be tougher on communism.

Containment was the preferred strategy of checking the Soviet threat. Rather than engage the USSR directly, the United States would intervene to prevent communism from taking hold in other countries (primarily through foreign aid), containing the Soviet sphere of influence as much as possible, and balancing each communist threat with an American counterthreat. The idea of fighting through funding was key to the broader strategy: providing civilian aid for reconstruction and military aid to groups that resist communism.

The **Marshall Plan**, put into place just after World War II, exemplified American civilian aid. In just four years, the Marshall Plan injected $18 billion into Europe's devastated economy; this was essential to preventing the spread of communism, to which the poorest tend to be more amenable. By providing food and money to literally rebuild the Continent, the Marshall Plan helped bring Europe back from the brink. In the next twenty years, Europe's economy grew at unprecedented levels and standards of living increased markedly. In 1947 the **Truman Doctrine** enabled the provision of American military aid to resist communism in Greece and Turkey. Many even date the beginning of the Cold War to the announcement of the Truman Doctrine because its pattern of aid was so fundamental to America's Cold War strategy. Containment also entailed **trade embargoes** and other **economic sanctions** — tools still used today — against communist nations.

A slightly more controversial notion was the **domino theory**, the idea that if one country in a region fell to communism, its neighbors would follow. The domino theory stated that America had to intervene, with force if necessary, to prevent any nation from becoming communist — and **Vietnam** was its prime application. Even the Vietnam War's once fiercest advocates, including its main architect, then secretary of defense **Robert McNamara**, now think it was a mistake. Essentially, US officials misunderstood the nature of the conflict: it was a civil war that had little to do with international communism and posed little, if any, threat to America or to international stability. It became a strategic and tactical quagmire (**strategy** in military terms refers to an overarching plan to attain goals, and **tactics** to the procedures and processes undertaken to implement a strategy).

Many aspects of Vietnam resonate today, especially for liberals. The conflict escalated under false pretenses: President Lyndon Baines Johnson's administration used a dubious naval incident to justify the **Gulf of Tonkin Resolution**, in which Congress gave Johnson the power to fight without a formal declaration of war. Americans were repeatedly told that US forces were winning, but the situation grew worse, with more and more fatalities. Ultimately nearly sixty thousand Americans died. McNamara and Johnson responded by sending more troops, then bombing, but no all-out land assault was ever ordered. A growing peace movement on the left strongly opposed the war and was further angered when President Richard Nixon's administration widened the conflict by bombing neighboring Cambodia. The lack of an **exit strategy** led to a messy withdrawal and loss of American prestige, and the postwar consensus was shattered. Unsurprisingly, then, a great fear of repeating the mistakes made in Vietnam continues to inform many Americans' views on foreign policy.

The Ideological Groups

Foreign policy is informed by ideologies that don't necessarily adhere to clear party lines, so it's necessary to understand something about the main camps that have fought for political control in the past century, including isolationists, paleocons, liberal internationalists, realists, liberal hawks, and neocons. Keep in mind that there are divisions within each group; for example, one ideological group may agree on outcomes but disagree on causes. But even these differences are important, because how you diagnose a problem informs how you propose to solve it.

Isolationists once dominated American foreign policy, but these days the only politicians who routinely preach this internally oriented stance are usually considered cranks, mostly because their ideology seems outdated. The United States is too big, too powerful, and already has its finger in too many foreign pies for old-school isolationism to be tenable. As conservative pundit Charles Krauthammer put it: "Classical isolationism is not just intellectually obsolete; it is politically bankrupt . . . its most public advocate, **Pat Buchanan**, ran for president of the United States, and carried Palm Beach. By accident."[1] The strongest isolationists these days are libertarians such as Republican Texas congressman **Ron Paul** and left-wing **pacifists** like Democratic congressman **Dennis Kucinich** of Ohio.

Isolationism began a long slide into political irrelevance during World War II. Isolationist sentiment was blamed for America's failure to neutralize Hitler sooner, and America's postwar dominance demanded a major evolution in foreign policy. The two main camps that arose after the war were liberal internationalists and paleoconservatives, who are currently rare and politically weak. Most liberal internationalists were Democrats, while most paleoconservatives were Republicans.

Paleoconservatives, often called **paleocons**, began as anticommunist interventionists — they approved of American intervention to undermine authoritarian regimes. Paleocons believe in democracy and limited government, and the necessity of promoting these values abroad. Their important institutions were mainly magazines, especially the *American Conservative*. The group is perhaps best represented by Republican president Dwight D. Eisenhower. As commander of the Allied forces in Europe, Eisenhower was no stranger to violent conflict, but nonetheless was a small-government conservative remembered in foreign policy circles for his farewell speech in 1961.

In it, Eisenhower identified core conservative tenets, stating that America's "basic purposes" were "to keep the peace; to foster progress in human achievement, and to enhance liberty, dignity and integrity among people and among nations." But Eisenhower worried about tactics as well as strategy, warning Americans to be humble, yet willing to fight: "Any failure traceable to arrogance, or our lack of comprehension or readiness to sacrifice, would inflict upon us grievous hurt both at home and abroad."

What most remember from the speech, however, was Eisenhower's warning about the **military–industrial complex**, the new American arms industry that emerged during World War II. Like many, Eisenhower knew that war would always be in the arms industry's interest, and that it had to be carefully controlled: "We must not fail to comprehend its grave implications. . . . Our toil, resources and livelihood are all involved; so is the very structure of our society. In the councils of government, we must guard against the acquisition of unwarranted influence, whether sought or unsought, by the military-industrial complex. The potential for the disastrous rise of misplaced power exists and will persist."[2]

Liberal internationalists helped build major international institutions, notably the United Nations. Its supporters — including its initial architects, Presidents Franklin Delano Roosevelt and **Harry Truman** and Secretaries of State General George C. Marshall and Dean Acheson — favor international, multilateral, diplomatic solutions to issues in foreign affairs. World War II convinced liberal internationalists that nations could not prevent violent conflict on their own, and they hoped large extranational sovereign bodies might be able to deter future violence. They wanted America to be engaged overseas, but stressed that America was a member of a multinational community rather than a totally independent actor. Calling force a last resort, they believed America should first rely on diplomacy and nonmilitary action — like containment — to combat hostile powers. Liberal internationalists have differed on their willingness to use force. Some supported Vietnam, but many did not. Under Democratic president **Bill Clinton**, they appeared more hawkish, advocating military responses in Bosnia, Kosovo, and Haiti. It struck many as strange that liberal internationalists called for the violent intervention they had traditionally resisted, but the key to their support was **humanitarian intervention**.

Opponents of liberal internationalism ridicule the ideology as unrealistic. They argue that international treaties, international law, and international institutions are worse than worthless. The agreements, they think, are only as good as the participating nations' will and ability to enforce them, and they see all international agreements as ties that primarily bind the United States to others' interests. They argue that liberal internationalists approve of intervention only when American interests aren't at stake. Liberal internationalists counter that acting for a moral good outside of direct national interests ultimately *helps* these national interests because America's reputation is extremely important to our influence in the world.

Realists are primarily concerned with immediate national interests — strategic and economic rather than humanitarian interests or promoting democracy for its own sake — and stress the importance of American independence. They believe that stability is fundamentally ensured by power and that international security is best achieved through the ability of the United States to deter actions we deem unacceptable. Realists therefore support a strong military and feel Americans must be willing to intervene in international affairs; they are more likely to embrace military action than the paleocons, and oppose disarmament plans championed by liberal internationalists. They distrust or dislike international institutions such as the United Nations, considering them not only useless but dangerous for creating a false set of expectations about how foreign affairs are managed. Realists are usually Republicans, and the most famous realist was Republican secretary of state **Henry Kissinger**, who held that post under both Richard Nixon and Gerald Ford. A growing group of neoliberals and liberal hawks accept parts of the realist argument, but nonetheless maintain the importance of multilateral cooperation.

Neoconservatives, or **neocons**, rose to prominence under President George W. Bush. Though originally Democrats, neocons eventually aligned with the Republican Party. Some key early figures were Jewish intellectuals, whose personal or familial history of escaping the Nazis or Soviets left them with a strong desire to fight totalitarianism — and an understandably deep aversion to appeasement. Neocons believe the United States has a moral and practical responsibility to intervene in international matters because America is the sole great power capable of stabilizing foreign affairs. They feel we have a moral imperative to spread democracy, and they advocate a more aggressive foreign policy than do paleoconservatives. Compared to realists, neocons are more ideological, willing to fight even when immediate national interests aren't at stake.

Irving Kristol is called the neocons' godfather; he favors few taxes, small government, traditional values, an expansionist foreign policy, and **national interest** — what neocons define as America's natural affinity for nations with similar systems of government. Other important neocons include writer and pundit **Norman Podhoretz**, former deputy secretary of defense and World Bank president **Paul Wolfowitz**, and chairman of the Defense Policy Board **Richard Perle**. Their most important institution is the **Project for the New American Century**, founded in 1997 by **William Kristol**, Irving's son. Many are also affiliated with **AEI**, the **American Enterprise Institute**, a conservative Washington, DC–based think tank. Many liberals take exception to the neocons' extreme form of promoting democracy. Some disagree that all nations ought to be democratic, or think that different nations need to develop into democracies rather than have the system thrust upon them. Liberals also tend to value other nations' sovereignty more than do neocons.

In the run-up to the Iraq War another group emerged, the **liberal hawks**. Liberal hawks strongly advocate American intervention to promote American values and/or to neutralize threats against American interests. Liberal hawks may support diplomatic and multilateral efforts abroad, but they generally merge the liberal internationalist desire to create a moral universe with some aspects of realist foreign policy. Liberal hawks favored invading Iraq, and most stand by that opinion. They argued America should intervene to control terrorism and to prevent the use of WMDs, as well as to remove Saddam Hussein because he was an oppressive dictator. They have continued to cite this last reason as a sufficient justification for the invasion. Important liberal hawks include journalists **Thomas Friedman** and **Fareed Zakaria**. Scholar **Kenneth Pollack**'s book *The Threatening Storm: The Case for Invading Iraq* is the single most important statement of liberal hawks' ideology to date and helped persuade many leftist intellectuals to support the invasion.

Background to the Iraq War

The early history of American involvement in Iraq is really the history of American involvement in **Iran**. After World War II, the United States supported Iran's pro-Western dictator, the Shah, as a check on the USSR. But Iranians grew disillusioned with the Shah's increasingly heavy-handed tactics, and by the mid-1970s the country was ripe for revolution. Originally secular in nature, the revolution turned religious after the United States made a series of strategic blunders, including killing a cult leader and razing a venerated mosque.

The rhetoric of the revolution came to haunt the United States, as Iranians took to burning American flags and calling America "the Great Satan." Their anger did not diminish quickly. Iran became a state sponsor of terrorism against America's key Middle Eastern ally, Israel, and attacked American interests as well. In 1979 Iran held fifty-two American diplomats hostage for over a year. In 1983 it helped bomb an American base in Lebanon housing peacekeeping forces, killing 241 Americans — until September 11, 2001, considered the deadliest terrorist attack on Americans in history.

In 1980, Saddam Hussein started the Iran-Iraq War; given the state of US relations with Iran, America aligned with Hussein, providing him with both military and monetary aid. It was a decision that would come back to bite us. It wasn't our first involvement with Hussein, however: throughout the 1970s, the United States, the United Kingdom, Italy, France, and Germany all helped Iraq build nuclear capability and chemical and biological weapons. Hussein used chemical weapons against Iran beginning in 1983. Though there was an international outcry over it, the US and the UK blocked a UN Security Council condemnation of the action. At **Halabjah** in 1988, Hussein killed thousands within Iraq with mustard and nerve gas. Hussein's willingness — not just ability — to use unconventional weapons worried the international community for decades.

By 1990, Hussein, financially and politically crippled from nearly a decade of brutal war, looked over the ill-defended border to Kuwait's lucrative oil fields — some of the biggest, most productive, and most efficient in the world. The temptation was too great, and Hussein invaded the tiny Gulf country. Developed nations were horrified, because any disruption in oil supply has a profound effect on the world economy. Hussein's invasion could raise prices by adding to uncertainty costs and lowering production — and if Hussein controlled a larger percentage of the world's oil, he'd be able to affect prices by removing it from the market. Many worried that Saudi Arabia, with the biggest oil fields of all, would be his next target. Many were also concerned about Hussein, period. Characterized by some as a dangerous madman, and by others as a highly rational sociopath, it would be difficult to overstate just how awful Hussein was. He once had his entire cabinet murdered at a meeting. The United States decided to punch back — Kuwait's small military could never have fought off the large, well-trained, battle-hardened Iraqi army.

Republican president **George H. W. Bush**'s administration gathered widespread international support and UN approval through an all-out diplomatic campaign and argued the case for war based on the inherent threat posed to developed economies as well as to the Gulf region. Bush built a domestic coalition of liberal internationalists, paleocons, neocons, and realists in the process. Public approval of the war approached 90 percent; the only opposition came from isolationists and pacifists. Bush launched **Operation Desert Shield** to defend Saudi Arabia and **Operation Desert Storm** to liberate Kuwait. Collectively these operations are known as the **First Gulf War**. Using bombers and cruise missiles to attack Hussein's military and infrastructure from the air, they quickly drove Hussein back into Iraq. But the administration went no further; officials decided not to depose Hussein, fearing it would destabilize the region and instigate civil war in Iraq or even a major regional conflict.

Though Hussein was thoroughly despicable, the Bush administration was concerned that getting rid of him was more dangerous than allowing him to stay in charge. Hussein had not allowed anybody else to gain real power within his government. With no clear successors, an Iraq suddenly Hussein-less would be a power vacuum — and a magnet for conflict. The biggest worry was **Iran**. Large, relatively developed, and ruled by a theocratic government controlled partly by Shiite religious officials, **ayatollahs**, Iran's history with Iraq combined with its heady Islamic revolutionary rhetoric made it a menacing neighbor. Iran's and Iraq's demographics further the potential instability: while Iran is ethnically and religiously quite uniform, Iraq is not; it's made up of Sunnis, Shiites, and Kurds. Sunnis and Shiites represent two ancient branches of Islam. When Islam's leader, the prophet Muhammad, died in AD 632, there was a bitter dispute over who should succeed him. **Sunnis** thought the leader ought to be elected, while **Shiites** felt any leader should be a relative of the prophet's. They've been fighting about it ever since.

Iran's population is nearly twice that of Iraq, and nearly 90 percent of Iranians are Shiite, while Iraq is about 60 percent Shiite. However, the 30 percent of Iraqis who are Sunnis controlled the government under Hussein. Without his iron fist keeping them in the Iraqi line, it was feared, Iraq's Shiites would ally with Iran against the Sunnis. Further complicating the picture, between 15 and 20 percent of Iraqis are ethnic Kurds. **Kurds** are also Sunni Muslims, but they're not Arabs — and Islam has never been their defining cultural characteristic. They are fiercely independent tribal warriors. Kurds in **Turkey** make up 20 percent of the population, and some of them have waged a guerrilla campaign for independence or autonomy against the government in Ankara since the 1970s; most Turks consider them terrorists. On the other hand, many think it's the Turks who have terrorized the Kurds.

In any case, because of the Kurds, foreign policy experts have always worried that destabilizing Iraq might draw Turkey into a war and upset our delicate relationship with this vital secular Muslim ally. Those worries were proven justified when Turkey sent troops into northern Iraq in 2008. Kurds undermined Hussein throughout his reign: they mounted the most viable coup attempt against the dictator during his career, and it was against them that he launched the infamous gas attack in Halabjah in 1988.

Due to long-standing tensions among Sunnis, Shiites, and Kurds, the first Bush administration was concerned about the real possibility of a civil war in Iraq if we ousted Hussein. Furthermore, officials did not want to spend a lot of money governing in a far-flung land. **Nation building** was not on their political agenda. One of the staunchest defenders of the elder Bush's policy was then secretary of defense **Dick Cheney**. Another was General **Colin Powell**, then chairman of the Joint Chiefs of Staff and the nation's top military officer. The first Bush administration also assumed that after a humiliating defeat at the hands of the United States, Hussein was open to internal attack. They thought — not unreasonably — that his government would quickly crumble.

Hussein, however, managed to stay in power. Though the United States made promises that we would help the Shiites and especially the Kurds mount an uprising, when the time came, we didn't deliver. For the Kurds there were serious consequences, including massacres by Hussein's forces. Kurds would remember the American involvement as a betrayal and were loath to trust us again. The United States also overestimated how badly Hussein had been damaged by the bombing campaign: the core of his power, the elite Revolutionary Guard, emerged largely intact. With no internally mounted coup or revolution, and with the guardians of his government in place, Hussein held on.

After the Gulf War, US policy toward Iraq shifted to containment. No-fly zones were established to ground Iraqi air forces in the Kurdish north and the Shiite south. Though the zones weren't very effective (anything could be moved by truck anywhere in the country, and was), they gave the United States and its allies a semblance of control, and they made any major Iraqi military buildup difficult.

Containment also focused on weapons inspection. Hussein's European- and American-assisted biological and nuclear weapon programs were well known. All fell under the heading of **weapons of mass destruction** (**WMDs**). America was not the first to try to contain Hussein's WMDs. In 1981, Israel bombed Iraq's nuclear reactor to prevent Hussein from developing nuclear weapons. Israel's interest was immediate: it is within striking distance of Iraqi rockets. After the 1991 Gulf War, Hussein was forbidden by the United Nations to develop or maintain nuclear, chemical, or biological weapons, and UN inspectors were to inspect facilities to confirm compliance. But Hussein was uncooperative, to put it mildly.

The **United Nations Special Commission on Iraq**, or **UNSCOM**, uncovered chemical and biological weapons programs after the Gulf War. Hussein was suspected of attempting to **weaponize** anthrax, smallpox, and ricin, among other deadly poisons and disease agents. The evidence was incontrovertible — one reason many would believe Hussein still had WMDs in 2001–3. Inspectors found these weapons and programs with no help from the Iraqis, who played what would become a deadly game of cat-and-mouse. Hiding weapons facilities, disguising weapons programs, and moving everything around the country to keep it from inspectors' prying eyes, Hussein's methods would lead many to suspect that he retained WMDs even when there was no clear evidence that they existed.

One skirmish over weapons inspections in 1998 led to a major US-led bombing campaign under President **Bill Clinton** called **Operation Desert Fox**. Desert Fox would later prove to be a watershed moment in American relations with Iraq. At the time, analysts and officials considered it merely one larger attack among the many bombing campaigns that had taken place since the Gulf War ended. Conservative scholars called it "a sham,"[3] and even moderate observers doubted its impact was lasting. Years later, we would discover that

Desert Fox so demoralized the Iraqis that they never again developed major weapons (though they did keep building conventional missiles).

In fact, Hussein's most feared arms were destroyed between 1995 and 1998. In 1995 **Hussein Kamel**, Hussein's son-in-law and former director of Iraq's weapons program, defected to the West. Hussein lured Kamel back to Iraq, where Kamel was promptly killed, but Hussein rightly suspected that Kamel had spilled the beans on Iraqi military practices to Western intelligence agents. To protect himself, Hussein destroyed the rest of his most controversial arms.[4] So there were three major moments when Iraq's WMDs were destroyed and arms development was halted: after the first Gulf War, after Kamel's defection, and after Desert Fox.

Desert Fox created pandemonium within Iraq. Hussein had people executed and arrested right and left, creating resentment, fear, and instability that greatly weakened his regime. An unintended consequence of Desert Fox and the purges that followed was a "cutoff in intel," as Iraqi sources previously informing Americans were either removed or shocked into silence.[5] Ironically, though Iraq was extremely weak after 1998, America didn't know it. Part of the American inability to understand the game Hussein played was surely cultural. To many of us, it seemed illogical that Hussein would keep out inspectors — risking further crippling economic sanctions and even violent intervention — if he didn't have any WMDs. But Hussein's defiance of UN regulations was a way to maintain his shaky post–Gulf War authority. Many Iraqis see intrusions into personal space — national, domestic, or physical — as mortifying attacks on personal dignity. Face can be regained only by an act of defiance. This is essential to understanding why Hussein kept out inspectors even though he eventually complied with regulations, halted programs and destroyed stockpiles.

Hussein's possession of weapons did not necessarily make him a threat. While most of the intelligence community believed that Hussein probably did have WMDs in 2001–3, only a few thought that they could prove imminently dangerous to America. Public and political opinion differed. Among those who thought Hussein posed little active threat was the commander in charge of Desert Fox, Marine general **Anthony Zinni**. Zinni was the most vocal insider opponent of the 2003 Iraq War, but his sentiments were echoed by others. Throughout the 1990s the majority of politicians and most of the intelligence community thought that containment was working in Iraq. A small but vocal minority disagreed. One of the dissenters was neocon Paul Wolfowitz, a distinguished scholar and diplomat, who believed containment was "profoundly immoral, like standing by and trying to contain Hitler's Germany."[6]

The most telling framework for understanding different officials' positions on Iraq may be which war most informed their thinking. Those like Wolfowitz, who lost family in the Holocaust, tended to see the situation in absolute and moral terms, and felt the United States should do more to stop Hussein rather than appeasing him as Hitler was appeased at Munich. High-ranking military officers and other officials, most of whom who were involved in Vietnam, tended to be wary of Iraq, eyeing it as a potential quagmire. Furthermore, most Americans who lived through Vietnam — including those who served — are generally averse to violent intervention and think military actions should be used cautiously, as a very last resort. In many ways, a conflict over worldviews shaped by fundamentally different moments in American history underlies the American experience in Iraq.

Wolfowitz, by all accounts, is intensely ideological; but other opponents to containment argued against it on practical grounds. For one, the no-fly zones and military exercises in Kuwait were expensive, costing about $1.5 billion a year. In retrospect, this seems cheap, since the war in Iraq cost at least $1.5 billion a *week* (and by early 2008 about twice that), but at the time many neocons thought containment amounted to wasteful spending. Secretary of Defense **Donald Rumsfeld** was broadly concerned about costs well before he assumed his post under President George W. Bush, and he made reducing the size and expense of the military his personal crusade.

Indeed, many who would hold high positions in the second Bush White House wanted to get rid of Hussein before September 11 brought that possibility to the public. In 1998, for example, Rumsfeld, Wolfowitz, Perle, George W. Bush's deputy secretary of state Richard Armitage, and others signed a letter to President Clinton advocating regime change in Iraq. They argued that Hussein's weapons programs were a threat "to our friends, our allies, and to our nation."[7] Part of their frustration stemmed not from Clinton's specific actions in Iraq but from the overall shape of his foreign policy.

During his first term in office, Clinton was criticized by both the right and left for his lack of an overarching foreign relations strategy. His ad-hoc style was derisively called **Band-Aid diplomacy**. In retrospect, many consider it a clever, moderate approach that frequently calmed choppy waters. Clinton's critics also believed that he was damaging America's interests and international standing by making the US appear weak, indecisive, and overly willing to negotiate with unfriendly elements. The most severe charge blames Clinton for not killing Osama bin Laden when the US had him under surveillance in Sudan in the 1990s. And many conservatives pointed to Clinton's disastrous first major foray into international affairs as evidence that America needed a more coherent foreign policy.

In 1993, on a peacekeeping mission in Somalia's capital, Mogadishu, American forces were ambushed and killed, and the soldiers' bodies were dragged through the streets by a mob — all caught on camera and broadcast worldwide. Clinton called for a withdrawal of troops within six months. The **Mogadishu moment** is a touchstone for conservative foreign policy wonks, who saw in it all that was wrong with liberal internationalism: reluctance to commit troops, fear of casualties, and willingness to intervene only in situations devoid of raw national interest. Clinton's defenders counter that the mission was initiated by President George H. W. Bush, and that Clinton withdrew as soon as he could. Whether or not we ought to have withdrawn once committed is likewise debated, as Osama bin Laden cited Mogadishu as his prime example of American spinelessness.

The Clinton administration's handling of the dissolution of the former Yugoslavia, however, was widely considered successful (though some right-wingers *and* liberals vehemently disagreed). After the death of longtime dictator Tito, Yugoslavia's leaders attempted to hold on to their apparently decaying power by inflaming long-term ethnic and religious divisions among Serbs, Croats, Muslims, and Albanians. Shocking violence escalated into **ethnic cleansing** — the removal of "others" from different areas, whether by threats, deportation, or death. A massive refugee crisis emerged.

The United Nations attempted to deal with the problem, but proved ineffective. After the fall of Srebrenica, which the UN had deemed a "safe area," to Serbian forces, the United States, through the **North Atlantic Treaty Organization** (**NATO**), took on a more active role. NATO bombed the Serbian army, effectively siding with the Croats; NATO soldiers attempted to keep the peace. The most impressive American effort, however, may have been the successful diplomatic campaign waged largely by **Richard Holbrooke** to facilitate a peace agreement, culminating in the **Dayton Accords**. Ironically, given today's geopolitics, American intervention was seen to draw the United States and the Muslim world together because Muslims in Bosnia were worst hit by the war.

The conflict represented the Clintonian brand of liberal internationalism, with its humanitarian bent, strong emphasis on multilateralism and diplomacy, and limited but frequent deployment of US forces, with more liberal use of air power. Against this backdrop, in 2000 George W. Bush and Dick Cheney campaigned for a more isolationist foreign policy. Bush explicitly rejected nation building in presidential debates with Al Gore, and in his first months in office Bush even decreased American involvement in Iraq. But in the words of President Bush, September 11 changed everything.

Soon after the attacks, the United States invaded Taliban-controlled **Afghanistan**, where **al-Qaeda** leader **Osama bin Laden** was thought to be hiding and where terrorist training camps were located. The effort focused on putting troops on the ground and relied heavily on Afghan warlords and tribal leaders opposed to the Taliban as well as on the highly trained Special Forces. **Special Forces** soldiers have local language skills and approach invasions from the ground up by integrating into communities and winning locals' trust; they are often the first ones into a conflict and the last ones out. Though the United States made quick headway in Afghanistan, many in the military privately worried about the administration's equation of capturing Kabul with winning the conflict. Indeed, their concerns were justified: though the United States has kept Kabul relatively stable, the hinterland of Afghanistan is still under the fist of tribal leaders and the official government's authority remains weak. An offensive near **Tora Bora** nearly caught up to bin Laden; critics argue that a larger American force would have finished the job, though perhaps with significant casualties.

Officials in the Pentagon were reportedly shocked when they were told to assess the feasibility of invading Iraq soon after September 11 and to prepare plans to do so. Many military officials and politicians worried that diverting resources from Afghanistan, where Osama bin Laden was thought to remain, was unwise. However, the first point to consider is why and how America decided to invade Iraq in the first place.

The Case for War

The Bush administration's public case for invading Iraq rested on three contentions: First, that Saddam Hussein was a direct threat to the United States because he actively supported terrorism toward America; second, that Hussein was developing WMDs; third, that America should help liberate Iraqis repressed by a cruel tyrant. In 2002 President Bush also broke with centuries of official foreign policy by declaring a new strategy of **preemption**, which states that the US can and should attack a country that poses a threat to the nation before it has the opportunity to strike us.

Almost all Republican politicians and a majority of Americans took the president at his word and supported invading Iraq. But from the beginning, the administration faced opposition from some of the American public, many foreign governments and citizens, and a surprising number of government officials and military analysts. Some of this insider dissent would only become public years after the war began, but there was more disagreement within the government than most knew at the time.

Left-wing liberals argued that the democracy rationale was a ruse, that the war was primarily over oil, and that war would hurt the Iraqis that Bush was purportedly rescuing. Liberal internationalists were upset by Bush's **unilateralist** approach: the administration did not wait for UN authorization or build a broad coalition such as George H. W. Bush had assembled before the Gulf War; Bush instead spoke of a "**coalition of the willing**," which included the United Kingdom and a number of less powerful countries, such as Poland. Some realists and liberals warned that Iraq would be a distraction from fighting the real enemy, al-Qaeda, and that the Bush administration was exploiting 9/11 for political gain; others restated concerns that removing Hussein would create chaos. Many Middle East experts agreed — and criticized the Saddam/al-Qaeda link as absurd, since Hussein was a secularist with nearly absolute power who had the desire and means to prevent Islamic fundamentalists from ever gaining a foothold in Iraq. Finally, they questioned the presence of WMDs because of Kamel's testimony. What was not clear was whether the programs had been restarted — and many believed they had.

The UN's Hans Blix and the **International Atomic Energy Agency** (**IAEA**) chair Mohamed ElBaradei declared that there was no evidence that weapons programs had been restarted or that leftover weapons still existed, but the Bush administration dismissed these reports. Given Hussein's earlier evasions, many believed — wrongly, in retrospect — that Hussein would be able to conceal most evidence. Though weapons inspectors did not think Iraq constituted a serious threat, the United Nations agreed that Iraq had breached the terms of its first Gulf War treaty. In 2002 it issued **Resolution 1441**, requiring Iraq to comply with its disarmament regulations, singling out WMDs, in addition to conventional missile capabilities. But the UN proved unwilling to commit any troops or peacekeepers to *enforce* the resolution. To some, this alone was justification for America to invade Iraq, since the UN's inability to ensure that its own laws were obeyed demonstrated that the contemporary international framework was fundamentally broken. They further believed that allowing UN authority to be undermined in this way would endanger any and all future UN actions — setting an extremely dangerous precedent.

Within the international community and the US government, though, there was resistance to the administration's claims that Hussein was linked to al-Qaeda or other terrorist groups, but less disagreement that Iraq possessed WMDs. Analysts contend that administration officials — in particular Rumsfeld — selectively heeded and ignored information in a process known as **stovepiping**, listening only to intelligence they wanted to hear. While Cheney and Wolfowitz advocated an invasion, Bush and Rumsfeld were reportedly unconvinced until an alarming — but mistaken — 2002 National Intelligence Estimate stated that Hussein posed a clear and present danger.

In 2003, President Bush brought the case to the American public in his **State of the Union** address, and Bush and Secretary of State Colin Powell both made presentations to the United Nations. As a staunch realist and highly respected moderate military leader, Powell's word carried great weight with Democrats, Republicans, and members of the international community. Powell testified that Hussein had "between one hundred and five hundred tons of chemical weapons" and "remained determined to acquire nuclear weapons," and that there was a "sinister nexus between Iraq and al Qaeda terrorists."[8] All these assertions were later disproved.

However convincing Powell's speech was to the public, it was met with disbelief by many intelligence analysts who knew the evidence he alluded to was shaky at best. The bipartisan Senate Select Committee on Intelligence later found that much of the intelligence provided for Powell's UN presentation was "overstated, misleading, or incorrect."[9] As military opposition grew, Vice President Cheney declared that there was "**no doubt**" that Iraq possessed WMDs, and he worked behind the scenes to "[dampen] skepticism in the intelligence community."[10] CIA director George Tenet assured the president that the intelligence was "a slam dunk."[11]

Most of the American public believed the Bush administration's case. The country had been traumatized by September 11. Security experts counseled that further attacks were likely. Americans of every political stripe were worried and wanted to prevent future acts of terrorism. As a nation, we were primed to accept violent conflict in our national defense.

But grave lapses were committed by the institutions intended to check presidential authority. The **media** were surprisingly unskeptical of apparent plans to invade Iraq; the paper many consider America's most reputable and/or most liberal daily, the *New York Times*, practically served as a running press release for the Bush administration. A series of articles by Pulitzer Prize winner **Judith Miller** asserted that Iraq had active "biological, chemical, and nuclear" weapons programs.[12] Miller's stories — and her editors' failure to fact-check them — would later prove a major embarrassment for the paper because it turned out they were almost entirely false. Miller relied on a few politically motivated informants and had no hard evidence for most of her claims. Eventually Miller was fired, but her articles helped pave the way for widespread public acceptance of the invasion.

Many say that Congress, too, was easily won over. Under the Constitution, Congress is supposed to declare war, but because the president is the commander in chief, the spheres of military power of these two branches of government overlap, often with confusing results. The Bush administration did not want to formally declare war, but it did seek political approval for the planned invasion. **A resolution authorizing the president's use of force** passed handily, with 296 representatives and 77 senators voting for the bill. The most vocal opposition came from the Democrats' Senate patriarch, **Robert Byrd** of West Virginia.

Many who voted for the resolution stated that they wanted to give the president the authority to use violence in order to prevent it — asserting that having more power would put him in a better position to bargain with the United Nations and Iraq. But opponents of the war countered that supporters made a political calculation: afraid to look weak in the war on terror, they thought a yes vote was politically necessary. Progressives especially fault congressional Democrats on this score. What was especially damaging for many in Congress was the revelation that most of them didn't read the intelligence assessment they were provided. Though dissent from the intelligence community was registered in the five-hundred-page document, it did not appear in the five-page executive summary.

Those who voted against the Iraq resolution did so for many reasons. Some didn't trust the Bush administration to make good decisions or run a war well. Others sensed that the intelligence they were provided had been "cooked." Some were concerned about setting a dangerous precedent for preemptive war, and many worried about waging war in a part of the world that has bogged down even the most powerful armies for decades. Many were concerned about costs.

The debate about the war has shifted to the Bush administration's intentions because abundant evidence has shown that its arguments for invading were false. There was no link between al-Qaeda and Hussein. There were no WMDs. Bush, Powell, and Wolfowitz all admitted as much in the fall of 2003.[13]

Bush's harshest critics believe there was a virtual conspiracy over oil, energy revenues, government contracts, and Iraq. They view Cheney's close ties with energy giant Halliburton as particularly suspicious. Indeed, Halliburton has made a lot of money from the Iraq War, but Cheney entered his vice presidency as a realist, not a neocon hawk; his supporters say that he became convinced by neocons. A more charitable view chalks up the administration's missteps to an unlucky confluence of personality disputes and confusion over how to navigate uncharted foreign policy terrain after September 11. Only a few right-wingers still maintain that Iraq under Hussein posed a threat and believe the United States — even in retrospect — should have invaded. Almost all who think we ought to have removed Hussein nonetheless agree the planning of the invasion was inadequate.

Perhaps the most troubling defense of Bush's invasion of Iraq was the administration's line that the outcome of the American foray was unpredictable. In fact, legions of military analysts, intelligence officials, and historians made astonishingly accurate predictions about how the war would play out. In particular, they anticipated the need for large numbers of troops, the necessity of a long-term occupation, and the very real possibility of a violent insurgency. However, the administration failed to plan for these contingencies, and until policy reacted to the deteriorating security environment in 2007, the situation went from bad to worse.

Planning the Invasion of Iraq

The Bush administration, along with many conservative pundits, thought invading Iraq would be a "cakewalk."[14] They made several assumptions about the intervention, most of which have proved inaccurate. Many of these beliefs were rooted in neoconservative ideology. First, they believed Americans would be gladly welcomed as **liberators** by Iraqis. Second, they assumed we would be able to hand over authority to an Iraqi government quickly. Third, they relied on Iraqi oil revenues for reconstruction costs, and thus assumed that the war would be inexpensive. Finally, and perhaps most devastatingly, key officials (particularly Rumsfeld) insisted that the invasion would require relatively few troops.

The idea that Americans would be welcomed by Iraqis came partly from neoconservative ideology and partly from evidence. Neocons believe that democracy is a natural good that all people actively desire. The breakdown of Iraq has undermined this notion, as many liberals and realists assert that, in fact, people want a secure environment and resent invasions by foreigners, even when those foreigners believe they are there to help.

In addition, a small group of Iraqi exiles living in the West convinced members of the administration that the United States would be welcomed by Iraqis who wished to be rid of Hussein. However, these exiles represented a small segment of the Iraqi population, and one that was necessarily amenable to American values — after all, most of them had left the country for political reasons. The administration also depended heavily on advice from **Ahmed Chalabi**, leader of the **Iraqi National Congress**, an exiled group opposed to Hussein's Baathist party. Chalabi was unreliable, though, and certainly not an American loyalist. He fell out of favor when it became clear he was passing on information to the Iranian government (Chalabi is a Shiite) in 2004. The administration seemed to think they could hand over Iraq's government to Chalabi himself. When that proved impossible, they were unclear on how to transition to a local government.

There was a major internal debate within the Pentagon over the **number of troops** that would be needed in Iraq. The military's top brass and distinguished military scholars all thought the force ought to number 300,000 soldiers at a minimum, and many wanted 400,000. Secretary of Defense Rumsfeld, who believed in a faster, lighter military, disagreed. It was over this debate that Army Chief of Staff **Eric Shinseki** broke ranks with the administration, publicly sticking to an estimate of 260,000 troops as the administration quoted much lower numbers. America and its allies invaded Iraq with 145,000 troops.

The administration lacked a well-formulated post-invasion plan, which worried many military officials. As Lt. Gen. Joseph Kellogg of the Joint Chiefs of Staff said, "There was no real plan. The assumption was everything would be fine after the war."[15] That assumption quickly disintegrated as Iraqis began widespread looting soon after the invasion. As American pundits and administration officials, including Rumsfeld, placed the blame squarely on Iraqi shoulders, many in the military took the looting as an ominous sign. Clearly, Iraqis did not think Americans were enforcing law and order. The United States was not only unable to maintain civic stability, we couldn't provide basic services. Electricity was not quickly restored. This inflamed Iraqi resentment, and made the American operation appear incompotent. The US also missed a huge PR opportunity just after the invasion by failing to provide sympathetic television content. Instead, Iraqis relied exclusively on Arabic programming — including the news network **al-Jazeera**, often accused of anti-American bias — for months.

But experts have concluded that the seeds of insurgency were really sown by two actions taken by Ambassador **Paul Bremer**, the second head of the **Coalition Provisional Agency**, or **CPA**, that ran Iraq from the American invasion until 2004, when the Iraqi interim government took control. First, Bremer carried out a deep form of **de-Baathification**, firing government officials, doctors, lawyers, and even teachers who were affiliated with Hussein's political party. The effect of this action was enormous. Not only were relatively knowledgeable bureaucrats removed from office, they were left without a job or pay, thus creating both the psychological and physical impetus for Baathists to lead an insurgency.

Second, Bremer **disbanded the military**, also sending the huge Iraqi army into unemployment and economic ruin. In other circumstances this might have been merely problematic, but in Iraq, a country awash in stockpiled arms, it had disastrous consequences. Experts think the ex-military supplied the foot soldiers for the insurgency, while disempowered Baathists organized and funded the operations.

American troops lived mostly apart from Iraqis, in much better circumstances, with electricity and running water. As violence against coalition forces increased, Americans grew only more isolated for security reasons. When it became clear that they would be there for a long time, troops were offered more and more services — though Iraqis by and large were not.

Iraqis were angered further by American tactics, which cut against their cultural values. For example, entering a house and intruding on the women of the family is taboo; shouting at men and taking them from their homes in the presence of their families is a great humiliation. The treatment of Iraqi prisoners at Abu Ghraib insulted the entire nation. And in Iraq, humiliation is cause for a violent reaction. To regain face, Iraqis were willing to fund and carry out insurgent operations against Western interests. Insurgents became especially good at creating **IEDs**, or **improvised explosive devices**, small bombs that would plague coalition forces.

Alarmingly, al-Qaeda now *does* have a foothold in Iraq, though there is disagreement over how powerful or threatening the group is compared to other violent factions like that of Shiite leader **Muqtada al-Sadr**. The Bush administration contended that the presence of **al-Qaeda-in-Mesopotamia** shows that the war was justified as the central front in the war on terror and **Islamofascism**, but critics counter that terrorism has grown *because of* the invasion of Iraq and that the continued American presence in Iraq nurtures the resentment that breeds more terrorism.

Bush and his advisers, as well as top military officials, did learn from their mistakes. After innumerable calls for his resignation, Donald Rumsfeld left office in late 2006 and was replaced by former CIA head **Robert Gates**. Bush and Gates then implemented **the surge**, committing 20,000 more troops (for a total of 160,000) under the control of General **David Petraeus**, a highly effective, respected, and intelligent commander who's considered an expert in counterinsurgency; during the preliminary invasion, his sector was the only area in which insurgents did not gain a quick foothold. The plan was to give Iraqi officials "breathing space," a respite from violence in which to create stronger infrastructure so the United States could soon withdraw troops. Though violence did not immediately abate, the surge did seem to work over time, with a marked drop in casualties in late 2007. Within the Pentagon, military officials who had correctly predicted the insurgency and the dangers of the occupation found a more receptive ear in Gates.

What's Ahead: Beyond Iraq

A broader debate over the direction of American foreign policy focuses on preemption. Conservatives, especially neocons, believe it is necessary to combat a new enemy that has merged radical Islam and terrorism in rogue states like Iran and Syria. Others think the Iraq War discredited neoconservatism and preemption. Many agree that if there's a clear and imminent threat to the United States, we have the right and responsibility to prevent an attack; but at the same time, more and more Americans are worried about our ability to accurately assess such situations. When is an attack *imminent*? How much evidence do we need to assess a threat?

Liberal internationalists have begun to articulate a different approach that treats disease, poverty, famine, and resource shortages as strategic threats because they are often the root causes of violent conflict. They also seek to repair what they see as the damage done to America's European alliances by the Bush administration's unilateral approach to Iraq. And everyone agrees that some resolution to the **Israeli/Palestinian conflict** is a key part of any strategic policy: America's support for Israel — and Israel's continued existence — remains one of the top stated reasons for anti-American sentiment among radical Muslims.

Iran and Pakistan worry many as well. In 2007 some reports suggested the Bush administration was preparing plans for war with **Iran**. Once again the issue was WMDs — specifically, Iran's nuclear program. Although the 2007 National Intelligence Estimate concluded that Iran had abandoned its nuclear program in 2003, in defiance of UN regulations, Iran continues to enrich uranium, the first step to building nuclear capability. Some conservatives maintain that because Iran appears to have been meddling in postwar Iraq, confronting Iran is necessary to achieve peace and stability in Iraq. Realists believe we risk dangerous overextension by fighting Iran; most liberals are staunchly opposed largely for the reasons they opposed invading Iraq.

Pakistan is more complicated. Pakistan has been a strategic partner since the Cold War, but after September 11, Pakistan became a key regional ally — partly because it has nuclear weapons. Now, more than ever, the United States thinks a stable government with strong authority is crucial in Pakistan to prevent nuclear proliferation and the spread of fundamentalist Islam. The main opponents to President **Pervez Musharraf** are pro-Western secularists, but we have continued to back the increasingly erratic military dictator, even after he put the country under a state of emergency and dismissed the Supreme Court's chief justice. When opposition leader **Benazir Bhutto** was assassinated in late 2007, the country appeared more unstable than ever — all the more threatening because the tribal areas in northwest Pakistan are thought to be the continued hiding place of Osama bin Laden.

Some foreign affairs experts think our preoccupation with the Middle East may be a distraction from even more serious matters: **Russia** is redeveloping rapidly, becoming an epicenter of wealth and ambition. As their tundra defrosts, Russians are taking advantage of their giant oil and gas fields and looking to those near the North Pole. The onetime superpower is still the second-largest nuclear power in the world. Most worryingly, it has a long history of repressive, violent, and expansionist leaders — of whom some fear Russian president Vladimir Putin is the latest.

China poses another quandary. Developing at an almost unimaginable clip, China is bent on strengthening its military and technological capabilities. And though the nation has shed its communist policies, embraced capitalism, and opened itself to the world, China remains profoundly undemocratic, with no civil liberties, no political opposition allowed, and no labor rights for its millions of workers. The United States lacks a clear foreign policy toward China, instead dealing with the giant nation as a trading partner and banker. Many worry that this lack of an overall strategy with China — to whom the US owes $600 billion — is dangerous. For example, the US has been exporting satellite technology to China with little oversight — and the Chinese have been using our machines to learn how to build new military devices. Let's not forget that China is also a nuclear power with the world's largest army of more than two million soldiers.

India also presents a need for a developed foreign policy. India has nuclear weapons, and as their economy becomes increasingly tied to America's, that nation will wield more influence. India is a traditional enemy of China, and may help contain any aggression by that country.

North Korea has long been a foreign policy concern. "Dear Leader" **Kim Jong-il** is rabidly opposed to the United States and heads the most closed society in the world. In 2006, North Korea announced it had successfully conducted a nuclear test, despite a 1994 agreement with the United States that forbade them to do so. The US reaction has been realist and liberal internationalist: we sent in diplomats, kept regional powers Japan, China, and Russia involved, determined what Kim was really after (money), and contained the threat.

As even the briefest of summaries shows, the world is a dizzyingly complex and often dangerous place. The old Cold War paradigm has broken down, China and India have become world economic powers almost overnight, Europe continues to unify and grow, Russia is suddenly awash in oil money, and the Middle East is a mess — what's a superpower to do? And is the United States really the only superpower? Many foreign policy experts, on both the right and left, already say the world is entering a new **multipolar** stage, driven by economic interdependence. Whatever the future holds, it's clear that US foreign policy will need to keep evolving as new challenges demand new approaches.

4

The Military

> The United States has an all-volunteer military. The draft was abolished in 1973.

> Some argue that a volunteer army makes it easier to start wars because it lessens politicians' and officials' accountability to the public.

> Others think a volunteer army makes it harder to start wars because soldiers will leave or not sign up during an unpopular conflict.

> A relatively small standing army coupled with a need for many troops in Iraq created strains throughout the entire military.

> The army, National Guard, and reserves all faced difficulty recruiting members after the invasion of Iraq; the standing army dropped entrance requirements.

> Liberals questioned some recruiting tactics, especially those targeting the young.

> There are serious concerns about veterans' health care, especially long-term mental health services; thousands of veterans are homeless, and most of these suffer from mental illness or addiction.

> Many veterans of Iraq and Afghanistan suffer from psychological trauma.

> Many veterans wounded in Iraq and Afghanistan need long-term rehabilitation because they have had limbs amputated or suffer from brain damage.

> Poor conditions in some areas of Walter Reed, the military's main hospital, provoked a public scandal in 2007.

> The use of military contractors is extremely controversial. Supporters say they are less expensive and more flexible, and allow for plausible deniability.

> Opponents argue that contractors alienate locals, decrease troop morale, are more expensive, and are too unaccountable for their actions.

Background to Current Debates

In America, unless you or your family work in the military, you probably know little about how it functions. That's unusual — in most developed countries, all men serve a period in the military; in many less developed nations the military is a powerful political force, often the power behind the throne. In times of war, however, public awareness of military issues grows. While some are strictly internal, others — such as the quality of veterans' health care — spill over into popular awareness.

The military was a highly respected institution throughout most of the past century, but the Vietnam War created a popular backlash against it. Many who were drafted deeply resented being forced to serve; some did all they could to avoid service. Vietnam veterans were the first to face obvious disrespect from a significant number of Americans, a fact that fueled the culture wars of the 1960s and '70s. The dissolution of the Soviet Union ended the Cold War and rendered the issue largely moot, however, as the armed forces were reduced. Recent conflicts in Afghanistan and Iraq have not heralded a return to earlier debates about the military; the troops have been unanimously supported, even by the many who did not or do not support the increasingly unpopular Iraq War. Debates on the military have focused on how we deploy and support our armed forces, rather than on the armed forces themselves.

What sets the American military apart from most other large national forces is that it is made up entirely of volunteers, and this system has widespread implications for recruiting, training, and deployment. The **draft**, or conscription, ended in 1973 amid strong public disapproval for the Vietnam War. Unlike World War II, in which there was little popular anger against the draft and a very high rate of volunteer enlistment, Vietnam did not inspire many young Americans to enlist. Young men often went out of their way to avoid being drafted, terrified that they would die or be wounded in an apparently losing war they didn't believe in.

A volunteer army, like a business, competes for employees, which means that the military must provide inducements to join. Politically, many think that a volunteer army is a liability — though how, exactly, is a matter of contention. On the one hand, some believe that using volunteers allows the government to commit troops without great popular support: the soldiers signed up for this, the theory goes, so they must be willing to fight. On the other hand, some argue that using a volunteer army makes it harder to wage war because soldiers have to be enticed with perks and can either sour on a mission and leave their service at the stipulated time or decide not to join up at all.

Iraq seems to have proven both points correct. Because soldiers were volunteers, they had no political iron in the Iraq fire; because Iraq has proven dangerous and grueling, few want to stay and even fewer are signing up. This has encouraged widespread use of contractors, questionable recruiting techniques, and the deployment of National Guard units that weren't really meant for combat operations. It's clear that the military must change to deal with emerging threats, but it's also apparent that when it does, it will have to provide better services to those in uniform — or resort to conscription. In 2003, over opposition to the Iraq War, Representative **Charlie Rangel** of New York and Senator **Fritz Hollings** of South Carolina, both Democrats, introduced legislation to **reinstate the draft**. They thought Americans would be less likely to support the war if forced to participate in it directly.

A major issue right now is how to help ease reentry into civilian life for those who have served in Iraq and Afghanistan. In 1944 the country faced a similar challenge on a much greater scale. To help ex-soldiers, Congress and President Franklin Delano Roosevelt created the **GI Bill**, a huge aid package that paid tuition at private and public universities and even included money for books and living expenses. More than eight million Americans received their education under the program; but as education costs rose, the GI Bill covered less and less. The military no longer offers a free ticket to outside education. Such contractions of services spur current debates.

Current Debates

The **Veterans Administration**, or **VA**, provides federally funded medical care to those who have served, through the **Veterans Health Administration**, which runs its own hospitals throughout the country. The VA has been criticized in the past for failing to provide adequate services — especially mental health services — but the outcry intensified as the Iraq War raged because more soldiers needed VA services and politicians, journalists, and the public paid more attention to the issue. By early 2008 more than four thousand Americans had died in Iraq and around thirty thousand had been wounded — presenting a huge challenge for the military health system. Estimates of the Iraqi dead hovered around eight hundred thousand.

Around two hundred thousand veterans are homeless, usually as a result of mental illness or addiction, which many maintain was caused or exacerbated by their time in the military — especially if they served in Vietnam. **Post-Traumatic Stress Disorder**, or **PTSD**, is often blamed for soldiers' lasting psychological damage, but it's nothing new: during World War I it was called **shell shock**, and many of its symptoms are described even in ancient military literature. Though we tend to think of PTSD as a form of mental illness, psychiatrists explain it as a reasonable and natural reaction to certain kinds of stress, at least in our society (it's not as common in other cultures). Partly because so many veterans from Iraq and Afghanistan suffer from serious psychological trauma, there have been many calls to improve mental health care for veterans — both in the short and the long term.

Many who work with the **homeless** are extremely concerned about veterans of Iraq and Afghanistan, who seem to be experiencing homelessness at a high rate and who are becoming homeless soon after they are discharged. By late 2007 more than 400 Iraq and Afghanistan vets were homeless, and experts predicted that they would eventually form a homeless "tsunami." Vets who suffer combat trauma are at greater risk of developing drug and alcohol problems, and the ready availability of street drugs like crystal meth and crack cocaine may exacerbate the problem.[1] More of the homeless vets than in the past were women, 40 percent of whom reported that they had been sexually assaulted by fellow soldiers while in the military. Sexual abuse is a risk factor for homelessness; the homeless are also at risk for sexual abuse. In 2007 President George W. Bush's secretary of housing and urban development (HUD) announced that a new program had helped move 20,000 vets into housing. A joint program with the VA developed 1,780 units for vets, and veterans advocacy groups called for drastic expansion of such subsidized housing. Homelessness and trauma are related, but combat trauma is leading to other problems, too.

In early 2008 the *New York Times* ran a special series on the 121 cases in which veterans of Iraq and Afghanistan were charged with murder. Combat experience was a common thread in the stories of their crimes — the accused often described their actions in terms of battle. One of the most prominent American experts on combat trauma, Dr. Jonathan Shay, points out that a soldier's skills have no place in civilian life. If a soldier doesn't learn to shut them off, those skills lead many to become unreasonably and unpredictably violent. Even more soldiers suffer severe mental distress, expressing feelings of "betrayal by those in power, guilt for surviving, deep alienation on their return from war."[2]

In 2007 the *Washington Post* broke a major story on conditions at **Walter Reed Army Medical Center**, the military's main domestic facility for treating wounded soldiers. While most of the hospital was clean and many wards extensively modernized, others were neither. In one notorious section, walls were literally falling down and covered in mold. The building was infested with roaches and mice. Problems went deeper than the dirt: an official investigation by an independent panel led by two former secretaries of the army criticized the hospital's entire system of outpatient care, citing a "breakdown in health services" due partly to "compassion fatigue."[3] The *Post* articles provoked a public scandal, but most of the problems cited had already been investigated in 2005 by the online magazine Salon, which continued to report on the situation at Walter Reed. But those stories had not garnered the national attention drawn by the *Post*. When it became clear in 2007 that these preexisting issues had been known to officials yet had not been adequately addressed, many were even more angry at the government.

Officials were swamped as they attempted to deal with long-term medical care, tried to arrange and maintain housing for wounded veterans and families, and confronted a complicated process to determine disability payments. Walter Reed was overwhelmed with patients for whom there was no established line of long-term care. National Guardsmen and reservists posed the greatest difficulties because the protocols for these soldiers were not well established. Outpatients, technically no longer hospitalized but kept in separate wards to receive medical treatment, outnumbered the hospitalized by 17 to 1. While inpatient care at Walter Reed was — and is — excellent, it's outpatient care — the longer, less visible part of a patient's care — that has proven so unworkable. Many wounded veterans of the Iraq

War, most of whom were hurt by exploding bombs, suffer from brain damage and/or have lost limbs, injuries that require months or years of rehabilitation as well as extensive psychological treatment. Walter Reed struggled with basic tasks such as assessing a patient's disabilities and determining whether or not they could be discharged. Caught in bureaucratic labyrinths of paperwork that had to be filled out several times, many soldiers languished for months. The center struggled to provide families with the necessary support. "If Iraq don't kill you," postulated one pithy wife, "Walter Reed will."[4]

Part of the problem was money. In 2006 the military faced a $530 million budget shortfall at domestic facilities because the war in Iraq was using up all of the armed forces' funding. In 2005 the government had decided to close Walter Reed and move its services to a different facility by 2011 as part of a long-term plan to manage costs and reorganize. Many argue that this decision led military officials to allocate even less money for the hospital — after all, why invest in a facility that's about to close? Finally, some maintain that Walter Reed fell prey to privatization. In 2006 hospital support services were largely handed off to IAP World Services, a company run by a former Halliburton executive (Vice President Dick Cheney was CEO of Halliburton for five years). One congressional investigation revealed that three hundred government employees were reduced to sixty staffers just before the privatization and only supplemented with another fifty new private workers — despite the fact that the five-year contract awarded the company $120 million.

In 2007 Walter Reed's commander, Major General George Weightman, was fired as the center's shocking dysfunction became public. The then Army secretary, Francis J. Harvey, was removed for his poor handling of the situation. The response to the Walter Reed scandal was less politicized than it might have been, since the anger was bipartisan. Democrats attacked the Bush administration for sending soldiers to war and then failing to provide them with adequate medical care, while veterans' services faced biting criticism from both parties, the military, and the general public. Republicans were likewise concerned about veterans' care, but were less antagonistic toward the administration.

Though the Pentagon promised to fix problems, change was slow. Walter Reed remained understaffed. Those in charge seemed unable to decide how to move forward. Congressional and presidential commissions attempted to provide guidelines, but popular ire persisted. Democrats held the administration accountable: an editorial in the *New York Times* singled out Bush and his former secretary of defense, Donald Rumsfeld, "who stubbornly insisted on going to war without sufficient resources — and then sought to hide the costs of their disastrous mistakes from the American public."[5] Republicans blamed the failures on Washington's broken bureaucracy rather than on senior officials.

All the bad press, however, only made recruiting harder for the already pressed armed forces. Faced with sinking recruiting numbers, the military **eased entry standards**, and in early 2008 the number of new recruits with high school diplomas — about 80 percent — reached its lowest levels in years. While liberals decried such changes, others emphasized that by far the majority of armed forces were adequately prepared. No more than 4 percent of those who scored between the 10th and 30th percentile on the armed forces internal aptitude test, for example, were allowed to join. The military also accepted those with criminal convictions, which previously would have disqualified them. Emphasizing that it looked at the "whole person," the military stressed that only 15 percent of new recruits needed to "waive in" because they had broken the law, and that 87 percent of those who did waive in had been convicted of small crimes and misdemeanors such as using a fake ID to buy alcohol before they were twenty-one.

By using the whole-person approach instead of automatically disqualifying some applicants, and by adding financial incentives like a $35,000 signing bonus for midlevel officers willing to reenlist, by 2007 the armed forces hit their recruitment goals: 80,000 army soldiers, 37,000 navy, 35,000 marines, and 27,000 in the air force. In

2005 the Pentagon instituted a five-year plan to enlarge the standing army to almost 550,000 soldiers, adding 65,000 soldiers in a $70 billion plan that represented the biggest military buildup since the end of the Cold War.

To meet their goals, recruiters looked to new venues, marketing the military at rock concerts and paintball tournaments. Some worried that recruiters became more aggressive, manipulative, and even dishonest, promising unrealistic financial and educational help. In early 2007 the **Department of Defense (DOD)** settled a lawsuit brought by the **New York Civil Liberties Union (NYCLU)** against the ways in which it mined a giant database of potential recruits. DOD bought detailed information from schools, marketing groups, and motor vehicle registries. The NYCLU wanted to prevent the DOD from sharing the information with either the police or intelligence agents; the DOD eventually agreed to this and other terms.

The need for troops pressured the reserves and National Guard, too. Though the Guard is fundamentally a militia and can be deployed for any purpose, in the past decades it has been used mainly to respond to natural disasters. With forty thousand guardsmen and guardswomen in Iraq, states that regularly rely on the Guard worried it wouldn't be available for relief work. The Guard, like the regular military, had a difficult time recruiting after the Iraq War began, but saw improvement in 2006–7. To boost troop numbers, the military also lowered standards for active duty soldiers by 2005. A drinking problem used to get you booted out of the army, and that decision would be made relatively low down on the chain of command, by battalion commanders. Instead, the military began forcing these officers to send reports higher up, and fewer soldiers were removed for infractions.[6]

Many of the issues the military faced were a consequence of the relatively small standing army and the high numbers of troops needed on the ground in Iraq and Afghanistan. "As Senior Army leaders have made clear," reported the *Post*, "without a bigger active-duty force, the only way they can maintain the intense pace of rotations in Iraq and Afghanistan is by relying more heavily on the reserves."[7]

Perhaps the most serious consequence of the small standing army, however, is DOD's heavy reliance on **military contractors** in Iraq and Afghanistan.

Gone are the days when rank-and-file American soldiers dug latrines or pulled KP to peel a thousand potatoes. Now, russet golds are likely flambéd by Filipino chefs, transported by Carolinian truckers, and guarded by South African musclemen from the dangers of a violent Iraqi insurgency. And none of these people — Filipino, American, or South African — are soldiers. They are all contractors, hired by a private company, paid by the day, and, critics claim, frequently beholden to nobody.

Though military contractors kicked up controversy during the Iraq War, hiring civilians for military purposes is old hat. Mercenaries were hired by both sides during the American Revolution; George Washington employed private teamsters to transport troops. For decades, the United States has used contractors for various tasks such as prosecuting the drug war in South America or shoring up faltering foreign governments considered vital to our national interests. In Afghanistan, the barely-there officially recognized government hangs on by the thread of President Hamid Karzai's life — protected by private security guards.

But the number of military contractors in Iraq — and the amounts they are paid — is unprecedented. In early 2008 an estimate calculated the presence of fifty thousand support contractors, twenty thousand non-Iraqi security guards, fifteen thousand Iraqi guards (hired to protect oil pipelines), and between forty thousand and seventy thousand construction workers.[8] No contractors hired by the United States are *technically* **mercenaries** (private soldiers or armies for hire), because their orders are not to find and fight an enemy, but to fight if and when attacked and then only for as long as it takes to get away. But these rules are frequently blurred, because Iraq is not a "traditional" combat zone: Westerners draw fire from civilians, militias, and other non-uniformed individuals (contractors aren't uniformed either, but are nonetheless highly visible in commando gear and SUVs).

Using contractors gives government **plausible deniability**, the credible ability to deny knowledge of or responsibility for an action. The **Central Intelligence Agency**, or **CIA**, was known to put short-term contractors under **deep cover** — never giving them any documentation that would allow these men and women to be traced back to the agency. Thus officials could claim that contractors were **rogue actors**, disconnected from official policy. However, in Iraq, the main reason cited in using contractors was cost, and, more immediately, lack of adequate numbers of active, highly skilled troops.

In the early 1990s, George H. W. Bush's secretary of defense, **Dick Cheney**, who was trying to build a leaner military after the end of the Cold War, commissioned **Halliburton** to run a cost analysis. The results showed that the government would save money by using contractors instead of hiring more military personnel: paying people more up front on a short-term contract with minimal long-term benefits such as health care would allow for lower overall costs. Reorganization of the military became the personal crusade of President George W. Bush's secretary of defense, **Donald Rumsfeld**, who served from 2001–6. The day before September 11, 2001, Rumsfeld gave a speech at the Pentagon, advocating the use of contractors in order to circumvent the Pentagon's vast bureaucracy, which he likened to that of the Soviet Union.[9] Contractors were also a neoconservative cause; in 2000 a report by the Project for a New American Century outlined a revolutionary overhaul of the armed forces by stressing market-based solutions — hiring private companies.

Contractors were employed, amid little debate, in 1991's first Gulf War; academics estimated that the United States "deployed about one contractor for every 50 active-duty personnel."[10] Democratic president Bill Clinton deployed so many contractors to peacekeeping missions in Kosovo that by 1999 the ratio had quintupled, with one contractor for every ten active-duty personnel — which by 2004 was "roughly equal to that of the recent war in Iraq."[11] In 2006 the first census of contractors showed the ratio approached one contractor for every single member of the military.[12]

There are three main branches of **private military firms**, or **PMF**s. First, and least controversial, **military consulting** firms provide management advice for the armed forces. Second, **military support** contractors carry out tasks such as cooking and cleaning for overseas troops. In Iraq, Kellog, Brown & Root, or **KBR**, a subsidiary of Halliburton, provides these services. Finally, there are **private security firms**, also called **PS**s, **PSF**s, or **PSD**s (for private security details), which operate elite guard units detailed to protect VIPs like ambassadors and generals and, sometimes, military or intelligence installations. PSFs also protect military support personnel and material — they accompany those Idaho potatoes from Baghdad to Basra. The most important PSFs are the American **Blackwater** and the British **Erinys** and **Aegis**.

Around fifty contracting companies — almost all founded after the invasion — operate in Iraq. Though it's unclear exactly how much they have been paid, it's at least hundreds of millions of dollars. Though many Republicans, especially those close to the Bush administration, argue that contractors save money, this is extremely debatable. Critics contend that the numbers fail to take into account **negative externalities** that are difficult to quantify. How much does it cost the army, for example, if a rogue contractor shoots an innocent civilian, thus sparking violent counterattacks against soldiers?

Most intangible, and potentially damaging, is the effect contractors may have on Iraqis' perceptions of Americans. There are numerous reports that contractors' aggressive posturing and procedures have alienated local populations. Contractors have been accused of everything from copping a bad attitude to the outright murder of innocent citizens. Their convoys' driving styles are routinely criticized: they drive at high speeds in vehicles equipped with several gunners, routinely forcing drivers off the road and even shooting along the sides of their SUVs to keep other vehicles at bay. Given the number of **IED**s (**improvised explosive devices**) on Iraqi roads, many say these practices are understandable and necessary. But they are definitely dangerous and possibly deadly, though nobody really knows because contractors don't stick around when they cause crashes, injuries, or other damage.

Technically civilians, contractors usually don't take orders from military personnel unless directly employed by them. Although operating outside the chain of command is never officially cited as an advantage of using private contractors, some consider it one, because depending on your point of view, the military is either overburdened or safeguarded by many levels of regulation. Commanders must choose engagements carefully, avoiding collateral damage and loss of any civilian life. But contractors need not be so careful. Critics contend that they are often reckless; a former Marine colonel who served in Iraq called some of them "cowboys,"[13] a sentiment echoed by many. Anchor Peter Jennings called PSDs "a second army of Americans," many of whom "look like they come out of a Sylvester Stallone movie."[14] It's been reported that some use steroids, drugs that can increase aggression and violence and impair judgment.

Furthermore, contractors in Iraq enjoy near-immunity from legal consequences. As America's first coalition leader, Ambassador Paul Bremer, left Iraq, he issued **Order 17**, exempting contractors from Iraqi prosecution. Nor can contractors be disciplined by the military, though they can be fired and removed by their employers. Congressional investigations in 2007 were the first official inquiries of any kind into the behavior of contractors, and as of February 2008, none had been charged with any crime. Some Democrats, mostly young progressives, think that Order 17 made Bremer nothing less than a criminal; others won't go that far, but are uncomfortable with the idea that contractors have no functional legal accountability. Then there are those who reason that wartime is ugly and inherently confused, and that rules about how people should treat each other are basically and fundamentally different in such circumstances. Some military men, though by no means all, take such a position, as did key officials in the Bush administration. However, many high-ranking officers believe the opposite and are convinced that contractors have severely damaged the military by decreasing transparency and accountability.

Contractors lack of legal accountability might protect them from prosecution, but it also prevents them from easily prosecuting any crimes against them. A young woman employed by KBR in Iraq alleges that she was drugged by follow employees and gang-raped, only to be locked in a shipping container when she reported the crime to superiors. Incredibly, KBR doesn't deny that she was imprisoned. Not only did she have no legal redress in Iraq, but a civil suit she brought in Texas was thrown out because her contract with KBR included a binding arbitration clause requiring any disputes to go to an arbitrator rather than a court.[15]

Some contractors' strong-arm attitudes has angered Iraqis. That anger turned deadly in 2004, when the killing and desecration of four American Blackwater guards in **Fallujah** exposed how vulnerable the military is to contractors' actions. The Blackwater convoy, which set out to pick up kitchen equipment, was understaffed: only four men, rather than the normal six, were detailed. Their cars were underarmored, the men had never worked together, they did not know their route and may not have had adequate maps. They also may have been set up by Iraqis working with Americans. Caught in an organized raid by armed residents, all four men were shot; the killings were videotaped, as was a gathering mob's disturbing mutilation of the men's bodies. Burned, assaulted, and dragged through the streets, the remains of two guards were hung from a bridge. The widely published images shocked many Americans into a new awareness of military contractors.

Although the armed forces were not responsible for the contractors' actions, they were forced to respond to the killings. The original plan of winning hearts and minds through reconstruction and face-to-face communication in the insurgent hotbed of Fallujah fell by the wayside. Instead, the Marines waged a major battle: seventy coalition soldiers were killed, along with hundreds of Iraqis (the number is disputed but was certainly much higher than the number of American dead). Fallujah now stands as a symbol of presumed American repression for many across the globe — and is used to help recruit terrorists and stir up anti-American sentiment. The fact that the American military must react to situations that contractors create disturbs many — not least the mothers of two of the downed Blackwater contractors, who have publicly and vociferously condemned the government for using contractors at all. Investigations stemming from their lawsuits challenging the company fueled the political debate.

Another serious problem exposed by the contractors' gruesome deaths was the **overextension of our supply lines**. While outsourcing such banal but vital tasks as food preparation might seem less controversial than the presence of paramilitary civilian guards, it, too, can spell trouble. Every bit of American infrastructure moved into or around Iraq must be accompanied by security forces. There's no question that American forces should be provided with necessary services, but all come at a cost. Though there has been much talk of the military receiving subpar equipment, their contractor-provided living, dining, and recreation facilities are relatively swank. They may not have body armor, but they do have flat-screen TVs, Pizza Hut and Subway sandwich franchises, even salsa lessons. While one can argue that such amenities are good for morale, many have pointed out that these services greatly exceed those usually offered in wartime.

There is another risk to outsourcing vital military tasks to private contractors: they can **walk off the job** whenever they want. After the Fallujah incident, more attacks left six truck drivers dead; two were taken hostage. Following these assaults, many drivers refused to go out until the roads were more secure. But the drivers weren't just ferrying around cupcake pans; some were detailed to carry ammunition, and various coalition forces were left running low until the drivers got back on the road. Members of the military would have had no choice but to carry out their orders.

Contractors' pay presents another dilemma. Depending on their job, experience level, and employer, contractors are paid from

$400 to $1,000 a day, with an additional per diem. This is many times the salary of a soldier with a similar level of seniority. There are reports that the higher pay of contractors bothers many in the military — and it also reduces the military's retention of employees. If you are a skilled soldier, why not quadruple your earnings overnight or once your term of service is up by working for Blackwater? However, contractors are offered almost no perks beyond their salary. They have no pensions, and are given minimal life insurance for which the maximum payout in case of death is $65,000 — many buy their own extra insurance. So private soldiers are expensive up front, but have few or no associated long-term costs — and gain no long-term benefits from their private employers. Military employees, on the other hand, entail higher long-term costs for greater benefits.

Complicating the financial assessment is the fact that many security contractors are ex-military, so the government not only paid for most of their training, it also provides them with medical benefits, pensions, and life insurance — without which a job as a high-risk military contractor might look less appetizing. But the military requires soldiers to retire, and there are very few jobs for which twenty years as, say, an Army Ranger qualifies a man. Retirees are relatively young, often miss the action and sense of purpose their military careers provided, and face boring, low-paying jobs as security guards or, if they are lucky, consultants. The prospect of making up to $160,000 a year is enticing, and many are lured by the promise of doing an exciting, purposeful job for which they were trained. Some simply want to make better money, and a few seem most interested in having the chance to shoot at things.

Also questionable is the **cost** of contractor-provided amenities. Contractors' bills are certainly high, but some counter that hiring contractors costs less than having the army provide the same services. Some say contractors like KBR are making a killing; others think they cut a minimal profit because costs are so high. This seems a little illogical — if KBR's extensive services were too costly, wouldn't they cut back? In fact, many contracts are awarded on a **cost-plus** basis, meaning that contractors are paid for their costs plus a guaranteed profit. Indeed, one way to deal with the issue of luxurious provisions could simply be more rigorously written contracts: the military could stipulate exactly what contractors would provide.

Some investigations of contractors' profits focus on the many **layers of contracting** that result from jobs assigned by the federal government because big contractors subcontract out various aspects of their agreements. But subcontractors also subcontract, and so on and so on. So a contract with Firm X to provide, say, meals to troops can spin off dozens of other legal agreements: Firm X hires Firm Y to supply utensils, Firm Y subcontracts out to Firm Z to stock forks; Firm X hires Firm A to make meatballs, and Firm A hires B to provide beef, C to get spices, and D to ship everything. It's amazingly complicated, and presumably profits are skimmed off at every level. And everything requires security. The State Department estimated that 16 to 22 percent of reconstruction costs went for security.[16] Other estimates are lower, from 10 to 15 percent, but as investigative journalist Jeremy Scahill points out in his exposé on Blackwater, "Given estimates of the total reconstruction cost from 2004 to 2007 of $56 billion, even a conservative 10 percent allocation for security would mean $5.6 billion."[17]

Contractors are making heaps of money. There seems to be plenty to go around. However, the federal **Government Accountability Office**, or **GAO**, has discovered numerous financial abuses. A Halliburton division greatly overcharged for fuel, leading to one of the first major public debates over costs in Iraq. It not only overcharged $16 million for meals on bases, Halliburton itself admitted to employees' taking $6.3 million in kickbacks from a Kuwaiti subcontractor.

One of the most serious criticisms has been that contractors often **do not compete**. Halliburton was automatically awarded the major support service contract because the government thought no other company was big enough to handle the enormous task. Blackwater's key contract was a $27 million deal to protect Ambassador Bremer, also a no-bid deal. Critics charge Bremer with abuses of contractor services; an internal audit showed that $9 billion in funds earmarked for Iraq's reconstruction was unaccounted for while he was ambassador.[18]

Critics believe the real reason contractors have proliferated is an intentional or tacit form of **corruption**. Dick Cheney's ties to **Halliburton**, of which he was CEO for five years, have been the subject of public scrutiny. Though he was forced to divest certain financial ties with the company when he became vice president in 2001, Cheney maintains close links to the corporation and is reported to receive a deferred salary until he leaves government, among other perks.[19] Many Democrats argue that Cheney's relationship with the company is inherently corrupt — and indeed, Halliburton has benefited from the Bush administration in general and the Iraq War in particular, receiving over $11 billion in contracts there.

Another controversial figure is former Pentagon inspector general **Joseph E. Schmitz**, who was forced to resign in 2005 after members of both parties accused him of turning a blind eye toward corruption. Republican senator **Chuck Grassley** of Iowa launched various investigations into Schmitz's conduct, including allegations that he had covered up criminal investigations of government officials. Schmitz went on to work for Blackwater.

Blackwater is headed solely by **Erik Prince**, an extremely wealthy, arch-conservative Christian who has almost no ties to any politicians except religious right-wing Republicans and their allies. He is personally connected to figures who have publicly written about the possibility of a Christian conservative revolution to overthrow the standing government.[20] In 2007, Blackwater's network of connections was officially investigated by Democratic congressman **Henry Waxman** of Florida, chairman of the House Oversight Committee.

In September 2007 the accountability tide finally turned against security contractors, when Blackwater employees protecting an American diplomatic convoy killed eleven Iraqi civilians. The Democratically-controlled Congress began an investigation. Another inquiry examined the possibility that "Blackwater employees illegally smuggled into

Iraq weapons sold on the black market that ultimately ended up in the hands of a U.S.-designated terrorist organization."[21] Some liberals are most worried about Blackwater operating in the **domestic sphere**. During Hurricane Katrina, the federal government sent Blackwater guards to New Orleans to keep the peace, which some felt ceded far too much authority to a private company.

To many, the possibility that anyone with enough money can buy an army to do whatever they want is terrifying. But in some cases, contractors have taken actions that no government would because they were not in any nation's raw interest but necessitated armed intervention. For example, as member states proved unwilling to commit troops, former UN secretary general **Kofi Annan** reportedly looked into hiring contractors to quell violence in the Democratic Republic of Congo. Given that contractors provide flexible options in politically sensitive areas of foreign policy, and have for many years, they won't just go away. But their role in the American military has received closer examination and reams of bad press, so it's likely that their function will be rethought and retooled in the coming years.

It would be difficult to overstate how challenging the next years will be for the American military. They must fundamentally adapt to many kinds of fighting and defense as new aggressors emerge and different threats predominate. They are in the process of building new weapons and reorganizing old structures to meet modern needs, and many aspects of military life are currently a work in progress. But at last, veterans' health is on the national agenda. Hopefully, this generation will follow through and provide the appropriate resources to those who bear the greatest cost in any military engagement — the soldiers themselves.

5

Health Care

➤ More than forty million Americans, or one in seven citizens, lack health insurance.

➤ The vast majority pay for health care through private insurance companies.

➤ Most buy insurance through their employer, who pays part of the premium; some Americans buy insurance independently.

➤ Medicare is a government health insurance program for the elderly.

➤ Medicaid is a government health insurance program for low-income citizens.

➤ The cost of health care has outpaced that of any other sector of the economy.

➤ Medical expenses are the most common cause of personal bankruptcy in the United States.

➤ Rising health care costs are due in part to the use of technology, drug prices, liability issues, and marketing to customers. Costs vary greatly by region and hospital.

➤ Controlling costs will be a key aspect of any new health care plan.

➤ Many think that pharmaceutical companies should be subject to greater regulation because the cost of drugs has risen, while profits remain very high.

➢ Most Democrats advocate some form of universal access health care. Most Republicans favor some version of the present system.

➢ A significant majority of Americans now support universal access health care.

➢ Opponents of government-provided health care argue that it is inefficient and unfair to business, and that it encourages irresponsible use of services.

➢ Proponents of government-provided health care counter that it is more efficient and less costly overall, and that it leads to substantial economic savings.

➢ Some believe health care is a human right, though few politicians argue this.

Background to Current Debates

Most of us are concerned about health care, and with good reason. Fifteen percent of Americans — more than **forty million people**, greater than the combined populations of California and Massachusetts — lack health insurance. It's a number unheard of in the developed world. Health insurance is a financial burden for many, and even those with insurance often cannot afford long-term or catastrophic medical care — they are the **underinsured**. Lack of adequate insurance is especially problematic in the United States because American health care is the most expensive in the world.

If you can pay for it, American health care is arguably the best. However, because so many Americans do not have good access to that care, the United States ranks low on lists of health care in the world's industrialized nations. The **World Health Organization**, or **WHO**, placed America thirty-seventh overall when a combination of five factors was considered. America ranked first only in per capita health care spending. France, which has an excellent comprehensive national health system, ranked first.[1]

Indeed, the United States is the only major developed country without **universal access**, or medical services provided to all. Because costs are so high, medical bills are by far the single **most common cause of personal bankruptcy** in the nation. Providers — doctors, nurses, and technicians — feel the pinch, too, because rising medical insurance and equipment costs, coupled with lower reimbursements, make medicine a less lucrative field than it once was. Many family physicians struggle to stay afloat, and the best paid doctors are those who refuse insurance, or work in fields where they are mostly privately paid, such as plastic surgery and dermatology.

While there is disagreement about the scale of the problem, most Americans, be they patients, doctors, or insurance reps, think our health care system faces serious challenges. If you know anyone in the health care industry, they will tell you that health care in America will change significantly in the next few decades because it must — exactly *how* is the question. Due to the huge scale of the health care beast, the specialized knowledge involved, disagreement over the nature of the problem, the sticky string of bureaucracy and legal liability, piles of money, and the literally life-and-death stakes, health care has proven to be one of the most intractable areas of contemporary public policy over the past few decades.

Until the first few decades of the 1900s, people directly compensated their physicians, nurses, and hospitals for health care, simple as that. If you needed a doctor, you paid him a fee. Possibly in chickens. There was no such thing as insurance. When the country plunged into the Great Depression, President Franklin Delano Roosevelt moved to create some kind of national health care, but was rabidly opposed by the **American Medical Association**, or **AMA**, the physicians' professional organization. Doctors then, even more than now, were highly respected and usually relatively wealthy members of their communities. They were deeply opposed to any program that might undermine their authority — or their pay. Because doctors were so influential, their lobbying efforts were extremely effective. However, during the Great Depression, hospitals faced ruin: they were practically empty because few could afford medical care. Hoping to take in a little money, some began to offer a rudimentary form of insurance. The premiums guaranteed the hospitals an income; the small monthly fees allowed more people access. The private insurance industry was born.

Most Americans buy **private health insurance**, which is a hedge against the future: we pay relatively small amounts of money each month to our insurer, say, Blue Cross Blue Shield, so that we won't have to pay huge amounts of money to doctors and hospitals if and when we get sick or hurt. We usually pay a fee for each visit to a doctor and some part of the price of prescription medication, called a **co-pay**. The absolute amount and relative percentage of the full cost of the services and medication for which one pays varies widely by plan. This is especially the case for pharmaceuticals. Women often pay for birth control because it isn't covered; most college and university plans, however, provide free or low-cost birth control.

Private health insurance plans differ widely in what they cover. Some will approve experimental treatments for major diseases such as cancer, but many will not. Some even include alternative treatments such as acupuncture. Major variance frequently occurs in the areas of mental health and substance abuse — both of which usually require long-term, often costly treatment. Some plans cover almost every cent of a therapist's bills. Most, however, limit the number of visits per year for which they will pay. Public health advocates often cite these programs as most in need of improvement because substance abuse and mental health treatment bring a high return on investment, allowing people to reenter the workforce or to become more productive.

Most working Americans receive private health insurance through their employer; both employer and employee pay part of the monthly dues. A significant minority, though, buy their own policies directly from insurance companies. Buying independent insurance is usually — but not always — extremely expensive. In Massachusetts a good plan might cost you $700 a month, compared to $300 for a similar plan through a large employer. In Wyoming, however, the same individual plan might cost only $150. It's incredibly variable.

Health Management Organizations, or **HMOs**, are an unloved form of private insurance that was created to encourage better medical outcomes through close management of an individual's health care. However, HMOs have evolved into cost management, rather than care management, bodies. HMOs usually include networks of doctors, and patients must receive a referral to see specialists. This gatekeeping may be irritating, but the original idea was to ensure that an individual's entire care was supervised by a central manager, the primary care physician. Having one doctor who keeps tabs on your care improves outcomes significantly, but not being able to choose their own doctors bothers HMO subscribers.

HMOs became infamous in the 1990s for heavy-handed attempts to control costs, including denying tests that administrators deemed unnecessary. HMOs are disliked by doctors, too, because they question a physician's medical authority. They have also been known to exert undue pressure on physicians to limit costs by minimizing testing, reducing time with patients, and prescribing cheaper treatments. However, HMO proponents point out that since theirs are much less expensive than traditional plans, HMOs make medical care available to more. Another form of managed care is the **Preferred Provider Organization**, or **PPO**, which arranges discounts with a set of health care institutions and professionals, but which offers greater choice among providers.

Health care reform began in the 1990s, partly in response to complaints about HMOs. In 2001, following earlier attempts during the Clinton administration, Republican senator John McCain of Arizona and Democratic senators John Edwards of South Carolina and Ted Kennedy of Massachusetts tried to pass a Patient's Bill of Rights. Perhaps the most important feature of the bill was a provision that would force HMOs and other forms of managed care to create an appeals committee to which patients could refer disputed decisions.

Bill Clinton campaigned heavily on health care reform in his 1992 presidential bid. Soon after coming into office, he created a health care task force headed by his wife, **Hillary Rodham Clinton**, an unprecedented public policy role for a First Lady. Republicans quickly questioned the legality of treating the First Lady as a cabinet member. Specifically at issue was her participation in secret cabinet meetings covered by executive privilege, a principle that allows some staff to be exempt from normal disclosure regulations meant to preserve the transparency of government. A court ruled that Hillary could enjoy executive privilege — but though they won the battle, the Clintons lost the health care war. Their health care plan foundered and never became law. The program rested on the notion of **managed care**, a heavily regulated, government-supplemented private insurance scheme that would, in theory, better cover more Americans without decimating the insurance industry. Opponents, including prominent Democrats, said that it would create an overly complicated system of payments and reimbursements. Ultimately, the plan may have died because its funding was complicated and unproven.

The government does provide some health insurance, including **Medicare**, which is **federal health insurance for seniors** that currently goes into effect at age sixty-five (people under sixty-five may receive Medicare if they are disabled or have kidney disease). Signed into law by Democratic president Lyndon Baines Johnson in 1965, Medicare passed congressional muster largely because private insurers were reluctant to cover elderly subscribers. Older Americans have more health problems and less income on average, so insurance buyers over sixty-five were a drain on the private insurance industry, which was happy to give senior care over to the government.

Medicare, though not perfect by any means, is extremely popular among its beneficiaries. Throughout your working life, you pay a compulsory tax — it comes automatically out of your paycheck — to help fund Medicare. That money is invested in a **trust fund** by the government, and when you turn sixty-five, Medicare will pay at least some of your medical bills. Medicare is federally funded but administered on a state level, so exactly what is and is not covered varies widely by state. In some states, for example, nursing home care is covered, but in others it is not.

Medicaid is government-provided **health insurance for low-income Americans** that began in 1965. Insurance companies and doctors did not strongly oppose it because, like Medicare, Medicaid didn't eat into their business. Those covered were too poor to buy health care or insurance anyway. Medicaid and Medicare are very different programs, though their names are similar. The administration of Medicaid is largely up to each state, so benefits, requirements, and systems differ. Some states subcontract to private insurance companies to provide services, while others provide services directly.

Many Americans qualify for both Medicare and Medicaid, and can receive both, though not full benefits from each. Medicare and Medicaid often pay physicians and hospitals less than does private insurance, partly because the programs have set payment caps, which is why many providers attempt to exclude Medicare and Medicaid patients. Medicare pays better than Medicaid, generally speaking, allowing a hospital to break even on costs, whereas Medicaid payments usually fall short by up to one-third the actual cost of treatment.

The **State Children's Health Insurance Program**, called **SCHIP**, is the most recent form of major federal health insurance; it provides health care for children in low-income families. Written mostly by Democratic senator **Ted Kennedy** of Massachusetts, SCHIP passed in 1997 under President Clinton, with major support from Republican senator **Orrin Hatch** of Utah and First Lady Hillary Clinton. SCHIP was opposed by many conservatives, who felt it was a first step toward a national health care system. SCHIP has faced budget shortfalls, and an attempt to increase coverage and expand its funding through a tobacco tax was passed by Congress but vetoed by President George W. Bush in 2007. Democrats continue to try to expand it.

Most Americans want some form of universal health care coverage. In the months leading up to the 2008 presidential elections, polls showed that health care was one of the top three issues for Democratic,

Republican, and independent voters alike. Republicans were more interested in reducing health care costs than expanding coverage, while Democrats were evenly split between the two goals.[2] Americans are increasingly worried about health care because it has become more difficult to get insurance, and both insurance premiums and out-of-pocket costs are growing far faster than either the rate of inflation or the rate of the economy overall — meaning that real expenses are rising fast.

Republicans attribute the problems to market failure brought on by the insurance industry, and think that fixing health care means enacting policies to restore the functionality of the market. Democrats agree there's a market failure, but think the solution is for government to either subsidize or run health care outright. The two terms that come up repeatedly in all debates over health care reform are **universal access** and **universal coverage**. "Universal access" refers to a system in which everyone has basic access to medical care, while "universal coverage" means everyone has some kind of insurance. Both terms refer to similar outcomes — expanded access — but indicate different ways to get there. A universal coverage system might require Americans to purchase insurance (which would be federally subsidized), while a universal access system might create free neighborhood clinics.

During the Democratic presidential nominating process in 2007 and 2008 a major debate erupted over **health care mandates**. A mandate would require citizens to purchase health care and implies the legislation of penalties to enforce the stipulation that everyone buy insurance. Mandates are relevant because of the problem of **free riders**, those who don't purchase insurance and therefore assume none of the financial burden of maintaining the health care system but who use services they don't pay for. Insurance works, after all, by spreading out risk among many people — so the greater the number of people who don't buy in, the higher the risk, and the cost, for those who do.

The debate on mandates is about both policy and politics. In terms of policy, some think that creating a legal requirement to have health care is the best way to ensure that everyone gets covered. Since proposals to create mandates invariably provide drastically increased government subsidies to purchase health care and/or to reduce costs, mandate supporters say that the requirement will not be financially onerous. They often liken the mandate to the current requirement to purchase car insurance.

Opponents counter that mandates are unnecessary and unfair. The reason people don't buy health insurance, they say, is not because they are being irresponsible but because they can't afford to buy it. If health care costs are lowered, they think mandates would be legislative and bureaucratic overkill. If the enforcement mechanism were the imposition of a fine for not purchasing insurance, many worry that the government would be adding financial insult to injury. Mandate supporters counter that the enforcement wouldn't need to be any more onerous than those used to ensure payment of student loans or car insurance — to which few object. Opponents also charge that mandates would be basically unenforceable and are therefore worthless.

Politically, however, mandates might be untenable because many people would reject outright the notion that the government would force them to purchase insurance. Some politicians, including Illinois senator Barack Obama, feel that including mandates in a health care plan will make any reform less likely to pass congressional — and popular — muster.

Key players in the health care debate include consumer interest groups and health care businesses, especially the insurance and pharmaceutical industries, both of which oppose attempts to expand government regulation and any universal access plans. Until the 2006 election cycle, Republican candidates were more heavily funded by the health industry, but in the 2008 presidential elections, the health industry favored Democrats. Since Democrats have been associated with health care reform, the health care industry was seen to be cozying up to politicians who might soon want to enact legislation that could interfere with their business. Making large campaign contributions, some suggested, was a way to lobby for their cause early on.[3]

On the other side of the ideological divide are groups like the **American Association of Retired Persons**, or **AARP**, which has campaigned for increased Medicare benefits, and America's largest labor organization, the **AFL-CIO**. A new group of business interests, the **Coalition to Advance Health Care Reform**, founded in 2007 and led by Safeway CEO **Steve Burd**, also advocates universal access health care and represents the increasing support of big business for government-provided health care and/or government regulation, a relatively recent trend.

Current Debates

The primary question in American health care is whether we should enact universal access care. Other issues circle this one: Should drug companies be able to make such big profits? Should they be able to advertise prescription medications? Should we privatize Medicare? The issue of **universal access health care** arises, however, because so many are uninsured or underinsured, and this is a problem not just for them but for the insured as well.

Some advocates argue that health care is a **human right** and that it is unconscionable for a nation as wealthy as America to lack national health care. These people are usually on the far left. Others, probably the plurality of those involved in health care policy, make practical arguments. They think that universal access is a good idea because it will save money overall: such a program will be expensive, but may reduce many health care costs by improving preventive care and lowering associated costs from administration and marketing. Others believe that increasing the health of the nation by providing national medical care could greatly increase the productivity of workers and therefore contribute to the economy. Democrats are the big supporters of universal access, though some Republicans, as well as many health care providers, support it too.

Many, however, are skeptical of any large government program and so oppose a federal health care system. A government that can give you everything you want, they say, can take away everything you have. They are also concerned that the cost of universal access would be crippling and lead to heavier taxation. Proponents counter that the United States' per capita GDP spending on health care is higher than anyone else's, including nations with national health systems like Japan and Canada, so it isn't necessarily the case that universal access would cost more in absolute terms. Indeed, we spend almost twice as much per person per year on our health care as top-ranked France. Supporters of our private insurance system maintain that competition and profit motive are good for any industry, including medicine, and feel that people have a right to profit from privatized services that the government should not monopolize. It must be said, however, that doctors, hospitals, and health care companies do make a profit in countries with nationalized health care. Many also argue that personal responsibility is at stake. Since one's health is partly the result of one's decisions, like what to eat and whether to smoke, many contend that those who make good decisions and therefore have better health should not be obliged to subsidize the bad choices of others who wind up with worse health. Proponents of nationalized care counter that many health problems are inherited or may be a matter of bad luck, so are not the soul responsibility of the sufferer.

Why do so many in America lack health insurance? The fundamental reason is the **rising cost of health care**. Costs began to rocket in the 1960s. In 1965 alone, daily hospital costs rose 17 percent, compared with 6 to 9 percent per year in the previous decade — and the trend has continued. Rising costs also reflect the use of new technologies. But costs aren't uniform: one hospital may charge twice as much for the same procedure as another. That might make sense if the hospitals offered radically different standards of care, but frequently, better hospitals actually charge less. Many health care reformers are focused on such disparities.

Medicare is partly to blame for rising costs because Medicare initially agreed to pay whatever fees doctors and hospitals set. As

Medicare and Medicaid changed their policies and negotiated fees with hospitals and health professionals, many providers raised their standard charges in order to falsely lower rates for Medicare and Medicaid, inflating health care costs across the board. Overcharging the government for medical services is a serious problem: enormous **fraud** has been committed by providers against Medicare and Medicaid, and several major insurance companies have paid settlements of hundreds of millions of dollars for overbilling Medicare and Medicaid. Individual fraud, though it occurs, does not entail such vast sums of money.

Another reason that the cost of health care has risen so quickly is medicine's extensive use of **technology**. Medicine in America now makes use of many new therapeutic and diagnostic procedures that were unavailable even twenty years ago, but most are extremely expensive. MRIs, for example, can see into soft tissue and help doctors find problems they would have been able to detect only through exploratory surgery before; an MRI machine, however, costs well over a million dollars to buy, and up to a million dollars a year to run. Each MRI may cost a patient or their insurance company $500 to $700. The machines are expensive because their cost factors in the research and development needed to create them, and since companies that make them are for-profit enterprises, they charge as much as possible for each machine. Still, an MRI is less expensive than surgery.

Insurance itself is partly to blame for rising costs, because it has made some providers and patients unaware of the prices being paid. If you have insurance, you might not notice the difference between a brand name and a generic drug, though generics are often much less expensive and equally effective. You probably won't worry about the cost of a $700 MRI, since you won't be paying for it, and you might get one even when you don't really need it. You are unlikely to shop around and find an imaging center that charges less. Even if it occurred to you to shop for your MRI, you'd have a hard time getting the relevant information. This is the kind of problem many Republicans zero in on. To them it indicates a failed market. Increased transparency, they say, would automatically lower costs without requiring the government to take over health care. In fact, they think patients should bear *more* up-front costs to force them to shop for services and to pressure providers to compete and thus lower prices. This, many believe, is the best way to fix the health care market.

Doctors, also often unaware of costs, frequently order unnecessary tests. However, it is important to note that doctors function at the intersection of public, private, and individual health interests. While limiting testing may be the responsible course for the health care system, overall, and for the profitability of health companies, conducting all possible tests on a patient might be the most responsible course for that individual. Thus doctors must constantly manage the competing interests of the public, private, and individual good. In any case, unnecessary testing has padded the nation's health care spending.

The increasing presence of law in medicine has also contributed to health care costs, though not necessarily in predictable ways. You may have heard politicians talk about **tort reform**, by which they mean **reforming medical malpractice laws** in order to cap payments to injured parties (*tort* is French for "wrong," and refers to harm done outside a contract). Malpractice has made the insurance that doctors carry increasingly costly and has certainly driven up physicians' rates. Some medical specialities are affected more than others. Obstetricians and gynecologists (ob-gyns) are probably hardest hit; the expense of insurance is a disincentive for many to go into the field. The resulting shortage of physicians further drives up costs.

People who advocate tort reform are almost always Republicans. They want to limit companies' liability; some politicians, business experts, economists, and legal scholars argue that tort reform can also spur competition. Medical malpractice reform, a subset of tort reform, has received some bipartisan support, and some Republicans have touted it as a way to contain health care costs. However, many argue that medical malpractice accounts for only a tiny amount — about 1 percent — of health care costs overall, and that tort reform is not a big enough bandage for America's health care booboos. Tort reformers counter that the problem is bigger than malpractice and point out sometimes ruinous insurance premiums doctors must pay to cover them from malpractice suits.

An even more pernicious way that legal issues have driven up medical care costs is via **liability laws**. Doctors are frequently forced to do every test possible to rule out even extremely unlikely conditions. Some of these tests kill more people than they save because they are invasive. For example, a doctor may do a test to rule out a treatable condition found in 1 in 10,000 people with the symptom that their patient has. But this test may lead to serious infection in 1 out of 1,000 who undergo the procedure, of whom 20 percent then die. If you do the test on 10,000 people with the given symptoms, statistically speaking, 2 people will die. If you don't do the test, 1 person dies — but it's probably a different person. This is a big issue in hospitals. Not only are the tests costly up front, but if they are at all medically risky, they can be even more expensive because they will cause adverse reactions in some people, who will then need even more treatment. Some tests do more harm than good to many patients.

Spending on prescription medication, as well as the cost of medications, has risen dramatically. However, since medications may also help prevent expensive procedures like heart bypass surgery, pharmaceuticals can help contain health care costs overall if used judiciously. **Big Pharma**, the nickname for large pharmaceutical manufacturers, is an exceptionally profitable sector of the economy. Merck, for instance, reported after-tax profits of $4.4 billion in 2006, their worst year this decade. Pfizer, the most successful American pharmaceutical company, made $19.3 billion in 2006.

New medications in America cost more than they do in many other countries because our patent laws extend a longer period of protection — seventeen years — but since the approval process takes so long, that often really means only ten or twelve years. After a patent expires, a drug is usually only slightly profitable for a drug company to make, or possibly not profitable at all because other companies **reverse engineer** the drug, or break down the chemical formula of the medication in order to make the drug themselves. These are called **generic drugs**. Older medications with expired patents are often less expensive in America, a fact often overlooked by critics of the US drug market. One of the most widely publicized by-products of America's expensive pharmaceutical market are the **busloads of seniors** who regularly cross the border into Mexico or Canada to buy less expensive prescription medications. The pills are usually exactly the same as those in the United States, brand-name medications rather than generics, but they cost much less across the border. In Canada, pharmaceutical companies price drugs within standards set by the government; these controls make their patented drugs less expensive.

Pharmaceutical companies argue that patents and no price controls are necessary to encourage the massive investment in research and development that each new medication necessitates. Without a reasonable chance that a new product will be profitable, it would be sheer folly for the company to develop it in the first place, given the cost to run large clinical trials and pass **Federal Drug Administration**, or **FDA**, muster. The scale of risk is huge, since a single drug that fails might cost tens of millions of dollars, and companies must test an average of three failing drugs for every one that goes to market. Thus the potential profit on any given drug must be extremely high to justify its research and development.

Critics of Big Pharma argue that pharmaceutical companies in Europe, where prices are more strictly controlled and less exclusive patents are offered, are still both very profitable and highly innovative. Therefore, the pro-patent argument made by American companies must be considered relative, not absolute. Many advocates for health care reform argue that pharmaceuticals cost so much because of marketing and high profit margins, not research and development. Indeed, most large pharmaceutical companies spend more each year on marketing than they do on research and development.

Another problem with the story the pharmaceutical giants like to tell, say critics, is that they are not as innovative as they might suggest. Many major new drugs are based on federally funded research originally done at universities or the **NIH** (**National Institutes of Health**). Indeed, patents may create incentives *against* innovation, because companies can patent new versions of old drugs. As the patent runs out on many drugs, new versions, like extended release formulas, are created. This is inexpensive lab tinkering that involves very little research, compared to totally new drugs, which are extremely difficult to develop.[4]

In 2003 new health care legislation expanded Medicare benefits to include prescription drug coverage. This is often referred to as **Medicare Part D**, after the section of Medicare under which prescription drugs are covered. Controversially, the bill did not contain a provision allowing Medicare to negotiate the prices of medications. Many health care reform activists believe Medicare, with its large buying power, should be able to leverage its market share and bargain down prices, much as insurance companies negotiate discounted rates from doctors and hospitals. Negotiating drug prices was opposed by most Republicans and supported by most Democrats. The Senate narrowly passed the contentious bill into law; some states received concessions that persuaded their representatives to vote for a bill they otherwise would have scrapped.

Another reason that health care in the United States is expensive is the astonishing number of administrators that we need to sort through complicated billing procedures. Those who advocate a universal access program say that health care costs would decrease with a good government program because it would be simpler to administer. Another cost is associated with the vast sums of money insurance companies spend on **marketing**, an expense passed on to the consumer. As for-profit institutions, hospitals compete for patients, leading to a costly **medical arms race**. An easy way for a hospital to communicate that it is on the cutting edge is to have impressive facilities full of the newest equipment. Practically speaking, this means that there are far more devices such as MRI machines in the United States than we really need, which drives up the absolute overall cost of health care.

Medicare is an interesting case study, and reformers quote Medicare statistics to argue that a universal access plan would be *more* efficient than our current patchwork system. Though many assume Medicare must be terribly inefficient, it isn't. In fact, almost 95 percent of Medicare's money goes directly to health services — administering it eats up only five or six cents of each dollar Medicare spends. Private insurance spends three times that amount — 15 percent — on overhead. It's counterintuitive for most Americans, who tend to be inherently skeptical of large government programs, but Medicare is more efficient for several reasons, one of which is its **economy of scale** — it's so huge that it costs less per person to administer. As a big buyer of health services, Medicare can also bargain down prices lower than can smaller private insurers.

The number of uninsured Americans is far greater than the number of unemployed Americans, so clearly there are many who work but still don't have insurance. No matter what your take on who deserves health insurance or who should provide it, there is no question that having so many who are uninsured is a problem. Lack of access to medical care for a significant portion of the population is especially worrisome in terms of infectious diseases. You simply don't want to be exposed to people who have something you can catch. In this sense, a healthier population is better for everyone.

Emergency care has been in crisis for years. Since 1986, federal law has required hospitals to provide emergency care regardless of an individual's ability to pay. Hospitals must also tell you that this is the case, so most uninsured people know that emergency rooms will treat them. This has led to an overuse of emergency rooms for what ought to be nonemergency care. But emergency care costs a hospital more than conventional care, and emergency rooms are packed, compromising the care they provide. Since most hospitals will go to great lengths to collect what a patient can pay, emergency rooms really provide free care only for those who are very poor.

An indirect effect of theoretically free emergency care coupled with a lack of insurance is that people who are uninsured or underinsured do not address health problems before they reach a critical stage. If a visit to the doctor costs $200 and you have no insurance, you might put off talking to a doctor about that pain in your side — and then show up at an emergency room a week later requiring open-heart surgery. Preventive care is less expensive than catastrophic intervention: it costs less to take even an expensive blood pressure pill than it does to have a stroke. The uninsured or underinsured often wind up in emergency rooms because they don't get preventive care or early interventions.

Indeed, the importance of preventive care — both medically and economically — is a potent argument for reducing or eliminating co-pays even for the insured. It's one that Democrats wield against conservatives who want patients to bear a larger share of the cost for most care so as to make those costs more evident to health care users. Opponents of reducing or eliminating co-pays argue that reducing barriers to care will lead to **overutilization**, a situation in which people will go to the doctor more than they need to. Others counter that since going to the doctor takes time and effort, few would actually go more than necessary.

Overused emergency rooms often have to divert traffic because they are so clogged, a serious problem when you are dealing with time-sensitive crises such as trauma wounds, heart attacks, and strokes. The problem is compounded when ambulances and patients are diverted from hospitals that specialize in certain kinds of care. If you are having a heart attack, for instance, you want to go to a hospital with an elite cardiac unit. If the hospital's emergency room is closed because it's simply too full, you may wind up with fewer treatment options. You might also spend so long in the ambulance that your condition will be significantly worse than it would otherwise have been.

The insured used to subsidize health care for the uninsured. The income from the insured's payments allowed hospitals and other providers to subsidize uninsured patients. Hospitals had to take in more money than they paid out, so if they accepted nonpaying patients or those who paid less, they had to make up the difference

somehow. Part of that shortfall would be made up by charitable donations, but not all of it. Excepting the use of the ER, however, the
uninsured or underinsured increasingly subsidize everyone else: as individual private customers, they are ineligible for the discounts that
insurance companies and programs like Medicare can negotiate. An
uninsured patient often pays significantly more for the same procedure than the insurance carrier of an insured patient.

Many believe that the best fix is universal access health care —
some form of government-provided or -funded health care that would
cover all Americans. When you hear politicians and pundits talking
about universal access health care, there are several terms that might
come up. The first is **single-payer program**, which is a form of insurance that is paid for by one entity — in this case, the government.
Instead of depending on many consumers, a single-payer system relies almost entirely on one. Another term is **one risk pool**. One risk
pool insurance means that all Americans would form a single insured
group, thus maximally spreading out the risk inherent in any insurance program. Like single-payer systems, one risk pool programs create a large group of people: however, in this case it's the beneficiaries
instead of the contributors (i.e., the government) who are grouped
together. Most health care scholars think one or the other of these
would be the best way to achieve universal coverage, but because private insurance is big business, neither is fully feasible.

Finally, you may hear the term **socialized medicine**, which
technically means government-provided universal access health care.
It's a politicized term because socialism is a very unpopular political
ideology among Americans. When politicians use the expression
"socialized medicine," it's meant implicitly as an attack. No viable
proposal to extend health coverage to all Americans is technically
socialized medicine because getting rid of private insurance altogether just isn't feasible. But using the term "socialized medicine"
isn't entirely inaccurate either, because any form of universal access
program in America would be funded by the government.

Many have worried that nationalized health care would provide a diminished quality of care. The word that comes up again and again in this debate is **rationing**. Countries with socialized medicine, argue opponents, wind up with long wait lists for services because care has to be rationed. Proponents of American health care reform argue that health care is rationed in the United States already. The obvious form of rationing is according to wealth: those who can pay for health care get it, and the more you can pay, the faster you can get it. A private doctor in New York who does not take insurance will see you whenever you want. You might have to wait for a bit, but it won't be for more than an hour. However, it frequently takes months to see a doctor who takes insurance for a routine checkup. Advocates for reform cite this as implicit rationing. They also point to emergency room services, which they say are effectively rationed because they are so overburdened. Supporters of reform also maintain that most services that are rationed in countries with national health services are elective (which is to say nonlifesaving) procedures such as cataract surgery. They support a universal access system that would be supplemented by private insurance, so that those who are wealthier or who want to invest more in health care could buy private insurance that would allow them to bypass some forms of rationing.

Increasingly, **Americans want a national health care system**. As costs for health care have risen, employers and health insurance providers have engaged in cost shifting — forcing individuals to pay higher premiums and a higher percentage of the cost for services. By the 1980s some businesses began to support a national program because health insurance was becoming so incredibly expensive. The most famous statistic is from Detroit, where employee health benefits add $1,400 to the cost of every American car. Manufacturers cite their insurance overhead as one reason Japanese cars can be priced lower than their American counterparts. Japan, after all, has national health care. But the auto industry isn't alone. Businesses would save a lot of money if the government picked up health insurance costs.

Small businesses, which lack the bargaining power of large companies, would benefit the most. Indeed, some reason that nationalized health care would be a boon for business.

One of the biggest changes that we might see soon in health care is the digitization of medical records. Converting paper records to electronic data will make some tech companies a bunch of money, but many advocates for health care reform believe that it will stream-line medical administration and leave less room for medical error by making it easier to compile a patient's full medical history. Some are concerned about privacy rights and worry that digital records might be susceptible to hacking or even exploitation by insurance carriers, who may be looking for reasons to drop people with high medical bills. However, helping health care providers move to digital record keeping is a point of bipartisan agreement in Washington.

Former Senate majority leader, South Dakota Democrat **Tom Daschle** has come up with an interesting idea to reform health care: the establishment of a **Federal Board of Health** that would deter-mine and oversee the nation's health care policy. In his book *Critical: What We Can Do About the Health Care Crisis*, Daschle says that Con-gress will never have either the political capital or will to create and implement good health care policy. He envisions an autonomous in-stitution like the Federal Reserve Bank, and asserts that the situation that necessitated the creation of the Fed is similar to that we now face with health care.

As a top domestic issue for all American voters, health care will be in the news for years to come, whether or not we get some form of universal access system. In the meantime, costs continue to rise sharply. Make sure you eat your apple a day.

6

Energy

> Oil, natural gas, and coal account for most of our current fuel consumption, but are finite resources located far from major markets, often in inhospitable areas.

> Republicans tend to favor extending supplies of current fuels, while Democrats tend to favor developing new sources of energy, but there is no neat policy division between the parties.

> Both major parties recognize the importance of finding new fuel sources.

> Coal, which is used to produce much of our electricity, is environmentally problematic.

> Nuclear power is increasingly popular and favored by Republicans more than Democrats. There are unresolved problems with nuclear power.

> Electricity deregulation has raised prices for consumers.

> Disruptions in oil supply have preceded all recessions since the Great Depression.

> Oil politics depends on supply, pricing, and consumption.

> America is the largest consumer of oil in the world, though India and China are catching up. This status makes us important players in the oil economy.

➤ Driving and agriculture account for most of America's high oil consumption.

➤ CAFE standards are a key policy debate and until 2007 were strongly opposed by the auto industry.

➤ Saudi Arabia is the de facto head of OPEC, the influential world oil cartel.

➤ America now buys more oil from Canada than from any other nation.

➤ No single alternative energy source can meet our fuel needs, though some combination of them can.

➤ All alternative energy sources face significant hurdles to development.

Background to Current Debates

Energy policy has been at the forefront of the American government's collective mind since at least 1946, when our oil production first fell behind our oil appetite. It would be hard to overstate the importance of energy politics: not only do our energy needs drive much of our controversial and expensive foreign policy, but energy issues can also trigger economic, manufacturing, environmental, and even public health problems. It may seem odd that the **Department of Energy (DOE)** considers itself primarily a national security agency, until you recognize just how important energy supply really is. Indeed, energy use underlies every aspect of our economic activity, and that's why the DOE, the **Senate Committee on Energy and Natural Resources**, and the **House Committee on Energy and Commerce** — which largely determine energy policy — are such important political institutions.

The background for American energy policy is a little strange because it's discontinuous. What we used for energy one hundred or two hundred years ago and what we use now, not to mention what we do with it, is quite different. You just don't need whale oil anymore. Until the early 1800s, power came from animals, and burning wood, animal fat, and modest amounts of coal provided all our heat and light. The **invention of electricity, the development of the internal combustion engine**, and **huge population growth** all fueled America's **growing energy consumption**, a hunger that in turn created many contemporary policy headaches.

These days we burn coal and natural gas to produce electricity, which is also supplied by dams and nuclear power plants. Electricity powers manufacturing and provides light and domestic power. We heat buildings with some electricity but mostly with natural gas and heating oil. Then there are our 230 million automobiles, run on gasoline, a refined version of petroleum, as is the diesel that trucks consume. Agricultural equipment is largely diesel-powered as well, and American farmers use large amounts of fertilizers that are produced with petroleum products. Together, coal, oil, and natural gas are known as **fossil fuels**; they're formed through intense pressure deep underground over thousand of years. They're **nonrenewable resources** because we can't just grow more of them — unlike, say, trees, cows, or corn. All of our fuels produce carbon dioxide, which experts believe is the primary culprit behind climate change, and mining and transporting them can also be environmentally problematic.

Whether or not the United States possesses the raw material to produce a fuel is a key measure of its national value, because it's less expensive and less politically challenging to use domestic fuels. America used to be the world leader in oil production. But by nearly all measures, the United States is running out of domestic oil reserves. Today, your best chance of finding black gold is in the Middle East, in such far-flung locales as Russia, Norway, Venezuela, and Indonesia, and (thankfully for us) in our next-door neighbors, Canada and Mexico.

Politically speaking, energy issues are unusual. While there is disagreement about the size and shape of the problem, everyone agrees on the basics: **the world is running out of oil**. It's becoming increasingly problematic and exceedingly expensive to obtain. It produces greenhouse gases, and there is no single good alternative to it. We need more electricity, too, but current technologies present challenges. Presently there is **no neat pairing of issue and party**. Generally, Republicans favor maintaining existing oil supplies and developing new ones through funding technology and increased exploration. They favor developing nuclear power and new coal technologies for electricity. However, many Democrats — mostly from states that produce and consume coal — are pro-coal as well. Most Democrats support conservation of current energy supplies and rapid development of alternative energy resources.

Many energy activists say most Democrats are too conservative, though, and want government to fund massive research and development programs. The environment is a big concern for most Democrats and many Republicans as well. Greenhouse gases, which have been released as a result of energy production, contribute to the climate change called global warming, so energy issues are intimately tied to environmental ones. But first, let's look at our major energy sources, the problems that surround them, and the possible solutions different groups suggest to deal with them.

Current Debates

Electricity is a somewhat homegrown amenity: **Benjamin Franklin's** famous death-defying **key-and-kite-flying experiment** was an early step forward, and it was Americans **Thomas Edison, George Westinghouse Jr.**, and **Nicola Tesla** who made domestic electricity commercially viable. Early electricity projects concentrated on hydroelectric power generated from dams. Dams have fallen out of favor because they can carry a high environmental cost and their number is inherently limited by topography. Their output, however, has steadily increased. The most famous US dam, the Hoover, was built under Democratic president Franklin Delano Roosevelt's Depression relief policies of the 1930s — which might be considered America's first attempt at official energy policy.

The **Tennessee Valley Authority**, or **TVA**, was created under Roosevelt for a wide variety of development purposes; it built dams and power stations across several Southern states, electrifying what was then the least developed region in the country. The TVA was **highly controversial**; private power companies were incensed that the government was supplying cheap electricity. In 1936 the fight went to the Supreme Court, with businesses arguing that the federal government was overstepping its constitutional powers by starting a public energy works. The Supreme Court upheld the government's actions, providing a green light to more active federal involvement in energy policy.[1] In the 1950s the TVA became a private company, but conflicts surrounding it expanded the federal government's mandate to subsidize development — just the sort of split decision that seems to recur in the energy sector, in which supplying power is both a private business and a public service.

In the 1960s the TVA, along with many other electric companies, invested heavily in **nuclear power**. In fact, one of the TVA's Depression-era board members, David Lilienthal, became the first chairman of the **Atomic Energy Commission** in 1946 under Republican president Dwight D. Eisenhower. Nuclear reactors harness the energy within atoms of uranium. It's a source of abundant power, but produces dangerous radiation. Because of the high risks and rewards involved in nuclear power, the Eisenhower administration helped create an international regulatory and information-sharing framework to ensure that other countries develop nuclear power safely. The Atomic Energy Act of 1954 paved the way for the modern-day **International Atomic Energy Agency**, or **IAEA**, which functions as the UN's nuclear watchdog.

In 2005 the IAEA and its director general, American-educated Egyptian **Mohamed ElBaradei**, won the **Nobel Peace Prize**. ElBaradei's third term as head of the IAEA was contested by the United States. The George W. Bush administration said that it opposed

ElBaradei because it was against anyone exceeding two terms in office and because it felt ElBaradei wasn't being tough enough on Iran, which has been accused of developing its nuclear program for military purposes. However, many suspected that the Bush administration was angry at ElBaradei for disagreeing with its official position on Iraq's nuclear capabilities back in 2002–3.[2]

Nuclear power is often muddled up with nuclear weapons because the materials for the former can be used to make the latter by **enriching fuel**, that is, processing spent uranium into weapons-grade material. **Pakistani scientist Dr. Abdul Khan**, the leading mind behind Pakistan's development of nuclear weapons, was widely denounced when it was discovered that he had sold technical secrets of fuel enrichment to North Korea, Iran, and Libya in contravention of international law — though Pakistan's military dictator, Pervez Musharraf, pardoned Khan. Dutch officials accused Khan of stealing nuclear secrets from them while he lived and worked in the country in the '70s. Khan helped North Korea create a nuclear weapon, which it did by enriching fuel from its **Yongbyon nuclear power plant** in 2006. The United States, United Nations, and IAEA are currently embroiled in a dispute with Iran due to worries over fuel enrichment there.

But even when we're not worried about other countries using nuclear power plants as a steppingstone to nuclear weapons, there's always the possibility of a catastrophic accident. American anxiety about domestic nuclear power crystallized in 1978, when there was a partial meltdown at the **Three Mile Island Nuclear Power Plant** in Pennsylvania, caused by a combination of equipment failure, human error, and lack of foresight. Nobody was killed, and it appears that the amount of radiation to which people in the area were exposed was minimal — less than that from a full X-ray (though there is disagreement on how dangerous this was).[3] But the accident terrified the public, fears exacerbated by the 1986 meltdown of a Soviet reactor in **Chernobyl**, in what is now Ukraine, where fifty-six died. There was also long-lasting environmental damage. However, a "2000 UN report [on Chernobyl] concluded that there is no scientific evidence of any significant radiation-related health effects to most people exposed."[4] While apocalyptic visions of Chernobyl's ghost town are haunting, the effects may not be quite as extreme as we think. Many, however, believe events at Chernobyl and Three Mile Island only hint at the problems with nuclear power.

Prominent in the 1970s and '80s, the antinuclear movement cites several major problems with nuclear energy. First, they claim that **nuclear energy is expensive**. Nuclear power has been highly federally subsidized, and activists argue that if the government didn't help pay for it, nuclear power wouldn't be affordable. Second, they point out that uranium is **scarce and nonrenewable**. Third, there is no system for managing **waste** produced by nuclear reactors, which remains dangerous for tens of thousands of years. The plan to bury it all in **Yucca Mountain** in Nevada has proved unfeasible, especially since it's an active seismic area. Oops. Fourth, some contend that **environmentally problematic emissions** result from nuclear power. Mining and processing uranium are energy intensive and release carbon into the air — something nuclear power is supposed to help limit. According to detractors, taking this into account makes nuclear power much dirtier than it otherwise appears. There are further claims that generating nuclear power produces other emissions that could contribute to cancer and other illnesses.[5] Fifth, nuclear power plants are vulnerable to being exploited for the **proliferation of nuclear weapons**. Not only could someone enrich fuel and make a nuclear weapon, they could steal (or in some parts of the world, buy) a bucket of uranium and make a **dirty bomb**.

A dirty bomb, also called a **radioactive dispersal device**, or **RDD**, refers to any kind of bomb with radioactive material in it. It's not a nuclear weapon, because no atoms are split — it just uses radioactive material.[6] The government is sufficiently concerned about a potential dirty bomb that it tested nationwide emergency response systems in a 2007 mock attack. Which gets us to the last major objection from the antinuclear camp: nuclear power is particularly **vulnerable to the threat of terrorism** — not only because of the immediate effects of a nuclear meltdown, but because a meltdown renders the vicinity uninhabitable for tens or hundreds of years. Opponents of nuclear power further contend that it is relatively easy to target nuclear facilities by cutting the power, interfering with the cooling systems, or sabotaging the equipment by infiltrating the staff. Antinuclear activism used to be closely associated with Democrats, and Democratic politicians have traditionally been less likely to support nuclear power. However, high oil prices have led many to reassess nuclear power.

The pro-nuclear side believes nuclear energy can be a viable, safe, and smart power source. They were especially active under President George W. Bush. Supporting nuclear power in the United States is generally seen as a right-wing position (although it currently has bipartisan support), but the nation that receives the greatest percentage of its power from nuclear reactors is the notably socialist nation of France, where almost 80 percent of electricity comes from nuclear power.[7] So left-wing politics are not necessarily incompatible with nuclear power. A recent study by an interdisciplinary group at the Massachusetts Institute of Technology acknowledged difficulties with nuclear power but concluded that these **problems may not be insurmountable in the future**. The problem of waste, for instance, may yet be solved by technological advances; the relatively high cost might drop as well. Proponents of nuclear technology fundamentally trust the ability of scientists and workers to design, maintain, and improve facilities and their operation, and believe it will become a more efficient industry. Those who are against it either feel the potential problems resulting from nuclear power are just too great, or that our money would be better spent developing other energy sources.

The Bush administration has been vocal in its support of nuclear power as a means to reduce American dependence on fossil fuels. Our use of nuclear power has risen steadily, and there might be a jump in nuclear production soon: nuclear power was a major component of the controversial but landmark **2005 Energy Bill** (once signed into law, it was technically the 2005 Energy Policy Act, aka EPAct 2005).[8] The bill included $1.25 billion to build a **new federal nuclear reac-**

tor, and guaranteed subsidies for new nuclear plants. It also contained a provision that would **allow nuclear plant employees to carry guns** — should the need to defend themselves and the plant arise. Let's hope those barrels of uranium are bulletproof.

America's electricity needs are growing rapidly, which is one reason **coal** is a big issue right now. Coal is surprisingly interesting because it spans economic, environmental, technological, and private/public debates; coal politics is a lesson in how the distribution of an economic resource can make strange political bedfellows. First, some basic facts: We have a lot of coal, almost all of which stays in the US and is used to generate electricity; about **half of our electricity comes from coal-fired plants**. Democrats are thought of as the more environmentally friendly party, and coal is probably the least environmentally friendly energy source, but many Democrats are pro-coal. Why? Because a significant number of congressional Democrats come from states that produce and/or consume a lot of coal. They're representing their states' industry, jobs, development, and if you want to get personal about it, their own campaign contributions.

Coal is dirty. Burning it produces **carbon dioxide**, a greenhouse gas, and releases chemicals such as **mercury**, which is damaging to neural formation, so it's especially bad for babies and children. Coal mining also takes a heavy toll on the environment, and can interfere with the health of waterways as well as challenge local communities. Finally, coal soot is an irritant. **Scrubbing technology** that makes coal cleaner isn't being used much because it's extremely expensive, while **coal is relatively cheap** — and it's hard to persuade power companies to lower their profits. When you get down to it, nobody really *likes* coal, but it's a trusty character in a scene with only a handful of unreliable actors.

When you see coal mentioned in the media or by politicians, you might hear the term **coal gasification**, which is a technical process for burning coal that greatly increases its efficiency. In theory, it can also be **less polluting**: a gasification plant may produce up to 40 percent less carbon dioxide than a conventional plant. And this carbon dioxide is easier to trap and keep out of the atmosphere. **Coal-to-liquids** refers to the process of making coal into fuel for vehicles. The upside of this is that the United States *has* coal, so using it as fuel would reduce our dependence on foreign oil; the downside is that the process is pricey and not very clean.

Clean coal refers to coal that has been purified and produces fewer harmful byproducts when burned. Clean coal technologies can mostly eradicate the production of **sulfur dioxide**, the noxious chemical behind **acid rain**. Clean coal technologies still produce carbon dioxide, just less than conventional coal burning, and the waste still has to be disposed of. All things considered, "cleaner" would probably be a better adjective to use. Clean coal systems are still being developed, and it's unclear how cost-effective they can be. The federal Department of Energy is currently planning a clean coal plant called **FutureGen**, which will hopefully produce near zero emissions. Coal promises to become more important because acquiring oil and natural gas is getting more expensive and risky by the minute.

Natural gas is flexible; we use it to fuel some vehicles, for heat and manufacturing, and to produce electricity. California pioneered this last use of natural gas in order to reduce emissions. During California's power crisis of 2001–3, however, natural gas use became a liability. In 1996, under Republican governor Pete Wilson, California became the first state to **deregulate** its electricity industry. The idea was to increase competition, and, in theory, create lower prices for consumers as well as bigger profits for companies. Private utility companies sold their transmission lines to other private companies called Independent Service Operators, or ISOs. The utilities were also encouraged to sell their power-generating capacity to other companies. Thus, the utilities would distribute to retail clients power that they bought for wholesale rates from energy generators. Wholesale prices were virtually unregulated, while retail prices — how much the utilities could charge consumers — were limited. Deregulation also allowed companies — notoriously, Enron — to bet on electricity prices. The bettors and the companies generating power were based outside California, so the state government had no control over them — they were beholden only to the **Federal Energy Regulatory Commission**, or **FERC**.

In the summer of 2000, California was hit with a heat wave, causing a spike in air conditioner usage; a drought decreased the usual supply of hydroelectric power, and since there had been little new investment in infrastructure, California's energy grid was strained to the breaking point. Wholesale prices went up, but retail prices could not keep pace because of price caps. Utility companies were caught in the middle. To acquire more fuel for the increased power demands, utility companies were forced to buy energy on the **spot market** — the moment-to-moment pricing of commodities — which was hugely expensive. Some of the generating companies drove prices even higher by making the shortages worse: they would shut down their generators during peak consumption hours, claiming maintenance work. This is one reason they faced legal proceedings later, but at the time nobody could stop them. Eventually utilities were allowed to raise rates on consumers, and **retail prices soared** to double what they had been the year before.

FERC refused to enact price caps; utilities had to be bailed out by the State of California and one eventually went under. Energy traders including Enron made loads of quick cash but were later charged with encouraging the withholding of power generation in order to reap the benefits of inflated prices in the energy trading markets, while power generators like Dynergy were sued for fraud because of overcharging. FERC's free market–oriented chair, Curt Herbert, was accused of everything from exacerbating the crisis to breaking the law by contravening his agency's mission. Supporters argued he was just "letting the market sort things out," in the words of Enron chair Ken Lay, who was indicted in 2004 for securities fraud.[9] As an independent agency, FERC did not have to bow to the Clinton administration's pressure to enact price caps nor to the entreaties of the California state government, but it eventually faced lawsuits. For some, the crisis demonstrated the growing pains of a badly planned but ultimately appropriate restructuring of the energy market, and the energy traders were just doing business. To many in California, though, the fiasco felt like the pillage of the average citizen by the already wealthy energy execs. It's a debate we see played out in different areas of the even more contentious but always exciting oil industry.

Ah, oil. Where do we start with our national bête noire? If we didn't have oil, many of us would have a hard time even buying groceries, which themselves would be impossible to produce in the same quantities because our farmers rely on diesel-fired machinery and petrochemical fertilizers. Indeed, **oil energy fundamentally underlies our national economic power**. Historically, nations that can harness a lot of energy dominate the world economy, and nations that lose their energy sources . . . well, tank. Oil is, for now and the foreseeable future, such a key resource that we simply could not function without it — a *lot* of it. Unless you live in a tree, walk everywhere, grow your own food from inherited heirloom seed stocks, and wear the fur of mink you shot yourself — with an arrow — you, too, are deeply enmeshed in the oil energy chain. The loss of our oil supply is quite simply the threat that ties together many of our national interests. And gets us in a lot of binds along the way.

We must understand a few things about oil at the outset. One is that it is a **finite resource**: the world will eventually run out. **How soon we will run out is a point of enormous debate**. What matters most in this argument, though, is not when we run out absolutely, but **when world oil production peaks** — because the subsequent decline will be sharp and demand will be growing. This moment is called the **Hubbert Peak**. Also, the cost of pumping an oil field increases as the field's reserves dwindle, so once you pass the peak, each barrel of oil costs increasingly more to produce. The most optimistic oil watchers, who tend to cluster in the oil industry but who can also be found in other sectors, forecast that the worldwide peak will occur as late as **2035**. Their confidence partly rests on the fact that the oil industry has gotten much better at extracting oil, enabling even once defunct wells to spring back into productivity.

Other experts predict we will see the peak around **2015**, while some think the peak already has passed. These groups fervently support finding, developing, and funding alternative energy sources — in fact, which policies you support politically are probably based on when you think the oil wave will crest. Why is the peak so important? Because it means either a **continuous or discontinuous adjustment** — the latter being potentially disastrous for the economy. If oil production peaks in 2035 and we maintain our supply lines over this century — a big "if" according to some — then we can probably transition to new fuels relatively painlessly. But if oil pipelines run dry and there's nothing to pick up the slack, it will be bad: **oil shortages triggered all three American recessions in the past thirty years**. Since the rest of the developed world is dependent on oil as well, if oil were to dry up more suddenly and permanently, it could lead to a global economic collapse much worse than the Great Depression.

Less and less "new" oil is being discovered, old oil wells are running low, and new oil costs more to extract because the easy, cheap stuff was pumped first. Another problem: due to the drop-off in domestic production, we need to get oil from other countries like Saudi Arabia. The Saudis have led the world in oil production because they have so much of it and because Saudi oil is very easy to extract. When the Saudis first began producing oil, they teamed up with American companies because they resented the Middle East's ex-colonial overlords, France and England, and because American expertise was simply the best. In addition, **America was — and is — the biggest consumer of oil** in the world. Even today we use **25 percent** of the oil produced worldwide; in 1955 we used 33 percent. This gives America enormous power over oil. **Saudi supply, American demand, and price have historically balanced the oil equation**.

Yet there are two dimensions to the politics of oil: *how much* oil is consumed and *where* oil is produced and consumed. Consumption has continued to increase, as the US appetite remains strong and China and India (with more than 2 billion people between them) have rapidly industrialized, siphoning more and more oil from world markets. But the biggest consumers of oil are not the biggest producers of oil. The United States used to be the top producer, but American supply has dwindled steadily since the 1970s, and we can no longer produce all the oil we need. China and India have almost no oil; neither does Japan or most of Western Europe. So most of the world's major economies are oil **importers** — including the United States, which now imports over 60 percent of our oil, primarily from Canada, Mexico, Venezuela, and Saudi Arabia. Major oil **exporters** include Russia, Norway, and the nations of OPEC.

OPEC, the **Organization of Petroleum Exporting Countries**, is a **cartel**, a group of sellers of the same or related goods who band together, usually to fix prices. **Pricing** is key to oil issues, and to understand how oil is priced, you first need to know that **oil is not sold in a free market**. The oil market is regularly interfered with, usually by Saudi Arabia and the United States, though other likely suspects include Venezuela and, before the American invasion, Iraq. OPEC, however, manages pricing unlike any other actor on the slick stage that is oil geopolitics. Formed in 1961, OPEC now includes Algeria, Angola, Indonesia, Iran, Iraq, Kuwait, Libya, Nigeria, Qatar, Saudi Arabia, the United Arab Emirates, and Venezuela, but **Saudi Arabia is the leader** of the Opack because it has more oil than anyone else. This means that if an OPEC member wants to curtail supply to raise prices, Saudi Arabia can flood the market to drive prices back down, thus cutting everyone's profits. **Lowering prices** is Saudi Arabia's ace in the borehole, their bargaining chip par excellence.

In fact, it's really their *only* bargaining chip, which is why some people say that OPEC isn't really a cartel: it cannot reliably enforce OPEC **quotas** — limits set on a nation's production. For price fixing to work, after all, everyone has to agree to limit supply to keep prices up. When prices are high, it's tempting for any one nation to sell a lot of oil, but since pumping more oil depresses prices, rates of production must be strictly controlled. But try telling that to Venezuela. They have been a South American burr under the Saudis' saddle for decades, frequently resisting their quotas. In addition, when nations want to buy political influence, they raise oil prices, usually by cutting supply. OPEC was formed to counter what many member nations felt was the economic imperialism of the **Seven Sisters**, six big American oil companies plus British Petroleum, but OPEC was also envisaged as a political bloc able to negotiate with the United States on foreign policy considered anathema to OPEC members — specifically, our support of Israel.

In the **Six-Days War** of 1967, Israel routed the combined forces of Egypt, Jordan, and Syria and occupied their territory in what the Muslim world considered a humiliating defeat. In 1973 Egypt and Syria retaliated with a surprise attack on Israel on Yom Kippur, the most solemn Jewish holiday. This war lasted three weeks, with similar results. OPEC raised prices and launched an embargo against any nation that supported Israel in the **Yom Kippur War**. The ensuing oil shortage caused skyrocketing gas prices. By 1977 Democratic President **Jimmy Carter** gave his infamous **sweater speech**: enumerating both the problems he saw with our energy situation and a plan to deal with them, Carter encouraged Americans to conserve energy by turning down the thermostat and wearing a sweater — like him.[10]

Americans resented what was widely perceived as a depressing lecture, and Carter became an unpopular president, though his energy policy now seems prescient in many ways, and oil consumption did *decrease* during Carter's tenure. In the same speech, Carter called fixing energy policy "**the moral equivalent of war**." He thought addressing the energy crisis was key to preventing war in the future, and now, many agree. But the 1979 Iranian Revolution further reduced oil supplies, leading to what has been called "the largest, most sudden redistribution of wealth in history . . . for a time, OPEC members were earning more money than they could spend, a bizarre situation that caused a temporary shortage of cash in the world's financial markets."[11]

A decade later, the effect of supply on prices triggered the **First Gulf War**. In 1989, Iraq had just ended an expensive war with Iran; **Saddam Hussein** wanted to capitalize on the high oil prices that resulted from the war's disruption of the oil supply. But none of Iraq's neighbors in the Gulf wanted Hussein to make money — he had already demonstrated just how ruthless and violent he could be. Kuwait flooded the market with cheap oil, driving down prices. Hussein took this as a national threat, accusing Kuwait of effectively "stealing" Iraqi oil revenue. Eager to stanch the flow and interested in gaining direct access to Kuwait's productive oil fields, Hussein invaded Kuwait.

Concerned that they would be the next target for Hussein, the Saudis buoyed up the unsteady market with extra oil as America, backed by a broad international coalition, pushed Hussein back with state-of-the-art oil-powered military machinery. As Paul Roberts writes, "The United States and Saudi Arabia had emerged as the managers of the global energy order. The Saudis would supply the oil; the Americans would supply the protection."[12] While many decry the use of violence to ensure a steady flow of the stuff (sometimes with slogans like "No blood for oil"), the uncomfortable truth is that nearly all of us participate heavily in the oil economy.

One could argue that low oil prices are in the interests of the developing world as much as the industrialized world; China's and India's rapid growth have been aided by the availability of relatively cheap oil after 1989. In America, driving and flying — whether to transport goods to stores, seeds to fields, or selves to vacations — fundamentally throttles oil demand. Another consequence of the Gulf War was unintentional, but triggered a new wave of United States fuel consumption: SUV fever. **SUVs** became popular after Americans saw images of muscular military vehicles broadcast during the Gulf War. SUVs are both heavy and powerful, so they need a lot of gas. More controversially, they were originally classified as **trucks**, and therefore weren't required to meet the more stringent fuel efficiency standards for cars. And fuel efficiency standards are the policy issue where the American manufacturing, oil, and environmental lobbies really lock horns.

Corporate Average Fuel Economy, or **CAFE, standards** are probably the most contentious policy you've never heard of. CAFE standards require that an auto manufacturer's fleet of cars achieve a certain average fuel efficiency, measured in miles per gallon (mpg); trucks are allowed a lower average mpg, which is why the classification of SUVs makes a big difference. When CAFE standards were first passed in 1975, the American auto industry gloomily predicted that the cost of meeting the standards would drive them out of business. It didn't, but it did allow Asian manufacturers to gain a big market share in the United States. Why? Asians were far ahead of Americans in developing fuel-efficient cars. So when the standards were enacted, they could quickly enter our auto market with consumer-tested goods. That said, Detroit dramatically improved fuel efficiency until the mid-'80s, when oil prices decreased and there was no longer a pressing need to make cars very fuel-efficient.

In 1987, under the Reagan administration, CAFE was frozen. CAFE standards were regularly debated over the years, but weren't increased because in addition to opposition from conservative Republicans, American car manufacturers lobbied hard against changes until late 2007. Then growing public support for measures that would curb global warming allowed a Democratic-controlled Congress to pass higher fuel economy standards. Though initially opposed by a section of the car lobby, eventually the entire automakers' association decided to support tougher standards. As written, the law requires both cars and SUVs to be 40 percent more fuel efficient, averaging 35 mpg by 2020. We can see how the domestic politics of oil breaks down: On the left, environmentalists, most Democrats, and some moderate Republicans including California governor Arnold Schwarzenegger favor reducing consumption by improving efficiency. On the right, auto and oil industries and conservative Republicans focus primarily on increasing production — and their top target for expanding production is ANWR.

ANWR stands for the **Arctic National Wildlife Refuge** and today is synonymous with the phrase "**drilling for oil in Alaska**." What this really refers to is the plan to open an area within ANWR to oil exploration. Many lawmakers from moderate or conservative states think their constituents will approve of only one vote in favor of the environment each year. Do they spend that single vote on something big business will complain about and which might put a dent in the American car industry — more stringent CAFE standards — or do they vote for something many constituents can sympathize with: protecting animals and wilderness? Predictably, they choose ANWR. However, the environment is an increasingly popular issue with voters, so greater numbers of lawmakers are more and more willing to vote for environmental regulations than ever before — even the once intractable issue of CAFE standards has seen important action on both the federal and state level.

Another reason CAFE standards didn't change for so long is that mandating better fuel efficiency would hit SUV production hardest, and SUVs provided Detroit with nearly all of its profits from the mid-'90s to around 2005, when soaring gas prices made guzzlers less attractive. Considering the floundering state of the American car industry, the SUV is a hero to the autoworker as well as the auto exec. SUVs kept a lot of jobs in America during the '90s, though their high fuel consumption has also sent lots of dollars overseas with each barrel of oil we import. When first introduced, SUVs were more expensive than most cars, and ate more gas, but gas was cheap. Then, the average SUV buyer didn't care that fuelling an SUV cost more. If you can afford to pay $40,000 for an SUV instead of $20,000 for a basic car, you probably aren't overly concerned about saving $1,000 a year on gas. However, as SUVs became more popular, manufacturers provided cheaper models — in 2008 many cost as little as $20,000 — pulling into the SUV market lower-income people, who did care about gas prices. Spiraling gas prices after 2005 put pressure on the SUV market, and SUV hybrids are now available. It's clear that consumer demand, not just government intervention, is forcing American automakers to develop more fuel-efficient fleets.

Oil is worth more than ever: on the first business day of 2008, it topped $100 a barrel, around five times its average price (adjusted for inflation) throughout the last century, which was remarkably stable. So what happened? Well, remember the peak production idea? The smaller the supply of oil, the more volatile the market becomes because it is less able to respond to disruptions in supply. Back in the days of oil yore, Saudi Arabia's huge fields, easy extraction, and close relationship with the United States could be counted on to quickly ramp up supply if oil prices got too high. Saudi oil quieted the market when Iraq invaded Kuwait in 1990 and kept prices below panic-button level after September 11. While high prices can really mess up the economy, the US government considers low prices bad, too, because low prices hurt America's oil industry (we are still the third largest producer in the world, behind Saudi Arabia and Russia). But in the past few years, our special relationship with Saudi Arabia has come under fire.

Many key government and policy strategists have increasingly questioned our reliance on Saudi Arabia. They note that Saudi Arabia maintains a repressive, unequal, sexist, and undemocratic regime — it still allows stoning, forbids females from driving a car without a male relative, and legally requires women (but not men) to dress a certain way. Furthermore, as the de facto capo of OPEC, Saudi Arabia is suspected to have engineered the high oil prices of the '70s and early '80s. The drop in oil prices in the '80s had more to do with the increasing availability of non–OPEC oil from Canada, Norway, Britain, and Russia than it did with OPEC price controls.

As the very real threat of terrorism loomed in the 1990s, it became clear that the Saudis were involved in that, too. Osama bin Laden is a Saudi, but more important, it's been shown that much of the funding for al-Qaeda flowed from and was funneled through Saudi coffers, implicating many Saudis in the attacks of September 11 and other al-Qaeda actions. These unsavory ties have made some strategists wonder if it wouldn't be better to divest ourselves of the moral and economic burden of having friends like the Saudis. Controlling Iraq, with its big oil reserves and very cheap extraction rates, would allow America to bypass or undermine Saudi's OPEC authority.

To some, the Iraq War comes down to this. To others, oil is part of the reason why someone like Saddam Hussein could ever be in power, but the Iraq War is more about the externalities of oil — dictatorship, violence, repression — than it is about oil per se. While the war is most reasonably described as being about different things to different people, oil is an undeniable factor. American forces were careful to protect oil infrastructure when Iraq was invaded. Liberals often cry foul about this, but once the Bush administration decided to invade, many have argued that it would have been irresponsible to American and even global industry *not* to protect Iraqi oil. If oil infrastructure had been damaged, oil prices would have gone even higher, potentially triggering a recession. Possibly even a worldwide recession.

Whatever the intention, one effect of the Iraq War has been to send oil prices to historic highs. That means that oil-producing nations, including Saudi Arabia and Russia, are making lots of money, as are those in the oil industry here in the United States. Losing out financially is anyone who depends on gasoline or diesel fuel. It's one reason the airline industry has suffered in recent years. Some say that the higher cost of oil is really a good thing. They think that the **real cost of oil**, subsidized for decades by the government, has finally been unmasked. For others, this seems like an unfair distribution of cost: the already wealthy oil industry is making more money while the average consumer is **pinched at the pump**. There are those who believe that keeping the oil industry booming is good for the economy because it creates jobs and more wealth overall. But many feel that it is our armed forces who are most adversely affected. Stranded for long, dangerous, extended, and sometimes unexpected deployments overseas, soldiers — and their families — are paying a higher cost for the geopolitics of oil and national security than anyone else. Except perhaps the voiceless millions in oil-producing nations who have little, if any, say in their governments' policies but who suffer the consequences.

Considering the complexities in the Middle East, it should come as no surprise that America's oil interest has shifted north: Canada is now our biggest oil supplier. Canada has a substantial conventional oil supply, but their even bigger reserves lie in **tar sands**, a misnomer because tar isn't involved: the name derives from the material's tarlike consistency. Tar sands have only recently become profitable with improved extraction technology and high oil prices. The United States has favored trading with our neighbor to the north because it's stable and friendly. Venezuela has lots of tar sands too, but our relationship with its government is problematic at best. Our options are simply limited: Iran is a no-go, Iraq is a mess, Russia is run by ex-KGB, and we're already in bed with the Saudis. It's enough to make us stomach natural gas.

Natural gas, or **methane**, has been touted as an alternative to the sticky situation of oil geopolitics. Natural gas, while much **cleaner to burn** than oil or coal, is nonetheless carbon emitting. The best way to transport it is in liquid form — called **LNG** for **liquid natural gas**, which can be piped or shipped, like oil. But you still have to transform LNG back into a gas before it can be burned, and the plants that do that are incredibly pricey. Then you have to bring the gas to the homes and factories that use it. Nonetheless, we have made such a big push toward natural gas that some experts predict it will be the dominant energy resource by 2025. Part of the enthusiasm for gas stems from the fact that methane usually comes mixed with other, more profitable gases such as ethane, butane, and propane, collectively referred to as **natural gas liquids**, or **NGLs**. Gas is attractive because it will make us less reliant on oil-producing nations like Saudi Arabia, but gas comes with its own **geopolitical issues**. The big fields are in **Russia, Turkmenistan, Iran**, and **Qatar** — nations that are far away and neither reliably stable nor friendly, and in the case of Iran, downright hostile. Switching to natural gas might get us out of the Middle East frying pan and right into the Central Asian fire. That's why so many people are keenly interested in alternative energy sources — particularly environmentalists.

The environmental issues surrounding oil, gas, and coal are difficult, but alternative energy sources also present challenges — ones we must face, however, because sooner or later we will have to switch to other forms of energy. How we manage that, with what degree of government guidance or intervention, economic disruption or invigoration, is the big question.

7

The Environment

➢ Environmental moralists believe that it is our ethical duty to preserve the earth. This is the traditional stance of many environmental groups.

➢ Environmental utilitarians think we ought to protect the earth to ensure human health and well-being. Most Democratic and Republican politicians are utilitarians; most environmental groups make utilitarian arguments.

➢ Environmental deregulators believe government intervention hurts the economy; this group includes the oil, gas, coal, and timber industries and Republican presidents Ronald Reagan, George H. W. Bush, and George W. Bush.

➢ Global warming is the biggest contemporary environmental issue; there is broad scientific and political consensus that the earth is warming and that this change is due in part to the release of greenhouse gases into the atmosphere by humans.

➢ The United Nations–sponsored Kyoto Protocol was the first major international attempt to cut greenhouse gases. The United States and Australia are the only developed nations that have not signed it; the United States thought Kyoto was unfair and overly optimistic.

➤ There is growing scientific consensus that the Kyoto Accords were highly flawed.

➤ George W. Bush pushed to open the Arctic National Wildlife Refuge (ANWR) for oil exploration; drilling there is generally unpopular but keenly debated.

➤ Companies are developing alternative and renewable fuels; but no one energy source can meet all our needs, and all new sources pose problems.

➤ There is an unstated consensus that new energy sources should be developed by private companies with some aid from the federal government. The political discussion is over the amount of aid and the projects that should receive it.

Background to Current Debates

Being green is in: Leonardo DiCaprio's been carbon-neutral for ages, soccer moms have gone organic, and tomorrow's tycoons may make their mints in ethanol. But environmental policy is often highly contentious, partly because those who argue over it attack the questions from radically different viewpoints. While political factions in Washington spat over the greens, the American public is not terribly divided. In a 2007 poll, 40 percent of Americans said a candidate's stance on the environment was extremely or very important to them; 71 percent were personally convinced that global warming is happening; and 62 percent think it requires "drastic action."[1]

Many Americans, however, are under the impression that the scientific community is split over global warming, though the vast majority of scientists are in basic agreement. Americans are also increasingly willing to bear the cost of environmental awareness: in 2007 a full 85 percent of Americans supported higher fuel efficiency ratings for cars, even it forced up the price of a new vehicle. What's most striking about these numbers is the extent to which they have risen in the past few years. Americans are simply much more concerned about the earth, and our place in it, than we used to be.

The American conservation movement began in the late 1800s when publicly owned and protected land was set aside, which eventually led to the national park system. However, it wasn't until the effects of industrial pollution began to be felt in the mid-twentieth century that most Americans really became aware of the environment as an entity that might deserve or require protection. **Rachel Carson's** 1962 book, *Silent Spring*, which demonstrated the destructiveness of the powerful insecticide DDT, galvanized the American environmental movement. *Silent Spring* alerted a wide audience to the persistence of toxic chemicals, popularized the idea of an ecosystem of which humans are a part, and reflected what was then seen as a conflict of interests between industry and the environment.

By 1970 it had become clear that America was getting more than a little filthy. Republican president **Richard Nixon** issued an **executive order** that created the **Environmental Protection Agency**, or **EPA**. The agency was designed more to protect humans from our own pollution than to preserve the environment from humans — a utilitarian view of natural resources. In 1970, Congress and Nixon passed an updated **Clean Air Act**, landmark legislation that helped radically reduce airborne pollutants worldwide. The first major institutionalizations of environmental interests occurred under Nixon but were **popular bipartisan efforts** with widespread public support. For Nixon, supporting environmentalism was a strategic political move because Ed Muskie, the Democrats' presumed 1972 presidential candidate, had made the environment his key issue. Nixon decided to beat him to the punch, and it worked: Nixon won.

Though today we associate Democrats more than Republicans with environmental issues, protecting the environment is — and historically has been — a relatively popular policy choice. The first environmentally minded president, Theodore Roosevelt, was a Republican. It wasn't until the Republican Reagan administration in the 1980s that Democrats became more closely identified with environmental protection. Reagan and his supporters wanted less governmental regulation of industry, a smaller federal government, and stronger states' rights, so they drastically reduced funding for federal programs and institutions such as the EPA, but with mixed results. Environmentalists called the Reagan years a "lost opportunity," but so did those who wanted various abilities and rights — more logging on federal lands, for example — turned over to private industry.[2]

Two early environmental issues addressed by the federal government, toxic waste and acid rain, anticipated many of the same fights that have played out over global warming. By 1980 perception of environmental issues had shifted away from aesthetics — smoggy skies and dirty rivers — and toward **public health** as researchers discovered that some chemicals had negative effects on people, as well as on animals and plants. The **Superfund** program was conceived to clean up **toxic waste**, which turned out to be pernicious stuff: fewer sites were treated than planned, partly because the chemicals proved more persistent than anyone expected.

In 1982 the EPA, citing executive privilege, refused to turn over thousands of pages of documents to congressional committees conducting investigations into allegations of fund misallocation. As executor of the program, EPA administrator **Anne Burford** was found in contempt of Congress and forced to resign in a controversy seen to damage the Reagan administration. The documents did show a political distribution of funds: the EPA would sometimes grant money to clean toxic waste sites for Republicans who were up for election and withhold funds from Democrats' districts. So even when both parties agree on the environment — declaring, for example, that toxic waste is bad and should be cleaned up — execution of policy can become politicized.

The controversy over **acid rain** provides important background on current debates. Acid rain is created when water vapor reacts with certain chemicals such as sulfur oxides and nitrogen oxides released by vehicles and industrial activity. While the basic problem had been known since the 1960s, awareness grew in the late '80s as plants and wildlife died from exposure to acid rain. When members of Congress introduced bills to curb acid rain–causing emissions, businesses that would be affected united to form a strong lobbying coalition. Utilities were the main players because electric plants, which are primarily coal powered, are a major source of sulfur dioxide, the prime contributor to acid rain. Business interests called for more research to definitively determine that acid rain resulted from their activity and not from natural causes before they would invest billions in cleaner technology. President Reagan funded research into the problem; the results led to the inescapable conclusion that acid rain was largely caused by industry. Utilities were forced to submit to a cap-and-trade system for reducing chemical emissions, a model that is proving important in the debate about global warming because it worked well to reduce acid rain while employing a market-based response to the problem.

The way the international community and the United States tackled the **ozone hole** may also shed light on future environmental solutions. In 1985 a group of scientists discovered that the atmospheric layer made up of ozone, which protects the earth from solar radiation, had a "hole." This was an area the size of Antarctica that drastically thinned each spring, letting in high levels of radiation that can cause cancer and contribute to global warming. Scientists knew that the use of **chlorofluorocarbons**, or **CFC**s, and other chemical compounds produced by humans posed a risk to the ozone layer, but nobody realized how drastic the situation had become. The worldwide response was swift; in 1987 the **Montreal Protocol** was approved by most nations to phase out the use of ozone-depleting substances. The statute was quickly written and globally adopted partly because new, economically viable technologies and materials were already available to replace ozone-depleting chemicals. Many scientists cite the Montreal Protocol as evidence that "curbing global warming will not be as hard as it looks."[3] In fact, awareness of the hole in the ozone went hand in hand with early warnings about global warming.

Finally, understanding the different interest groups is important to decoding environmental policy. Some believe that it is our moral duty to protect and preserve the environment and the life within it — I'll call these people the **environmental moralists**. They think that human behavior toward other species and the earth should fundamentally alter. While many in this group are political liberals, some are apolitical, and there is a growing contingent within a group usually associated with conservative political views: evangelical Christians. What would Jesus drive? Not an SUV, they say.

Old-school environmentalists suffered a **schism** in 2005, when **Ted Nordhaus** and **Michael Shellenberger** published an essay entitled **"The Death of Environmentalism,"** in which they argued that "modern environmentalism is no longer capable of dealing with the world's most serious ecological crisis,"[4] by which they meant global warming. Shellenberger and Nordhaus called modern environmentalism "another special interest," and argued that the entire framework for environmental policy needs to change in order to win a culture war over core American values. Their contention inflamed environmentalists, who were either deeply offended or highly supportive. The newer, more radical environmentalist wing thinks that environmentalists must entirely change the way they operate; many are also environmental moralists, but are cutting a new path in what they see as practical means to a vital end.

Most environmental moralists also belong to another group who frame environmental issues in practical, human terms. They warn that unless we do something to preserve the environment, we are going to face serious problems. I call them **environmental utilitarians**. Nearly all environmental groups, as well as most Democrats and Republicans with environmental concerns, employ utilitarian arguments. On the extreme end are **Amory Lovins** and the **Rocky Mountain Institute**. Lovins maintains that being environmental is usually more efficient, that you can save more money being environmentally friendly. The institute stresses entrepreneurial, market-based solutions to environmental issues.

The **Natural Resources Defense Council**, or **NRDC**, is one of the largest and most influential environmental groups; its mission statement stresses **sustainability**, a word often used by utilitarians to express their desire to maintain and manage the environment as a system of which humans are a part. While the NRDC is a respected institution, in 2007 progressives charged it with offering favorable concessions and government handouts to polluters. The utilitarian viewpoint has become the dominant voice in the political debate because many years of research have taught us that pollution can be harmful to our well-being and because of the potential dangers of global warming. In other words, you may not be worried about spotted owls going extinct, but you'll worry if your beach house is going to be underwater.

Another group of people don't agree with the moral or scientific premises of the first two groups. They tend to distrust environmentalists and scientists, suspect that most scientists are tacitly in cahoots with environmentalists, and accuse both groups of pursuing a political agenda. They are more likely to be found in the interior than on the coasts, and a surprising number work the land as farmers or ranchers. They tend to support the use of natural resources by agriculture and the mining, timber, and extraction industries and to frame arguments in terms of property rights, states' rights, small-government policies, and economic development. I'll call this last group the **environmental deregulators** since they call for less or no government regulation of resource use.

This group grew under **Ronald Reagan**, was prominent under **George H. W. Bush**, and has become powerful under **George W. Bush**. They are usually Republicans, though many Republicans are not deregulators and some Democrats — notably the Michigan congressional delegation — sometimes support deregulation. Finally, there are notable Republican environmentalists such as California governor **Arnold Schwarzenegger**.

Increasingly, most Americans feel that business and industry are not necessarily in conflict with environmental protection. Generally, we see the earth as a complex system and feel that resources need to be managed properly in order to be available in the future: the **utilitarian viewpoint dominates**. Of course, the big question that has shaped much of our recent thinking on the environment is global warming, a phenomenon that was debated in the 1990s but is now almost universally recognized as a serious — and potentially disastrous — fact.

Current Debates

In 1987, Republican senator **John Chafee** of Rhode Island introduced early legislation to phase out ozone-destroying substances, partly over concern about global warming, deeming them "monumental problems with a doomsday effect."[5] Nowadays his concerns are widely echoed; even the once doubtful, including President George W. Bush, have recognized that global warming is real, is at least partly caused by humans, and is a critical problem that needs to be addressed. The old debate over whether climate change is occuring is dead; the current debate focuses on what to do about it.

First, the terms. **Climate change** refers to any change in the earth's climate — natural or human-caused. **Global warming** refers to the trend toward higher mean temperatures seen recently worldwide. It's important to note, however, that "global warming" refers only to an average — some places, in fact, seem to be getting colder, and the incidence of violent weather appears to be on the upswing. Technically, the terms "global warming" and "climate change" don't imply human causes for the temperature increase, though we tend to interpret both that way. Climate change per se was never really contentious, since the earth's climate has changed both drastically and moderately over time. Global warming was once a matter for scientific debate, but now the trend is indisputable: things are heating up. Scientists think current global warming is partly due to the **greenhouse effect: greenhouse gases**, including methane, water vapor, and especially **carbon dioxide**, trap energy in the atmosphere and warm the earth, as the glass panes of a greenhouse warm the air inside it. There is more carbon dioxide in the atmosphere now than ever before in human history because we have been burning coal, oil, and gas for the past couple of hundred years, releasing their stored carbon. Scientists predict that various areas will be **affected differently by global warming**: Asia, Africa, and South America may be worst hit, with more violent weather, both longer and more frequent droughts, and catastrophic floods. Europe could become significantly colder. Climate change skeptics often interpret data showing cooling trends as evidence against global warming — but because of the asymmetric effects of global warming, such local cooling is, in fact, in keeping with the theory. Seas will rise from melting ice caps and glaciers, a process happening much faster than initially expected, and if enough ice melts, coastal areas could be inundated — especially problematic in places where it's hard for people to relocate or where coastal property is highly valuable. Russia might be the biggest winner: warming could thaw the vast tundra in Siberia, thereby increasing agricultural output and easing extraction of oil and gas, much of which are currently locked under permafrost that is expensive and difficult to drill.

The first major legislation on global warming was the international **United Nations Framework Convention on Climate Change**, or **UNFCCC**, a legally nonbinding treaty that the United States signed in 1992. It didn't impose any standards for emissions, but rather established a framework in which those controls would be created. In 1997 mandatory international limits on greenhouse gas emissions were set in the **Kyoto Protocol**, which stirred up a storm of controversy when the United States refused to sign on.

The protocol required emissions reductions in six greenhouse gases among signing nations. There were two main groups of signatories: developed countries, called **Annex I countries**, and developing nations, called **non–Annex I countries**. The latter, including China and India (which both signed the treaty), were **not required to reduce emissions.** The United Nations thinks people who don't have, say, electricity, should have access to it before they worry about reducing their greenhouse gas emissions, while those of us who have basic amenities and can afford the technology to reduce emissions, should. Some find this asymmetry ideologically or economically unfair. China, after all, now has the world's third-largest economy and, by one measure, nine of the ten most polluted cities in the world.

Possibly because it is expected to suffer the earliest consequences from global warming, **Europe has taken the lead** in reducing emissions. For **Annex I** countries, a group that includes Europe, Kyoto established a **cap-and-trade system**. This means that each nation agrees to an absolute standard for emissions, but the obligation can be met in several ways: by **reducing emissions**, purchasing **carbon credits**, or creating **carbon offsets**. Cap-and-trade systems work like this: Let's say all of Europe agreed to a 10 percent reduction of carbon dioxide. But instead of an absolute cap, with each country reducing emissions by 10 percent, some will reduce emissions more than others — but the total reduction will amount to 10 percent.

Pretend Sweden and Italy both produce 100 tonnes of carbon dioxide per year, and both have to reduce their emissions by 10 percent. Sweden finds it can economically reduce emissions by 15 percent, but Italy can only reduce emissions by 5 percent. Maybe Sweden uses cleaner-burning fuel, or has newer power plants, or can build the technology more cheaply. Sweden has reduced its emissions below what the cap requires, and Italy needs a carbon credit to meet the cap. So they can make a deal: Italy could buy Sweden's "extra" 5 percent emissions reduction. Both Italy and Sweden meet the cap, both get to choose how they do it, and Sweden makes some money on the side.

Cap-and-trade systems often include **carbon offset** provisions: a company or nation can meet its emissions goals by reducing carbon in the atmosphere through doing things like planting trees. The Kyoto Protocol included a **clean development mechanism**, or **CDM**, whereby a developed country can invest in clean technologies in poor countries and thus "reduce" its emissions by lowering someone else's. This could work because installing cleaner technologies is cheaper in, say, Pakistan than it is in Germany. Plus, a CDM might allow poor countries to avoid polluting technologies altogether and develop clean ones early on — called **leapfrogging**. Some carbon-offset companies are facing suspicion, though: people think they might just be taking money and doing little or nothing to actually create carbon offsets. So far there has been little oversight.

There are advantages to a cap-and-trade system: it **fixes a predictable ceiling for emissions** and allows participants to meet obligations in a **flexible and relatively cost-effective** manner. Cap-and-trade systems also create a whole new business by establishing a **market** for carbon credits. In fact, losing out on this might be one of the worst immediate effects America suffers from not signing Kyoto: **London** has emerged as the global center for the new carbon-trading commodity market, already so gigantic that some analysts predict it will be worth more than the oil commodities market by midcentury. We will probably wind up with some kind of cap-and-trade system in the United States because industry likes the flexibility and the potential for profits in trading carbon credits. Some environmental groups, however, advocate a carbon tax. It's increasingly popular with politicians, too: independent New York City mayor **Michael Bloomberg** endorsed a carbon tax in 2007.

A **carbon tax** would tax each unit of carbon dioxide a person or business emits via their use of electricity, gasoline, and diesel. Some prefer a tax because it would affect decisions an individual or a business makes about power and fuel use. Advocates argue that it is simply **easier to conserve energy** than to find and develop new energy sources, and they believe a carbon tax would encourage this. Most groups who want a tax think it should be **revenue-neutral** (meaning the government doesn't keep it): they want the carbon tax money paid back to all of us, or they want to credit the amount of carbon tax each person pays toward other taxes. Counterintuitive? The idea is that we would see how much energy really costs, and those who use less might actually make money from those who use more. Carbon tax advocates also worry that cap-and-trade systems are open to manipulation — that utilities will negotiate overly high emissions caps or will be allocated too many credits. They also like the transparency of a tax: consumers know exactly how much they pay for their carbon emissions, whereas cap-and-trade plans can pass along costs as a "hidden tax." However, unlike cap-and-trade systems, carbon taxes put no cap on emissions, are less favored by business, and are difficult to popularize because, quite simply, nobody likes taxes.

Kyoto was very controversial in the United States. Al Gore, then vice president, pushed hard for the treaty, but President Bill Clinton did not send it to Congress to sign, and when George W. Bush was elected in 2000, he made it clear that he wouldn't support Kyoto either. President Bush further opted out of most 2007 United Nations climate change meetings and convened his own panel for advising on emissions reductions. His administration stressed its desire for each nation to make its own decisions, which speaks to its relative distance from the international policy framework. Bush also called for voluntary reductions from businesses and utilities because he favors less government regulation, but since businesses rarely undertake costly changes without some coercion, nobody has taken this suggestion very seriously.

The **main objection to Kyoto** was that it set **unrealistic goals** for US emissions reduction — and failure to meet goals would have resulted in a substantial fine. Individuals in both the Clinton and Bush administrations objected to the goals, and so have important environmentalists. In fact, there is growing consensus that Kyoto is the wrong framework for emissions reductions, and many now assert it has done nothing to reduce emissions since it was passed. Other major objections to Kyoto included the fact that it demanded no reductions from developing countries. Some felt that reducing emissions in the United States would be costly and might hurt our economy or at least slow it down, especially in relation to those of fast-growing countries like India and China, which are exempt. To many, this seemed like an unacceptable cost, but it was a difficult argument to communicate. Our rejection of Kyoto angered many other nations partly because **the United States is the biggest producer of greenhouse gases**: we spew out fully one-third of the world's carbon dioxide emissions. This is due to our manufacturing sector that produces goods that are consumed worldwide and our high individual use of carbon-emitting gasoline and electricity.

The main American supporter of Kyoto and an early political activist on **anthropogenic** (human-caused) global warming was **Al Gore**, who won an Oscar for the documentary about climate change, *An Inconvenient Truth*. Gore and the **UN Intergovernmental Panel on Climate Change** were awarded the **2007 Nobel Peace Prize** for their work to combat global warming. Why the Peace Prize? Because many people think that global warming will drastically alter the worldwide availability of resources and ultimately lead to **resource wars**. The crisis in Darfur may be an early example. **Darfur**, an area in western Sudan, has been hit with bad droughts, resulting in desertification. Groups looking for water (mostly for agriculture) entered areas traditionally controlled by others; violent militias on both sides and government collusion with some factions escalated the armed conflict to levels some called genocide. The intensity of **Hurricane Katrina**, which caused a humanitarian crisis in New Orleans, has also been blamed in part on global warming, since hurricanes get stronger over warmer water.

Disappointed by the lack of environmental action on the federal level, in 2003 nine northeastern states banded together and formed the **Regional Greenhouse Gas Initiative**, or **RGGI**, to create their own regulations, centered on a cap-and-trade system modeled on Kyoto's. Moderate Republican governor **Arnold Schwarzenegger** of California spearheaded a similar effort called the **Western Climate Change Initiative**, which became an international effort in 2007 when the Canadian province of Manitoba joined. Schwarzenegger has been an effective environmental advocate, demonstrating that climate politics aren't necessarily party-oriented, but involve factions within political parties.

In 2007, Massachusetts led an effort to **sue the EPA**. The EPA claimed that states had no legal right to regulate carbon dioxide, arguing that carbon dioxide was not a pollutant and therefore could not be regulated under the **Clean Air Act**. Rather, the EPA asserted that the agency held the sole authority to regulate the substance. The matter went to the Supreme Court, which sent down a split decision in favor of the states. The Court ruled that carbon dioxide was a pollutant, and could be regulated under the Clean Air Act, in a move seen to be a slap in the face to the Bush administration. But the fight didn't end there. California also set the **first greenhouse gas emissions standards on vehicles** in the nation, requesting a waiver from the EPA to do so, which was denied. California's CAFE regulations were tougher than those passed in a national bill in 2007, and the state decided to fight the decision, filing another lawsuit with the EPA in 2008. By then, twelve other states had adopted California's standards.

States took action largely because President Bush was less interested in environmental issues than were previous presidents. In 1999, for example, his predecessor Bill Clinton attempted to toughen standards for the amount of **arsenic** allowed in drinking water. After Bush took office, he insisted that meeting the levels would be difficult for small communities with limited means to install new filtration technologies, but he faced a firestorm of negative press. He relented, and Clinton's law was adopted; however, research now shows that even these measures may be inadequate because arsenic is more carcinogenic than previously thought. On the other hand, in 2005 the EPA strengthened standards to control levels of **lead** in drinking water after a scandal over public water in Washington, DC.

In 2001, President Bush's EPA head, ex–New Jersey governor **Christine Todd Whitman**, was in the eye of several political storms. She first questioned a government report on the human causes of global warming and then assured New Yorkers that the air in Manhattan after September 11 was safe; both positions have been largely discredited. Whitman resigned in 2003, and later publicly stated that she left because she personally disagreed with Vice President Dick Cheney's desire to soften air pollution standards. Whitman now faces a class-action lawsuit brought by people sickened by post–September 11 air quality in New York.

Bush's **Healthy Forests Act**, passed in 2003, has also been controversial. Advocates say that it will reduce destructive fires by allowing forests to be thinned, while detractors claim that not only will it make fires worse, it's really a sop to the timber industry. New evidence from the Forest Service suggests that the thinning allowed by the Healthy Forests Act may indeed contribute to the severity of fires.

It's burning of another nature — oil, gas, and coal — that produces most greenhouse gases, so finding alternative, renewable resources has become a new focus for environmentalists. As reserves of conventional fuels are finite, renewable resources are becoming important to the auto, extraction, and utility industries as well. Although the interests of both groups will at some point align as petro reserves dry up, environmentalists and the extraction industry currently butt heads like caribou in rutting season — and one of the main battlegrounds has been the **Arctic National Wildlife Refuge**, or **ANWR**. Called "**anwar**," it is synonymous with the phrase "drilling for oil in Alaska."

In 1987 the results of a survey conducted by the Department of the Interior led to the recommendation that an area within ANWR be opened to oil drilling. The area is small compared to the size of ANWR, comprising **8 percent of the territory**. But ANWR is gigantic, and 8 percent of gigantic is still huge: **1.5 million acres**, an area bigger than Delaware. ANWR provides one of the best chances (but not the only one) for developing new oil fields in US territory, and the potential reserves are substantial.[6] Advocates cite the importance of domestic oil for national security, and say that developing ANWR would create thousands of jobs. They contend that only a tiny portion of the land would be taken up by any oil facilities, leaving plenty of room for local wildlife. The two small Native American populations in the area, who are financially dependent on the oil companies, support drilling, as does most of the Alaskan government because it equates oil with economic development. Alaskans are mostly pro-drilling and have historically been distrustful of conservationists. However, conservationists report that this suspicion, along with the pack ice, has thawed in recent years, perhaps partly due to corruption scandals involving Alaskan politicians taking bribes from the oil industry.[7]

Those in favor of preserving ANWR argue that drilling produces oil and waste spills, which are hard on the particularly delicate arctic wildlife. Environmentalists also contend that the "footprint" of oil drilling is much bigger than what drilling advocates assert, because the numbers cited do not account for enclosed areas or the space under pipelines. Some biologists also argue that animals maintain a wide distance from drilling installations, thus shrinking their habitat beyond the area taken up by an oil site itself. This may be especially true for the internationally protected herd of caribou that migrate through the coastal plain.

There's also an efficiency argument against exploration: ANWR would take perhaps fifteen to twenty-five years to produce oil at high yield, whereas alternative energy sources could be developed more quickly. Experts estimate ANWR would produce at most around 1.5 million barrels of oil a day, which is practically a drop in the country's gas tank; we use more than 19 million barrels a day — 7 billion a year — now. Proponents say that ANWR oil would significantly reduce our dependence on foreign oil. Anti-drilling groups counter that by the time ANWR could produce 1.5 million barrels daily, we would be using even more oil than we do now, so ANWR would reduce our dependence on foreign oil by only a relatively small percentage. Nobody seems to factor in future use of alternative energy. So what *are* our alternatives? Nuclear, wind, and solar power might provide electricity, while biofuels and hydrogen may supply transportation fuels.

Wind power creates no emissions, is totally renewable, and leaves a very small "footprint" on the land; but it depends on something that is not always there — wind. Since energy is very difficult to store, given current technology, wind power's **intermittency** can disrupt power grids, so wind must be used in conjunction with other power sources. Wind power is currently slightly **more expensive** than power derived from coal or natural gas, though not by much.

But wind is **scaleable**: you can derive electricity from one windmill or eight hundred, whereas coal-fired power plants have to be big to be cost-effective, requiring millions in up-front investment. Government policy has slowed down wind power development by not providing predictable extensions to its funding, making it risky for wind entrepreneurs to invest further in research, development, and production.

Even environmentalists are split over wind power. Some think wind is an excellent form of alternative energy, while others are concerned that wind power may damage ecosystems. Offshore wind farms have been criticized for disrupting coastal habitats, while land-based farms may reduce bird and bat populations. Bat loss is a serious problem for wind farms on farmland, because as pollinators and natural insecticides, bats are critical for agriculture.

"Biofuels" refers to any fuel made from organic material. **Ethanol**, which is plain old ethyl alcohol, is the best biofuel candidate: it burns cleanly, isn't toxic (except to your liver), and is renewable because it's made from plants. The United States allows up to **10 percent ethanol** in gasoline mixtures, which are called **E10**, and about half of US gas contains some ethanol. High ethanol use requires different engines; those currently available burn up to **E85**. The ethanol industry got a big boost from the **2005 Energy Bill**, which led to the development of sixteen new ethanol-producing facilities. The 1992 Energy Policy Bill required the federal fleet of cars to be **flex fuel vehicles**, or **FFVs**, capable of using E85 gas, while the 2005 bill required the federal fleet to run on E85 all the time. This has led to unforeseen shortages of E85 gas and resulting price spikes, although these should level out over time.

But ethanol isn't perfect. American ethanol is **made from corn**, which is sown and harvested with diesel-burning farm equipment. In theory, these could run on ethanol, but for now they only consume more fossil fuel. The chemical process of converting corn to ethanol produces loads of carbon dioxide, too. Some scientists calculate that these factors make ethanol even more emission-producing overall than gasoline, though there are ways to avoid this. Brazil uses sugarcane to make ethanol in special low-emissions-producing plants, but it can't be imported here in usable quantities because the US ethanol industry is protected by high tariffs. Plus, all biofuels require a lot of space; it's estimated that even if all US soybean and corn acreage were used to produce ethanol, we would satisfy only 9 percent of our fuel needs.[8] And if you use corn to run cars, you can't use it to run bodies; in a world where approximately 25,000 people die of hunger daily, the food-for-fuel use might be too morally costly. In 2008 record-high food prices worldwide were partly blamed on the use of acreage for growing fuel instead of growing food. Furthermore, the viability of ethanol is reliant on high crop yields, achieved through bioengineered crops and lots of fertilizer that itself produces greenhouse gases. Finally, detractors point out that ethanol relies on government subsidies, which some contend amounts to corporate welfare for large agribusinesses such as Archer Daniels Midland. Most politicians from states that produce crops that can be used for ethanol are strongly in favor of using the biofuel, regardless of what party they belong to.

Cellulose, the largely indigestible fiber that makes up much plant matter, can be used to make ethanol with the aid of enzymes (special proteins that help jump-start chemical reactions). The technology, however, is still being perfected and made more cost efficient. The resulting **cellulosic ethanol** is far superior to conventional ethanol because it requires almost no fossil fuel to produce. **Switchgrass** is a terrific source of cellulosic ethanol: it produces more than twice as much fuel per unit as corn, and as a native perennial plant, it requires less fertilizer and pesticides. Many environmentalists advocate major funding to research cellulosic ethanol production. The good news is that **switching to ethanol is cheap** for consumers — it could cost only about $100 to install simple new equipment in your car.

Another biofuel is **biodiesel**, which is made from renewable resources such as vegetable oil. The problems with it so far are, one, it's costly because not only do you have to outfit a car with a biodiesel system, but the fuel itself is more expensive than gasoline; two, it's hard to find; and three, like all biofuels, it requires a great deal of land area to produce. A plant called **jatropha** could revolutionize biodiesel because it can grow cheaply in marginal areas. Though not cultivated in the United States, it is being tested in India and China.

Hydrogen is a much-touted but so far mostly unavailable new fuel. The simple gas is renewable, can be made anywhere, is clean to use (it produces only water vapor), and can be relatively clean to make as well. Hydrogen cars would run on electricity generated from hydrogen, but generating hydrogen itself takes energy. Hydrogen can be produced as a by-product of coal gasification and nuclear power plants; however, using natural gas, coal, or oil to make hydrogen somewhat defeats the point of making it in the first place, since the process still uses nonrenewable and emission-generating energy sources. You really need to use **electrolysis**, the process by which electricity is used to split water into hydrogen and oxygen molecules.

Notice the circular quality of hydrogen power — hydrogen can make electricity, but to make hydrogen, you need electricity. If you want to move from fossil fuels to hydrogen, you must also use wind, solar, hydroelectric, wave, or geothermal power to generate hydrogen — plus you need more available electricity overall. The next issue is storing and distributing hydrogen, which is difficult. And once you have a hydrogen car, where do you get the fuel? That's another circular problem: people won't buy the car if the fuel isn't readily available, but companies won't build hydrogen stations if nobody has hydrogen cars. In theory, this is where government investment might make a real difference: it could build, or encourage others to build, hydrogen stations. There have also been concerns about the safety of hydrogen, but these diminished as engineers designed better carrying mechanisms. Basically, anything that can make a car go can be dangerous, and hydrogen is dangerous in a different way than gasoline or diesel.

BMW is producing a commercially available hydrogen car, though some claim it is worse for the environment than a diesel truck because it has poor fuel economy when run on gas and requires a lot of water when using hydrogen. All the talk of hydrogen would be quenched if someone developed a really **good rechargeable battery** that could provide enough electricity to run a car for a day or so — eliminating the need for hydrogen in the first place. Current **hybrid cars** use both gas and electricity; the car runs on electricity at some times and gas at others, greatly increasing fuel efficiency. The first widely available hybrid car, the **Toyota Prius**, was developed in Japan, which has been way ahead of America in developing fuel-efficient cars since the 1970s. More than half a million have been sold. A **significant hybrid car tax break** offered by the federal government has been phased out; advocates of cleaner energy believe it should be extended.

Solar power uses only the sun, but solar cells are very expensive, are made with toxic chemicals, and produce electricity only when the sun shines. One important possible application for solar power would be to **produce hydrogen**; another would be to create **peaking stations** that provide extra power only when electricity use is at its highest. **Blackouts** and **brownouts** (when voltage drops and lights dim) have become more frequent on peak usage days because the United States has not invested in new electricity infrastructure. The problem is that electricity cannot really be stored — you have to make it as you consume it. That's why you can't just rely on solar power all the time. Peak usage usually occurs on hot days when people use air conditioners, which require a lot of electricity — as opposed to most home heating systems, which are typically powered by heating oil or natural gas. Since peak usage days usually coincide with sunny weather, solar power is ideal for peaking stations.[9]

One of the big questions in the development of alternative energy sources — and in environmental policy in general — is what role the government should take. Right now, there is a combination of public and private investment in new technologies. Billionaire founder of Virgin Records and Airlines **Richard Branson** decided to invest $3 billion in renewable energy; the **X PRIZE Foundation** is planning a new set of lucrative prizes for the development of commercially viable cars that run on clean and renewable energy; and many power and car companies are developing new technologies (often with some federal subsidies) as well. The 2005 Energy Bill pumped more federal money into developing cleaner and renewable energy sources, though many feel that it was a case of too little, if not too late.

Given the problems with traditional power sources, renewable energy is definitely the wave of the future. There is a tacit consensus that cutting-edge technology will be developed by private industry subsidized in part by the government, but if we ever reach a national energy crisis, the government might take the helm. And while many environmental issues are argued every year, major policy debates will likely focus on issues surrounding energy for the foreseeable — warmer — future.

8

Civil Liberties

> Civil liberties exist to protect the individual against state intrusion.

> An individual's or party's positions on civil liberties often appear inconsistent.

> Some think the right to bear arms gives individuals the right to own guns, while others believe it refers to the collective ability of the community to raise a militia.

> Urban and rural populations interpret issues of gun control differently.

> Generally, Republicans more strongly support gun rights, and Democrats advocate gun control. Notable exceptions include former New York mayor Republican Rudy Giuliani.

> Warrantless wiretapping of international communications began under George W. Bush. Republicans are split on the practice; most Democrats oppose it.

> The power of eminent domain allows the government to seize private property for public use. A 2005 Supreme Court case expanded eminent domain, leading to a popular backlash.

> Detention and rendition practices used with terrorism suspects have been criticized for violating constitutional guarantees of a prisoner's rights. Some say these practices are legal, others think

they are unfortunate but necessary, and others find them completely incompatible with American values.

➤ There are arguments over what constitutes torture, if and when it is legal, if and when it is morally acceptable, and whether the United States has tortured prisoners.

➤ The loudest critics of American rendition, detention, and interrogation techniques have been civil liberties groups and human rights organizations.

➤ Some think capital punishment is cruel and unusual and should be abolished.

➤ Some methods of capital punishment have been found unconstitutional.

Background to Current Debates

America's system of civil liberties is unique. Civil liberties guarantees are meant to protect the individual against the action of the state, especially political attacks brought by a government against its enemies. Our most famous civil liberty, the right to free speech, is not even guaranteed in England, where most of our notions of individual liberty originated. Civil liberties place both procedural and substantive limits on governmental power and serve as a check on behalf of the citizen against powerful groups, institutions, and individuals. Put another way, they protect individuals and smaller groups from being dominated by majority rule. But where do these rights begin and end? Under what circumstances can they be denied? Our civil liberties are primarily enshrined in the Bill of Rights — the first ten amendments to the Constitution, which were passed in 1791 — and the Supreme Court has played a vital role in determining the boundaries of those rights.

However much our early government valued civil liberties, they are rights that have been debated throughout American history. Many historians feel that President John Adams's otherwise outstanding career was marred by his enactment of the 1798 **Alien and Sedition Acts**, which suspended free speech and led to the imprisonment of newspaper editors who criticized the Adams administration. In the 1950s and '60s, civil liberties issues took center stage as the United States underwent a series of major cultural shifts. Since September 11, 2001, new questions about civil liberties have arisen, as fighting terrorism became a key part of the national political debate.

The current debate over civil liberties is the latest version of a division that has existed throughout American history. The conservative camp — mostly Republicans, and especially powerful under President George W. Bush — argue that concerns over security should be paramount. They favor changing laws to allow authorities to work with the least bureaucratic and legal oversight possible. Yet this has split the contemporary conservative movement into two groups: conservative **libertarians**, who are staunch supporters of civil liberties and limited government and who feel that many new policies erode important protections, and those we might call **executivists**, who think that the president and the executive branch can best do their job — keeping America safe from its enemies — if they have a free hand to operate as they see fit.

The unofficial leader of the executivist group from 2001–8 was former Wyoming congressman, secretary of defense, and Halliburton CEO, Republican vice president **Dick Cheney**. Conservative libertarians, who generally agree with the Republican Party on economic issues, criticize the executivist position on civil liberties. They are joined by the liberal camp, mostly Democrats, although Democrats themselves are also divided: some are more vocal supporters of civil liberties and human rights, but others argue that certain expectations of liberty and privacy must be downgraded to deal with the war on terror. Human rights advocates and civil libertarians, who may belong to any party, but who usually identify more closely with groups that advocate civil liberties than with whichever party they support, have been vocal opponents to recent changes in policy on civil liberties.

Most Americans are somewhere in the middle, willing to give up some protections for enhanced security. Though partly due to the secrecy surrounding much national security policy, it's unclear at times whether or not reductions in civil liberties buy us much security. Some say it's too high a price to pay; others believe that our liberties would be worthless if we can't defend them aggressively. Other civil liberties issues such as capital punishment or gun control versus gun rights are domestic matters but involve similar anguish over balancing individual rights with community security.

One of the interesting things about civil liberties is that an individual's position on any given issue may seem **philosophically inconsistent** with her position on other civil liberties issues. Many liberals, for example, value the collective over the individual when it comes to gun control, but favor individual rights over collective rights when it comes to torture or wiretapping. Many conservatives support individual rights of gun ownership over collective rights to safety, but feel that breaching an individual's rights by using torture might be acceptable to protect communities. Both Democrats and Republicans have libertarian views on certain issues, but they differ over the areas in which they think government should intervene.

Libertarians are really the only ones who have a consistent ideological viewpoint when it comes to civil liberties, and because of where Democrats and Republicans stand on these issues, libertarians sometimes agree with Democrats and sometimes with Republicans. Many of the major civil libertarian organizations are independent and nonpartisan, the most well known being the **American Civil Liberties Union**, or **ACLU**. While the ACLU is widely perceived as liberal, they've also supported the rights of political conservatives, including the late Reverend Jerry Falwell, and reactionary groups such as the American Nazi Party. And many libertarians pride themselves on being political independents.

As a group of issues, civil liberties show us that almost nobody — politician, scholar, or average citizen — adopts a predictable, coherent view. Positions on civil liberties are often decided not by a broad rule but on a case-by-case basis. Our positions are almost never absolute, but relative and contingent, because we weigh values differently depending on circumstances. And that makes for interesting politics.

The Second Amendment: Gun Control versus Gun Rights

The debate over gun control laws has often been framed in terms of the culture wars, pitting rural, suburban, and small urban communities who want to keep guns (usually for hunting) against centers of urban violence where many support tough gun control. There is a cultural divide, to be sure, but the issue ultimately boils down to legal questions about civil liberties and the extent of certain rights as embodied in the Second Amendment: "A well-regulated Militia being necessary to the security of a free state, the right of the people to keep and bear arms shall not be infringed." That's the whole amendment. It's not much to go on. The debate centers on who exactly the Constitution says can have a gun, if different kinds of guns can be regulated by different laws, and even whether it matters what the Constitution says about guns in the first place.

If you are a strong supporter of gun rights, you think the Second Amendment provides plenty of guidance: it says you can bear arms. Period. Others maintain it's not quite that simple. Supporters of gun control believe that the amendment refers to the right of the citizens as a body to form a militia or a military. They say that this is clear from the mention of the militia and the phrase "bear arms," which, they contend, was clearly a military reference in the late 1700s, not a personal one. You didn't bear arms to shoot a deer for dinner. You bore arms as a citizen fighting in the Revolution. As is the case with most civil liberties issues, one aspect of the debate is between the individual and the community. Can we as a group bear arms, or can we as individuals keep guns? Gun control advocates point to the use of the word "people" to argue that this was intended as a collective right. Some strike an ideological middle ground by saying that the right to bear arms was meant as an individual right to act within a collective. These people may therefore support many gun control laws but also the basic right of an individual to own weapons. Some gun control supporters also argue that the right granted inherently had to do with maintaining a militia, the need for which no longer exists. Thus, they think the right has lapsed. Gun rights advocates insist that the initial phrase of the amendment doesn't matter and that it simply grants a right. Gun supporters also say that the phrase "shall not infringe" means that government has no ability to regulate gun ownership, while gun control supporters respond that infringement and regulation are different things. After all, we have a right to free speech, but it is regulated: libel and slander laws punish people for unfairly dragging each other through the mud.

Those who support individual weapons rights also make historical arguments, referring to the old common law right to self-defense. Many gun rights advocates contend that it's safer for more individuals to carry weapons because they may defend themselves or others if threatened. This isn't just an assumption. In 2002 two legally armed students stopped a shooting at Virginia's Appalachian School of Law. In 2007 armed Omaha shoppers stopped a teenage shooter in a local mall. Also in 2007 an armed megachurch security guard shot a heavily armed man who had already shot six people and killed two. Gun control supporters, on the other hand, reply that this reveals the need for stricter regulations. If the shooter hadn't had a gun, they reason, he wouldn't have been able to hurt anyone in the first place.

There is another historical argument that few today actually make, but that certainly lurks behind both the enthusiasm of some gun rights supporters and the discomfort of some gun control proponents: a citizen's check on the government. America is now quite politically stable compared to most nations and groups throughout human history, but our nation was born from an armed, violent rebellion. The Revolution had many causes, from economic to social, but its rhetoric was expressly and almost entirely political. The founders fought against a system of government and sought to establish a new one that would be more just. They were fully aware of the excesses of tyranny, and went to great lengths — the separation of powers and our system of checks and balances — to ensure that no one group or individual could easily dominate. The idea that a citizens' militia could defend the government in a time of invasion or insurrection — or, alternatively, could defend the people's rights against a tyrannical government — is implicit in the Second Amendment, say some respected legal scholars. While the Supreme Court has been active in many areas of civil liberties, it has been relatively quiet regarding how to interpret the Second Amendment. A 1939 opinion held that the amendment creates a collective right, not an individual one, which opened the door to contemporary gun regulation.[1]

There is a strong division between urban and rural attitudes toward guns. In rural areas, they are often part of everyday life. Many Americans hunt; on ranches and farms, guns may be considered necessary. Guns are prevalent in low-income urban areas as well, whether they protect against or inflict personal violence. Urban gun violence in America has decreased dramatically since the 1980s, plummeting after 1993 (though it's still high compared with other developed nations). Gun control advocates think that reductions in violent crime are a direct result of gun control laws enacted in 1993, while gun ownership supporters trace the decline to the 1980s and tie it to other factors like a strong economy, more law enforcement officers, and changes in policing techniques. Gun violence affects blacks more than whites: African Americans suffer nearly twice as much violent gun-related crime as whites in America.[2] Gun control is also considered a women's issue, because most women who are victims of homicide are killed with a gun by someone they know. Consequently, a federal law was passed in 1994 barring anyone with a domestic violence, harassment, or stalking restraining order from buying a gun.

The **National Rifle Association**, or **NRA**, supports the right of all Americans to own weapons of any kind. The NRA considers its cause particularly patriotic because it sees itself as a defender of constitutional rights. A pillar of the conservative coalition, it's also an extremely effective lobbying institution, which often serves as a political guidance counselor to its members. Since Republicans are much more likely than Democrats to support gun rights over gun control, however, the NRA overwhelmingly supports Republican politicians.

Republican politicians who deviate from the gun rights platform usually hail from urban areas. Former New York City mayor **Rudy Giuliani**, for instance, aggressively prosecuted gun manufacturers and distributors in his successful effort to reduce crime rates. Later in his career, he maintained that urban violence and hunting are very different issues, indicating that gun control laws that differently affect urban and rural areas are acceptable. Conversely, Democrats from rural areas — such as former Vermont governor and Democratic National Committee chairman Howard Dean — tend to be more favorable to gun rights, pushing for limited regulations that help distinguish between law-abiding citizens and potential criminals.

The **Brady Handgun Violence Prevention Act**, America's best known gun control law, was passed by Congress and signed by Democratic president **Bill Clinton** in 1993. Known as the **Brady Bill**, this law stipulated a waiting period and background check for all purchasers of handguns, though there were many loopholes. Background checks are now conducted digitally in an FBI database. The provisions do not apply to private sales of handguns, because the federal government cannot regulate intrastate trade — trade within a single state. The Brady Bill was named for **James Brady**, the White House press secretary who was severely wounded and permanently disabled during the 1981 attempted assassination of Republican president Ronald Reagan. His wife, Sarah Brady, has been a force behind gun control laws ever since, through the **Brady Campaign to Prevent Gun Violence**.

In 1994, Congress also passed the **Federal Assault Weapons Ban**, which automatically **expired in 2004** because it contained a **sunset clause**. A sunset clause means that a law will expire unless actively renewed; it's a common legislative technique that allows policies to be reconsidered over time and as a result often makes controversial measures more politically palatable. The ban was created to eliminate semiautomatic firearms from public circulation (semiautomatics fire one round per pull of the trigger and automatically move the next round into place; automatics keep firing as long as the trigger is depressed). While gun rights activists campaigned against the law, most politicians were convinced that semiautomatics were too dangerous to be sold publicly, and were simply unnecessary for hunting. After the Columbine High School shooting in 2003, in which two students killed twelve others before killing themselves, Congress unsuccessfully attempted to pass legislation creating a background check and waiting period for sales at gun shows. The assault weapons ban has not been renewed; Republicans generally favor this status quo, while most Democrats favor closing the gun show loophole and extending the assault weapons ban.

The Fourth Amendment: Warrantless Wiretapping — Executive Power versus Citizens' Privacy

The Fourth Amendment states, "The right of the people to be secure in their persons, houses, papers, and effects, against unreasonable searches and seizures, shall not be violated, and no Warrants shall issue, but upon probable cause. . . ." Fourth Amendment issues are associated with the **Warren Court**, the Supreme Court under Chief Justice Earl Warren, who sat from 1953 to 1969. The Warren Court first articulated the constitutional necessity of obtaining a warrant for a wiretap, based on a citizen's "reasonable expectation of privacy" in a telephone call.[3] In 2005 controversy erupted when the *New York Times* revealed that President George W. Bush had issued a secret executive order authorizing **warrantless wiretapping** on American citizens. Wiretapping of foreign communications is not covered by the Fourth Amendment; the Bush wiretapping program involved conversations between at least one person within the United States and at least one person outside the country, not two parties in America.

In early 2002, President Bush allowed the **National Security Agency**, or **NSA**, to eavesdrop on conversations involving American citizens without fulfilling existing legal requirements to do so. Many think this was illegal, endangered civil liberties, and/or constituted a usurpation of powers by the executive branch. Some who defend the action argue that it was legal, while others say it was a reasonable breach of existing law because it was necessary to preserve national security in the wake of September 11.

Civil libertarians — mainly journalists, lawyers, and academics — fought the executivist Bush administration on warrantless wiretapping. Classic conservative Republicans who want small government and strong privacy rights split with the Bush administration over it, joining many Democrats. The public has not rejected warrantless wiretapping, but it's questionable how many understand the specifics. Almost all congressional Republicans supported the practice, though one of its strongest critics was the Senate Judiciary Committee's lead Republican senator **Arlen Specter** of Pennsylvania. Democratic senator **Russ Feingold** of Wisconsin has also been a vocal opponent and attempted to pass a motion of censure (basically a slap on the wrist from the Senate) over the issue.

On the other side of the fence, former attorney general **Alberto Gonzales** was a staunch defender of the program, which he claimed "did not invade anyone's privacy, unless you are talking to the enemy in this time of war."[4] Gonzales's efforts to continue the program when he was White House counsel (the president's official lawyer) led to a hospital room showdown with a postoperative Attorney General John Ashcroft, Ashcroft's acting attorney general (who legally had taken over because Ashcroft was sick), and the FBI. The incident may have been the decisive factor in Gonzales's downfall when it became clear that he had lied about the events in his testimony to the Senate. The Bush administration assured the public and Congress that warrantless wiretapping was stopped in 2005, but the legal ramifications of the program may take years to sort out.

The United States has long intercepted conversations between one foreign party and another, since non-Americans are not protected by the Constitution. Communications involving citizens, however, were considered subject to Fourth Amendment protection. In 1978 the **Foreign Intelligence Surveillance Act**, or **FISA**, required authorities to get a warrant from a special court — the Foreign Intelligence Surveillance Court, which operates in secret — for wiretapping involving Americans. Warrants can be obtained retroactively, as long as the court is informed within seventy-two hours of the start of a tap.

However, the Bush administration argued that the rules were unacceptably restrictive given the circumstances. It also sought phone and e-mail records of thousands of Americans, and most telecom companies they approached handed them over, with the exception of **Qwest**. There has been disagreement over whether the telecom companies are liable for this action, which could cost them billions of dollars in litigation and settlements; conservatives proposed a bill that would grant the companies retroactive immunity, which progressives oppose. The administration thought secrecy was key to the program; Bush personally accused the *New York Times* of endangering national security when it broke the wiretapping story, and some right-wingers agreed. The paper had been concerned about security, too, and only ran the story after sitting on it for a year while attempting to figure out what to do.

The problem, say many critics, is bigger than the wiretapping that has already occured. They see the system of warrantless wiretapping as an **erosion of checks on power** that were created to prevent abuses by the executive branch. This has been the main argument of the professional organization of lawyers, the **American Bar Association**, or **ABA**. During the Vietnam War, the government spied on Americans frequently — not because these citizens were directly engaging with the enemy, but because they were antiwar activists. John Kerry, a decorated war hero turned antiwar activist who eventually became a Democratic senator from Massachusetts, had his phone tapped. Earlier, the government spied on Martin Luther King Jr. The

FBI under J. Edgar Hoover was notorious for wiretapping citizens Hoover personally considered subversives; concern over Hoover's illegal spying grew in the 1960s. In 1972, Republican president Richard Nixon's order to break into the Democratic National Committee's Watergate offices to place a wiretap led to his resignation and revealed to the American public the extent to which our leaders may go to preserve their power.

Those who are most against the wiretapping program argue that the ability to spy on citizens, with no check, is **open to abuse** and therefore cannot be allowed. Start secretly listening to the phone calls of a suspected al-Qaeda operative, they say, and soon you'll be reading the e-mails of your political opponents. Critics maintain that the system of obtaining warrants is not onerous, but is necessary. After September 11, the number of warrants granted by the **Foreign Intelligence Surveillance Court** (**FISC**) skyrocketed, and according to its published reports, the court has denied a warrant only five times, while more than twenty thousand warrants have been granted.

Executivists countered that obtaining warrants is time-consuming. In 2007 the director of national intelligence, Michael McConnell, stated that each warrant took two hundred hours to prepare. A *Wired* blogger multiplied the number of warrants FISA granted in 2006 by two hundred and found that McConnell's numbers added up to fifty thousand workdays spent on warrants, or the full-time work of 218 employees with top secret clearances.[5] While McConnell may have exaggerated, it's probably true that applying for warrants is annoying and takes up time, though opponents of the program point out that the inconvenience is well worth the stronger guarantee of privacy and the checks on power that obtaining a warrant entails.

Some executivists, however, maintain that the warrantless wiretapping program was legal in the first place. They say that as commander in chief, the president is allowed to conduct operations against the enemy as he sees fit. There are also some who argue that Congress specifically allowed the president to bypass FISA when it passed the **USA PATRIOT Act**, which included provisions allowing for lower standards of evidence to be met in order to conduct certain kinds of surveillance. Most members of Congress, however, did not think that their vote for the PATRIOT Act amounted to a vote to override FISA, and many were outraged when it was suggested that they did.

The PATRIOT Act's full name is a mouthful: the **Uniting and Strengthening America by Providing Appropriate Tools Required to Intercept and Obstruct Terrorism Act of 2001**; its provisions were likewise lengthy. The PATRIOT Act was controversial from the moment it passed; civil libertarians felt it unnecessarily eroded many important protections against government intrusion. The act lowered barriers to intelligence gathering while restricting foreign financial transactions, as well as immigration and visa regulations. One of the better known provisions allowed the government to search library records to see what materials patrons requested or checked out. Numerous lawsuits have challenged the PATRIOT Act, and some provisions have been found illegal. The act was, however, the result of a strong bipartisan effort in Congress, and while there have been political debates on certain provisions, especially as the bill has been amended, most politicians supported it.

Everyone in the Bush administration who defended the wiretapping program maintained its legality; pundits and political supporters, who aren't bound to meet the same legal standards, argued that whatever rights warrantless wiretapping violated, if any, were negligible compared to the additional security it provided. To many, it is a choice between a high level of privacy and national security. Opponents counter that this reasoning presupposes a **false choice** because the issue is not whether the government should be able to spy on Americans, but rather whether it should have to obtain a warrant to do so. They further contend that the process of obtaining warrants does not decrease the number of taps that are put in place, while proponents of easier spying respond that bureaucratic delays must be kept to a minimum in order to speed intelligence gathering and devote time to investigations.

Another worry for many civil libertarians is **data mining**, the practice by which the government culls data from various sources, including police databases. What is most troubling about such mining is that almost nobody is aware it's happening. Furthermore, the data considered include not only crimes of which people have been convicted — or even charged — but even such banalities as traffic accidents. Because these systems have such a broad sweep, concerns are growing that information on one's political affiliations or practices may be subject to scrutiny. Civil libertarians contend there is little oversight on such mechanisms, and think that if the government engages in such actions, there should be someone making sure these powers aren't abused.

The Fifth Amendment: Eminent Domain versus Private Property Rights

Eminent domain refers to the seizure of land by government and allows federal or state governments to take private property for public use. The government may either purchase property (almost always land) for its own use, as is the case for, say, a site for a sewage treatment plant, or it may turn over the property to a third party to develop. In all cases, the owner is compensated, and the price is typically stipulated by law at fair market value or more. Eminent domain is addressed in the Fifth Amendment, which states in part, "nor shall private property be taken for public use, without just compensation." The Supreme Court originally interpreted this clause narrowly, ruling that property claimed by the government had to be used by the public. Eminent domain was largely limited to land acquisition for roads, bridges, tunnels, military installations, and public works such as water and sewage facilities.

In 1954 the definition of eminent domain was expanded when the Court allowed decayed and violent urban areas, called **blighted property**, to be razed and sold to private companies for development purposes.[6] The controversial case targeted areas of Washington, DC, that were basically slums. The majority decision stated that getting rid of the buildings in question benefited the public good because they posed a threat to public safety, while economic development was in the public's best interest. Many fiercely condemned the decision as explicitly racist because the property was almost exclusively occupied by African Americans. Libertarians were upset because they support private property rights. The strongest critics, however, were liberal groups and Democrats.

In 2005 the Supreme Court handed down a highly contentious ruling on eminent domain for the purpose of **economic development**. This ruling further expanded the notion of public use to property in good condition, where there was no violence or other endemic social problems, allowing it to be claimed by the government on behalf of private developers. The case centered on an area of **New London, Connecticut**, that was seeking investment from pharmaceutical giant **Pfizer**, which built a major research facility there in 1998. New London was in an economic downturn, so the city was keen to attract Pfizer's business and ride the company's economic coattails. New London planned a large development around the Pfizer facility that would include a conference center, hotel, apartments and condos, and retail space. One hundred fifteen homes had to be destroyed to build the desired project, but fifteen owners declined to sell, of whom ten were residents and five were investors. The Supreme Court decided against the homeowners, ruling that any activity that would increase jobs, growth, and tax revenue is a legitimate form of public use.

Most who followed the case were outraged; primarily, they objected to the implication that a private company could buy whatever it wanted, including a family's home, with impunity. *Kelo v. City of New London* may be the single most unpopular Supreme Court decision in a generation. Surprisingly, given that liberals are less closely associated with business interests than are conservatives, the pro-business decision was made by the liberals on the Court, who argued that a small number of holdouts should not be able to prevent a project that would be beneficial to a community; the conservatives opposed the expansion of eminent domain, citing their support of individual property rights.

Other opponents of the ruling included the American Association of Retired Persons (AARP), the National Association for the Advancement of Colored People (NAACP), and the Libertarian Party. Groups such as the AARP and NAACP protested the expansion of eminent domain on the same grounds that Justice Sandra Day O'Connor stated in her dissenting opinion: it historically disadvantages politically weak groups such as the elderly and racial minorities. Many liberals and Democrats agreed, as did those who oppose the ability of the wealthy to deprive the less economically advantaged. The concern is realistic: eminent domain has even been proposed to take over public golf courses and give them to gated communities.[7]

President George W. Bush strongly disagreed with the court's decision as well, and issued an **executive order** in 2006 to limit its ramifications. The order stated that the federal government could not take private property for purposes of economic development. In the wake of *Kelo*, at least forty-two states passed laws limiting eminent domain, and Republican-led coalitions attempted to pass limits in Congress. The impact of eminent domain for economic development is widespread, as eminent domain is invoked with some regularity. The number of eminent domain cases in the past ten years has been estimated at anywhere from the low hundreds to the thousands (the numbers are politicized). Some of the cases are particularly troubling to many because they involve completely unblighted private property — usually with water views and other desirable features — being taken over by private companies.

The upside of the Court's 2005 decision for supporters of individual property rights was the enormous popular and political **backlash** it unfurled. In 2006 the Ohio Supreme Court ruled for homeowners in a major case that pitted working-class residents of a Cincinnati suburb against developers who wanted to create a huge retail and office complex worth $125 million. The Ohio court ruled on the basis of state law, and considering the new provisions limiting eminent domain that were enacted by most states after the 2005 decision, the indication is that state governments may indeed limit governments' ability to seize property for economic development.

The Sixth Amendment: Rendition and Rights of Detainees

Guaranteeing certain rights for those detained by the government is considered a foundation of the American justice system. The Sixth Amendment to the Constitution assures a speedy trial by jury and provisions to ensure fair hearing of a case in court. Rights of detainees fundamentally rest on the writ of **habeas corpus**, which is protected in Article I of the Constitution. "Habeas corpus" is Latin for "[we command that] you have a body," and it allows any detained citizen to appeal in court his or her incarceration. Habeas corpus recognizes the self-sovereignty of an individual to maintain control over his or her own person. Originating in medieval England and long considered a cornerstone of modern judicial systems, it is seen as a vital means of protecting individual rights against abusive or arbitrary state action.

Habeas corpus became a key political issue after September 11, when the government began a widespread crackdown on al-Qaeda. Opponents of the Bush administration's policies have criticized everything from the capture of prisoners to how they are released. **Extraordinary rendition** is defined as the extrajudicial kidnapping of a suspect in a foreign country and the transfer of that prisoner to either the nation that carried out the abduction, or a third party. "Extrajudicial" merely means that the process exists outside the conventional legal system. Many progressives and human rights activists argue that rendition is used to circumvent regulations against torture by handing over prisoners to countries with less than stellar human rights records or to secret US prisons abroad. Rendition is different from **extradition**, the legal removal of a suspect from one country to another in which he will be tried or sentenced; extradition follows international treaties and is often a lengthy process.

Rendition has been used by many nations to capture notorious criminals. The most famous cases of rendition include the removal of Nazi war criminal Adolf Eichmann from Argentina to Israel in 1960 and the transfer of Carlos the Jackal from Sudan to France in 1994. The first known American rendition was authorized by Republican president Ronald Reagan to bring a Lebanese hijacker to justice. Many renditions occurred under Democratic president Bill Clinton. One of the bombers responsible for the first World Trade Center attack in 1993 was arrested using rendition. A few far-left liberals are opposed to rendition in every instance; most believe there are times when it is acceptable to breach the laws of a given nation in order to apprehend a criminal, especially if it has a shaky rule of law or is run by an unfriendly dictator.

Many have criticized the United States and the Bush administration for its use of rendition after September 11. The problem, some contend, is that the United States has been using rendition too frequently, and often on people who are not proven terrorists. Critics point out that lower evidentiary standards of rendition mean a higher margin of error in identifying suspects. **Maher Arar**, for example, a Syrian-born Canadian engineer, was detained in New York on his way home from a vacation. Arar says he was taken to Syria, where he was tortured and held for a year, never charged, and returned to Canada. Arar sued in the United States, but a federal court dismissed the claim, in part because the judge maintained that high-level Canadian authorities had approved the detention. Similar lawsuits have been dismissed on the grounds that hearing the case would necessarily entail disclosure of state secrets.

Another point of concern for many is rumored **black sites**, secret prisons and holding centers outside of American territory. The government initially denied their existence, but now admit that at least a few exist in Eastern Europe and/or the Middle East. Many are worried that secrecy is being misused — not to preserve important intelligence information, but to conceal the use of torture and the denial of rights such as habeas corpus to which a prisoner in the United States is entitled. Civil libertarians and human rights advocates insist that, one, prisoners should have access to legal counsel, and two, nonpartisan international groups such as the **Red Cross** should be allowed in to ensure humane conditions — impossible if these prisons remain secret. Some speculate that the centers were kept secret because information on their existence helps terrorists recruit new members by preaching the brutality of the United States. Others counter that rumors of torture and secret detention centers aid the American military effort by serving as a deterrent to terrorists who may fear the treatment they could receive; they also may respect a system that employs methods as vicious as those of the terrorists themselves.

Bush's second secretary of state, **Condoleezza Rice**, stated that the United States refuses to transfer prisoners to countries where we know they will be tortured — a statement picked apart by detractors, who pointed out that her phrasing left a loophole for any torture that the United States learns of after the fact. European governments, specifically the United Kingdom, were the target of intense internal criticism when it came to light in 2005 that American rendition flights passed through their airspace and airports. Indeed, one argument against using rendition frequently is that it may create a disincentive for allies to support American interests, especially judicial ones such as requests for extradition. For their part, US officials were reportedly annoyed that their European counterparts had benefited from intelligence gathered from suspects through rendition, and then attacked its use.

One safeguard for rendition used during the Clinton administration is to require the target country to have some sort of procedural safeguard for the suspect (what's often called **due process**), such as an issued arrest warrant. The American use of extraordinary rendition is ironic in any case, because an early form of rendition used by the British was considered an intolerable act that spurred colonists to revolt. Britain's 1774 Administration of Justice Act, passed after the Boston Massacre, was meant to force witnesses and defendants to undergo trials in England rather than in the colonies, purportedly to guarantee a "fair" trial — meaning one favorable to the British government.

The American base in **Guantánamo Bay**, Cuba, nicknamed **Gitmo**, has been the source of much debate over what some consider the immoral or illegal treatment of prisoners held there. Some insist such detentions are legal and key to protecting the nation from further terrorist attacks. There are several facilities at Guantánamo, the most infamous being the now defunct **Camp X-Ray**. Gitmo was used to house detainees shortly after September 11, and the first people brought there were captured in Afghanistan. Gitmo detainees are classified as **enemy combatants** rather than prisoners of war, or POWs. Common **Article 4** of the **Third Geneva Convention** — the four Geneva Conventions being the major body of international law that is supposed to regulate the conduct of war — identifies POWs as members of an army, militia, volunteer corps, or other organized resistance group, commanded by a superior, who are physically recognizable at a distance as military personnel.[8] The Bush administration reasoned that Common **Article 3** of the Third Geneva Convention, which guarantees fair trials and prohibits torture as well as "outrages upon personal dignity, in particular humiliating and degrading treatment,"[9] does not apply to those held in Gitmo. In 2002, President Bush signed a memo designating detainees as enemy combatants.

Detainees have been held outside US territory in order to circumvent American protections or the rights of a prisoner inside the country. Those who support the program contend that the circumstances of the war on terror are such that the old rules cannot be applied; others see a willful and wanton disregard of constitutional principles. There are two main sides: those who believe that both holding prisoners at extraterritorial sites and the conditions there are legal, and those who think neither is legal. There are also some who maintain that the programs may not be technically legal but are necessary. Again, this is not an argument made by those responsible for the programs, who must work within the law; rather, it's the reasoning of some pundits, commentators, and even officials outside the executive branch. The moral arguments follow a similar pattern: some say that the conditions are moral and justifiable, while others believe they are neither. Then there are those who feel the situation is immoral but justifiable, and consider that though the detainees' rights are being violated, these breaches are less important than national security.

Detainees were first installed in Cuba in 2001, and Guantánamo became the major holding center in 2002. A public outcry began soon thereafter, when many civil liberties advocates grew increasingly concerned about conditions and procedures at prison sites outside US territory. Many were upset that, one, Americans were holding prisoners without charge in contravention of habeas corpus, and two, that trials were planned in military courts, which require lower standards of evidence than do US civil courts. From 2001 to late 2007, more than seven hundred people had been detained at Gitmo, and more than four hundred released. Government officials announced that fewer than one hundred of the remaining detainees will be tried.

Amnesty International, an international human rights organization that is especially active in cases of political imprisonment, has been a particularly vocal critic of US policies concerning alleged terrorists, calling Gitmo "a human rights scandal." The **ACLU** and **Human Rights Watch** are other important organizations that maintain campaigns against extraterritorial American detention centers. They believe detainees at times have been denied counsel, held for long periods without charges, and subject to unfair trials — all in violation of constitutional guarantees. Testimony from former Gitmo detainees alleges abusive treatment; there is also a high rate of attempted suicide in the facilities.

The subject of **military tribunals** received increased attention in the fall of 2007, when self-described political conservative reservist Colonel **Stephen Abraham** became the first high-ranking military official to publicly criticize Guantánamo procedures. Abraham specifically alleged that the intelligence used to detain inmates was fragmentary, unsubstantiated, or irrelevant.[10] Indeed, civil liberties supporters say that many detainees were held because they came into contact with suspected terrorists, though there is no evidence that they themselves were ever involved with terrorist organizations.

Guantánamo detainees attempted to challenge the tribunals by filing habeas corpus petitions in federal court, but the controversial 2006 **Military Commissions Act** removed federal courts' jurisdiction over habeas petitions from Guantánamo, which angered many. Some contended that the act thus violates the constitutionally guaranteed right to habeas corpus, and the Supreme Court agreed to rule on the issue. Though many in Congress who voted for the act actually opposed the removal of habeas corpus, the bill passed because of other measures that Congress was convinced were important to secure the country, and they expected habeas to be reinstated soon.

The Eighth Amendment: Torture and Capital Punishment

"Excessive bail shall not be required, nor excessive fines imposed, nor cruel and unusual punishments inflicted," states the Eighth Amendment. But what constitutes cruel and unusual punishment is not spelled out. As with so much of the Constitution, interpretation of the text — both the words and the framers' intentions — is key. **Torture** clearly cannot be used by the American government on its own citizens, and international law to which the United States has been a party — namely, the **Geneva Conventions** — states that prisoners of war cannot be tortured either. Torture has been debated heatedly since September 11: what does or does not constitute torture, and whether torture is ever justifiable.

The debate includes both moral and practical strands, which sometimes conflict. Some believe that torture is inherently morally repugnant and is never justifiable. Others think that there may be some very restricted circumstances in which torture is morally acceptable, while still others contend that those conditions are broader. If, in theory, torture might sometimes be justified, then the question is: under what practical circumstances?

All of these points have been questioned publicly since September 11; the issue does not divide neatly between Democrats and

Republicans. While more Democrats are against torture, many Republicans are opposed as well. Most notable among these is Senator John McCain of Arizona, who was tortured during the five years he endured as a POW in Vietnam. However, many Democrats criticized McCain for not supporting measures to prevent Americans from waterboarding suspects. Some Democrats feel torture in certain instances may be justified, as do many Republicans. Perhaps the highest-profile advocate for the use of torture — a position few publicly take — is legal scholar **Alan Dershowitz**. He thinks torture works and that outlawing it is unrealistic, so it should be regulated to prevent abuses.

The issue of torture has arisen in the past decade because of the nature of the **war on terror**. Whether or not you agree with this terminology (and many do not), it is clear to all that the rules of violent conflict have shifted. Terrorism may involve a few individuals supported by a larger network of people they never meet, all of whom are bent on killing civilians without warning. For Americans, terrorism is a new danger, but, sadly, many throughout history have had to deal with it. During the late 1800s and early 1900s, terrorism was embraced by anarchists the world over, though they were especially influential in Russia and Eastern Europe. An anarchist set off World War I by assassinating Archduke Franz Ferdinand of Austria. More recently, Ireland, England, Lebanon, and Israel have all had to confront domestic terrorism. The scale of the threat today is greater than ever. Weapons are more destructive, terrorist networks are global, and terrorists are bent on killing large numbers of civilians.

To prevent the kind of violence that Americans experienced with the 1983 bombing of the Marine barracks in Beirut, the 1993 attack on the World Trade Center, the bombing of the USS *Cole* in Yemen, attacks on American embassies in Africa, and of course September 11, information and intelligence are key. Intelligence agents were chastened by the revelation that September 11 plotter **Zacarias Moussaoui** was on the FBI's radar before the attack, but was not sufficiently searched or interrogated. Some FBI agents tried repeatedly to get a warrant to search Moussaoui's belongings after he was arrested in

August 2001 on an immigration violation, but were denied by higher-ups within the bureau. Moussaoui's computer contained important links to terrorist networks, which were not discovered until after September 11. In this case, even a conventional investigation would have revealed valuable information, but it illustrates how time-sensitive the discovery of information can be.

The easiest position to communicate in the debate over torture is the outright rejection of torture in all circumstances because it degrades the perpetrator as much as or more than the victim and erodes the moral high ground of a legitimate war. In this view, terrorists commit moral outrages, but torturing even a known terrorist would lower both the torturer and any who condoned the action to the terrorists' ethical level. While many organizations and individuals take this position, its most eloquent proponent may be the Nobel Prize–winning author J. M. Coetzee, especially in his famous book *Waiting for the Barbarians.*

The argument that torture is wrong because it debases the moral position of the torturer is particularly strong in the case of the war on terror because some American values and systems seem to be pitted against those of a certain branch of radical Islam. Some think torture decreases our ability to **win hearts and minds** — the phrase often used to describe a conflict's larger ideological battle — because it demeans American morality. Others (mostly conservatives) counter that terrorists respect strong leadership, which in their world is often marked by brutality and violence — an argument that has been made frequently in regard to Iraq. Torture, therefore, could even be seen as a way to deter others from attacking an enemy who is willing to use it.

Others reason that torture is not just wrong but useless because it leads to **bad intelligence**. This is John McCain's main argument, borne out by his own experience. When McCain was tortured, his captors asked for the names of his flight squad. Instead, he told them the lineup of the Green Bay Packers, knowing that any information would be enough to make his assailants leave him alone. The **Israeli Supreme Court**'s ruling on torture is often cited by proponents of the bad-intelligence argument. Israel openly experimented with torture to prevent violence against its citizens, but by 1999 their supreme court ruled against its use because the court found that information obtained under torture was no better than that gathered through conventional means.

Canadian politician and prominent legal scholar **Michael Ignatieff**, among others, has argued otherwise. He says torture must work, or it would not be used.[11] This may be naïve, however, as more and more psychological research shows that almost anyone will be abusive to almost anyone else, given a particular situation, even if there is no payoff for such behavior. In 1971 the infamous **Stanford Prison Experiment** demonstrated that context may give rise to abusive behavior. Stanford's psychology department randomly assigned students as prisoners or guards, and found that the guards quickly became "sadistic,"[12] which much subsequent research has confirmed. The psychologist behind the Stanford study, **Philip Zimbardo**, calls this the **Lucifer effect**: evil circumstances make people behave evilly. Much psychological research supports the civil libertarian idea that safeguards are necessary to ensure that human behavior does not descend into brutality. Some arguments against torture are this prosaically practical. Some say that prisoners shouldn't be hit, for example, because allowing physical contact obscures the line between acceptable and unacceptable treatment and makes it much more likely that any given prisoner will be abused.

When pictures of American guards abusing detainees at the **Abu Ghraib** prison in Iraq surfaced in 2004, with shocking images of smiling female soldier Specialist **Lyndee England** giving a thumbs-up to naked hooded prisoners, it's fair to say that most Americans were sickened and disturbed. Some deemed the treatment torture; others felt it was not torture per se, but rather degrading or abusive treatment. To many, this distinction was pointless, but others saw it as important. *The New Yorker*'s **Seymour Hersh**, who wrote a series of articles on the subject, contends that abuse of prisoners was widespread and part of a military program; he is probably the single strongest mainstream critic of the Bush administration's policies concerning terrorism. Indeed, it was the military itself that broke the Abu Ghraib story, though it is rumored that it did so because the photographs had already been leaked (probably by a senior officer), and the military decided that releasing the story might control the damage by making it appear that it wasn't trying to cover up anything. That said, only a very few of the images were made public. Reportedly, those released were the *least* disturbing and didn't show the grossest violations, including sexual abuse of female prisoners.

Abu Ghraib was investigated by General **Antonio Taguba**, hence the name of the major document on the scandal, the **Taguba Report**. Taguba says that his report, which described sexual, physical, and emotional abuse, was met with disapproval by then Secretary of Defense **Donald Rumsfeld** and Deputy Secretary of Defense **Paul Wolfowitz**. Taguba maintains that though he briefed many military leaders and submitted his report well before a Senate hearing, Rumsfeld lied about how much information he had received and when he had received it, in order, Taguba claims, to be able to play innocent during investigative hearings.[13] Finally, Taguba felt that many of the practices at Abu Ghraib constituted torture and were unacceptable. On this score Taguba has been notably vocal, given that military officers are generally closemouthed about any personal disagreement with official policy — at least while they're still serving.

Those who do not dismiss torture altogether consider it a valid option because they think there may be times when it could yield information that might help prevent an attack. To some, preserving the dignity of a potential or proven terrorist and his or her torturer is less important than protecting innocent lives. The classic thought problem on torture is the **ticking time bomb scenario**: there is a terrorist in custody who knows the location of a bomb that will go off in some period of time and that is sure to kill at least one hundred innocent citizens. The authorities know the terrorist knows the information, and know that they have the right person. The terrorist won't give up any information. Is torture in this circumstance justified? Indeed, the ticking time bomb scenario persuades most that torture in some cases might be acceptable, and the notion rests on basic theories of justice that seem intuitive to many. Most people, when confronted with this situation, can understand a moral justification for torture: in this case, many agree, it's better to deny the rights and dignity of one or two individuals in order to save the lives of many.

Increasingly, politicians and commentators refuse to deal with this thought experiment because it is admittedly far-fetched. If you had the terrorist and knew you had captured the right person, how likely is it that you would have no idea where the bomb was? How probable is it to have someone in custody who knows a lot of information about a specific, imminent attack?

Reality is rarely quite so clear-cut, and the only ticking time bomb scenario that occurs with any regularity happens when authorities manage to pick up someone who has abducted a still-missing victim. In matters of war and terrorism, however, one can easily imagine a situation in which police may be trying to prevent an imminent attack. Indeed, wiretapping — a less extreme violation of rights than torture — has been crucial in capturing important figures involved in European terror plots. Many in the Bush administration argued that their post–September 11 procedures, whatever they were, greatly increased the security of Americans and seriously crippled terrorist groups.

Finally, there are some who think that rejecting torture in all forms at all times potentially endangers national security, but nonetheless believe that we should not torture prisoners. Ignatieff is a proponent of this view and has argued that most who oppose torture are not honest about the costs involved. To him, torture may yield important information that could save lives. Some feel that's worth torture; others counter it's better to potentially endanger the innocent because the moral consequences of using torture are actually worse than letting some people die.

Other debates have centered on what constitutes torture: the practice of waterboarding has received the most attention. In **water-**

boarding, a victim is restrained while the nose and mouth are covered with a towel and water is poured over the face. The process simulates drowning, and those who have undergone it (including some elite American soldiers for training purposes) almost invariably describe it as a form of torture. First secretary of homeland security Tom Ridge, among many others in the military and intelligence communities, agrees.[14] The CIA reportedly stopped the practice in 2003 and banned it in 2006.

In 2007 the question of whether or not waterboarding is torture slowed Attorney General **Michael Mukasey**'s Senate confirmation. Mukasey stated that he found waterboarding repugnant, but evaded questions about whether or not it was legal or a form of torture. Mukasey may have been protecting the chain of command. In 2008, President Bush vetoed a bill that explicitly outlawed the CIA from using tactics such as waterboarding. Later it was revealed that high cabinet officials, including Secretary of State Condoleeza Rice and Vice President Dick Cheney met secretly but with the president's knowledge to outline and approve methods of interrogation. The level of involvement by senior officials in interrogation measures was extraordinary.

The national debate over torture raised another important question about government power when President Bush added a signing statement to the Detainee Treatment Act of 2005, John McCain's amendment to the 2006 DOD appropriations bill that banned the torture of detainees. Signing statements are legislative postscripts that are added onto a bill by the president when he or she signs it into law. Historically, most have been political or rhetorical, but since the 1980s, constitutional signing statements, based on the president's interpretation that a law is constitutionally defective, have become more common. Under Bush the number exploded. Constitutional signing statements allow the president to instruct government agencies how to apply a law. This fundamentally arrogates some power reserved by the courts — the ability to determine and interpret constitutionality — to the executive branch. It is impossible to overstate how revolutionary this is, and it is not at all clear whether it is legal.

Bush's signing statements mostly eluded notice until the **McCain Amendment**, which was followed closely by the press. When Bush signed it into law, however, he stated that the executive branch could interpret it "in a manner consistent with the constitutional authority of the President . . . as Commander in Chief and consistent with the constitutional limitations on the judicial power."[16] Basically, the statement asserted that the executive branch does not have to follow the law, based on the president's role as commander in chief, on which there is no constitutional check. McCain made no comment on Bush's evisceration of his plan, for which he was attacked by many progressives. Congress (like most Americans) has always assumed that Congress *does* have a check on the president's powers as commander in chief: the War Powers Act would be pointless if that were not the case.

Who rightfully controls the use of force abroad has long been a political issue among the different branches of government. Article I of the Constitution gives Congress the power to declare war, but the fact that Article II designates the president as commander in chief muddies the legal waters. Furthermore, many think that the framers did not mean to require Congress to declare war for any military action, but only for **total war**, which has no formal definition but which is considered war on the scale of the world wars. This view gives the president considerable leeway, which, by the Vietnam era, many considered far too broad. As conflict in Vietnam escalated and American involvement in Southeast Asia increased, many in Congress became furious that both Presidents Johnson and Nixon waged war without a formal declaration from Congress.

·   Their solution was the **War Powers Act** of 1973, which allowed the president to commence a military action and allocated a grace period of ninety days before the matter had to be brought to Congress for a vote. The idea was to give the president some flexibility, while asserting Congress's role in any military action by requiring a vote over the **use of force**, and not just the **declaration of war**. However, many presidents have treated the War Powers Act dismissively, instead arguing that as commander in chief they have the right to direct the military more or less at will.

Signing statements represent the same conflict between the executive and legislative branches. The idea that a signing statement can explicitly circumvent a congressional law to which it is attached is so counterintuitive that it took politicians two hundred years to attempt, although not all constitutional signing statements oppose the spirit of the law they affect. The watershed moment was a 1986 memo written by **Samuel Alito**, then deputy assistant attorney general. Alito argued that based on the fact that legislation must be signed by the president in order to become law (or be passed by a congressional supermajority to override the president's veto), the framers must have recognized that presidential intent — how the president envisioned a law being implemented — was important.

Alito described possible legal issues: "In general, is presidential intent entitled to the same weight as legislative intent or is it of much less significance? . . . What happens when there is a clear conflict between the congressional and presidential understanding?"[17] Nobody has actually answered these questions, but President Bush nonetheless issued an unprecedented number of constitutional signing statements that clearly seek to exempt the executive branch from various laws. Since the executive branch has functionally removed Congress's power to legislate on the matter because the president could add a signing statement to a law, or veto it outright, it is probably up to the Supreme Court to decide how to deal with signing statements. Considering that Alito is now on the Court, we must assume that he, at least, will rule in favor of the executive branch.

Like torture, **capital punishment** is an Eighth Amendment issue because the amendment specifically forbids **cruel and unusual punishment** — but how we interpret that is an open question. The death penalty has been ruled legal because it hasn't been considered an unusual punishment; however, certain applications of the death penalty, as well as various methods of carrying it out, have been ruled unconstitutional because they are deemed cruel. The movement for abolition of the death penalty was inspired by Cesare Beccaria's *On Crimes and Punishment* of 1767, and was influenced by Quaker thought and the political philosophies of Montesquieu, Voltaire, and Bentham.[18] Thomas Jefferson attempted to pass capital punishment reform in the Virginia legislature but was narrowly defeated. In the first half of the 1800s, Wisconsin outlawed the death penalty, and other states reformed its use. Six states outlawed capital punishment in the early 1900s, but by 1920 they'd all reinstated it. After World War II, the death penalty lost favor, especially in traumatized Europe. Indeed, the European Union requires abolition of the death penalty as a condition of membership. In 1972 the US Supreme Court invalidated most death penalty laws; but statutes were rewritten, and executions resumed in 1977. Current opinion seems again to be moving against capital punishment, however. In 2002 the Supreme Court ruled that mentally retarded prisoners could not be executed because such punishment would be cruel and unusual.[19] In 2005 the same verdict was given in cases in which the prisoner is under eighteen.[20]

Opponents of the death penalty argue that execution is inherently a cruel and unusual punishment. Twelve states have outlawed it for this reason, and others have ruled certain execution methods illegal. Critics also contend that executions are arbitrary in that many people who commit the same crime receive different punishments. Many maintain that race is also an issue because blacks are more likely to be placed on death row than whites.

Opponents of capital punishment also question the accuracy of capital convictions; these arguments have reshaped the death penalty debate. DNA evidence has led to many releases; capital punishment opponents cite the numbers of mistakenly imprisoned inmates as evidence for judicial fallibility and warn that capital punishment is far too risky because some innocent people may be executed. And while a wrongfully imprisoned person can be freed, capital punishment isn't something you can take back. In 2000 then Illinois governor George

Ryan, a Republican, declared a **moratorium** — a delay until further notice — on all state executions pending a report on the accuracy of such convictions. In 2007, New Jersey's legislature was the first in over thirty years to abolish the death penalty. Death by lethal injection, long considered the most humane form of execution, was stopped in 2007 when it became apparent that it can cause intense suffering.[21] Such executions resumed in 2008 when the Supreme Court upheld lethal injection.

Supporters of the death penalty make both moral and practical arguments. Many believe that it is morally correct, for example, to claim a life that has taken a life. Some feel that those who commit certain crimes simply deserve to die. Often cited are particularly heinous cases of torture, rape, and murder. Many also think that capital punishment is a deterrent, dissuading people from committing serious crimes like murder out of fear of being executed. Recent studies that appear to support this theory have been hotly debated, but the effect seems most significant in states like Texas, which has a relatively high and frequent rate of execution. However, these results remain controversial.[22] Another practical issue, much touted in the 1980s though less current today, is cost. Keeping prisoners is expensive, since the state must not only house and feed them but provide medical care and other services. Some believe that the burden prisoners place on taxpayers should be minimized and that it is inappropriate for the state to provide for people who have committed serious crimes.

At various times, certain states passed capital punishment requirements, effectively forcing a jury to hand out a death sentence with a guilty verdict for specific crimes. This was found unconstitutional, but some softer sentencing guidelines have been upheld.

The tension between individual rights and government authority is fundamental to our democratic system of government, but the fight against terrorism has recast many old debates in a new light while bringing them to the forefront of the national conversation. On Capitol Hill, in the courts, and on the campaign trail, civil liberties will remain hotly contested for years to come.

9

Culture Wars

> ➢ "Culture war" is a term popularized by Republican and conservative politicians.

> ➢ Culture war issues split Americans along religious as well as rural versus urban divides.

> ➢ Most Americans hold moderate positions on culture war issues.

> ➢ Abortion has been the frontline of the culture war; a majority of Americans do not think that *Roe v. Wade* should be overturned.

> ➢ People who oppose legal abortion think that a developing child has a right to live that is stronger than any claim the mother may have against having that child.

> ➢ People who support legal abortion think that a woman's right to decide whether bearing a child will be harmful to her trumps any rights her fetus might have.

> ➢ The right to die and physician-assisted suicide are new fronts in the culture war.

> ➢ Most Americans support stem cell research; opponents believe that it is wrong to use any embryo, even one created outside a human being, for research.

> ➢ Scientists think stem cell research could help treat an untold number of diseases.

➢ Same-sex marriage is opposed by a narrow majority of Americans, but civil unions are slightly more popular.

➢ Supporters of same-sex marriage think that it is a civil rights issue; many of them oppose civil unions because they do not provide the same benefits as marriage.

➢ Those who most adamantly oppose same-sex marriage do so on religious grounds.

➢ The Defense of Marriage Act defines marriage as a contract between a man and a woman and allows states to disregard same-sex marriages performed in other states.

➢ School prayer cannot be required by the state; the Pledge of Allegiance has been challenged as unconstitutional, but the Supreme Court has not ruled on the matter.

Background to Current Debates

Journalists and pundits have used up a lot of ink and airwaves writing and talking about America's internal clash of civilizations, often called the **culture war**. In both 2000 and 2004 the presidential election was very tight, coming down to a few "swing states." The country's coasts went Democratic, the interior voted Republican, and the map of America was divided up between conservative **red states** and liberal **blue states**. But the colors may have been deceiving, and the country might be more accurately imagined in various shades of purple, with pockets of primary colors scattered throughout. Increasingly, though, commentators and some politicians have begun to question whether Americans are actually very divided.

Some pundits have countered the claims of a split country by pointing out that hair-thin electoral margins indicate a relatively close, and centrist, political consensus among Americans, with a few strenuously committed to the hard right or far left. This is borne out by the polling data, which indicate that most Americans currently hold centrist positions on many culture war issues including abortion, embryonic stem cell research, and same-sex marriage. But we seem to enjoy antagonism more than moderation, and besides, conflict makes for better copy.

The idea of a culture war has its roots in the changing social mores of the 1960s and '70s: the supposed clash between the more traditional culture of the 1950s and the so-called **counterculture**, in which many Americans embraced civil rights, women's liberation, open sexuality, cultural and moral relativism, and skepticism toward the government, especially the war in Vietnam. Others were appalled by hippie counterculture; these people largely redefined the field of political debate in America as a question of underlying values, pitting progressivism against orthodoxy.

Starting in the 1980s, social conservatives in the Republican Party increasingly attempted to frame political debate between two sets of values — one, which they characterized as libertine, and the other, which they often called traditional — creating the culture war. This was the era of politicians avowing their **family values**. Pat Buchanan's prime-time speech during the 1992 Republican National Convention brought the term **culture war** home to millions of Americans, and the media have used it ever since. Buchanan identified several threats to "traditional values": radical feminism, legal abortion, the separation of church and state, and openly gay lifestyles. Many Republicans are not deeply offended by gays or secularism, but those who are — social conservatives — have controlled the Republican message since the '80s. Liberals argue that the culture war is really a campaign strategy, producing a set of **wedge issues** designed to anger middle- and working-class white voters so that they'll vote for pro-business Republicans.

Current Debates

Abortion has been the single biggest battleground in the culture wars and the motivating force behind the **Christian Right** — politically active evangelical Protestants and conservative Roman Catholics — since the 1980s. It became a key issue for many women's rights activists in the 1970s. Abortion is a very emotional issue for many, and it's long been highly politicized. Even the terms are contested: **right to life** and **right to choose** represent the two main sides of the political debate. I'm going to use scientific terms like "embryo" and "fetus" when referring to early stages in human development. Be aware, however, that some opponents of legal abortion find these terms offensive. They call a fetus an **unborn child** and say they support the rights of the unborn. Two sets of debates surround abortion: popular and legal. It's necessary to deal with the legal question because changing or upholding current laws is a basic goal for many who disagree over abortion.

But let's start with some numbers. As of late 2007, about half of Americans thought that abortion is morally objectionable, while 40 percent found it morally acceptable — and at the same time a significant majority agreed it should be legal.[1] This disparity may show that fewer people really do morally object than say they do, or that some consider abortion morally problematic but think it ought to be legally available. The opinions of men and women in general are similar, and those who oppose legal abortion seem to hold their opinion more strongly than do supporters of legal abortion — though this may be because the former are in opposition to existing law.

Americans appear ambivalent on abortion overall: about half say they support limits on abortion, such as parental notification or twenty-four-hour waiting periods, but a significant majority of Americans do not support overturning *Roe v. Wade*, the 1973 Supreme Court case that affirmed the existence of a constitutionally protected **right to a legal abortion** in the United States. Abortion during the first trimester is least controversial. Only a small number of Americans think that abortion should be illegal even in cases of rape, incest, or threat to the mother's physical health, and only about 15 percent would support or reject a political candidate primarily over his or her views on abortion.

Abortion is about **values** because it raises the question of whose rights are primary: those of the mother or of the fetus. For many, abortion also raises profound questions about the nature of life itself. Those who most oppose legal abortion believe that a new life begins at the moment of conception. They also believe that an embryo has the same basic rights as all humans, in particular the right to have one's life protected — hence the political terms **right to life** and **pro-life**. They think that abortion is murder, and therefore wholly morally repugnant under all or almost all circumstances. Most right-to-lifers are religious, and the concept of a soul often figures heavily in their thinking. Those who are against legal abortion and are not particularly religious do not believe the soul has anything to do with the issue; to them, human life is sacred and must be protected.

Some who oppose legal abortion also make a **slippery slope argument**: abortion devalues life and may lead to the **state-sanctioned murder** of those whom society deems less worthy than others, such as people in a vegetative state, or even the mentally ill. Those against legal abortion often make secondary moral arguments about the law's effects on society. They think that the availability of abortion makes women more likely to engage in risky or inappropriate sex; they argue that legal abortion implies that the government finds certain attitudes toward sex and parenthood acceptable that they find objectionable. Finally, some claim that the availability of abortion actually contributes to teen pregnancy and single-parent households because it lessens the impact of sex and therefore removes a deterrent from engaging in it.

The question of the mother's well-being and right to choose whether to have a child is paramount for supporters of legal abortion — hence the term **pro-choice**. Many supporters of legal abortion think that a woman's rights, needs, or wishes take precedence over those of her fetus; others do not believe that a fetus has fundamental rights until some point in development; and some do not agree that conception immediately results in a full human life but that life develops as a fetus matures. On the extreme end, some do not think that a baby has its own life until it is born. Most, however, recognize a fetus as an independent being when it can survive outside its mother's body without intensive medical intervention — sometime in the last trimester. Pro-choicers reason that women have a right to maintain the integrity of their own bodies and reproductive processes without government interference or the imposition of others' moral standards.

Advocates of legal abortion also make practical arguments for available abortion, maintaining that women often suffer unduly — economically, emotionally, or socially — with children they do not want or cannot support. When a pregnancy jeopardizes a woman's health or life, pro-choicers feel that compelling her to choose between an illegal abortion and her own health would be a gross violation of that woman's fundamental right to medical care. Indeed, *Roe v. Wade* focused on the rights of doctors, patients, and the practice of medicine as much as it did on notions of privacy and the right to choose.

Pro-choicers have further argued that abortions will always be available no matter what the law — but safe abortions may not be. Were abortion to become illegal in America, women with enough money would be able to travel to Europe or Canada to receive medically safe abortions, but at least some lower-income women would probably resort to the backroom abortions that were quite common before 1973. Abortions not performed in medical facilities by trained professionals have a high rate of life-threatening complications, which is why many felt that abortion legalization was largely a public health issue. Finally, illegal abortion raises criminal justice concerns: those who receive, pay for, or perform abortions could be thrown in jail.

There are important lobbying organizations on both sides of the issue. The biggest pro-choice group is **NARAL Pro-Choice America**. One of its founders was **Betty Friedan**, a prominent feminist activist. **Planned Parenthood of America** has also been a staunch backer of pro-choice legislation and candidates. **EMILY's List** is an organization devoted to electing feminists to office; support for legal abortion is one of their primary issues for determining whom to endorse. All of these groups lean heavily Democratic.

Major pro-life organizations include the **Christian Coalition**, powerful especially in the early 1990s under **Ralph Reed**, and **Focus on the Family**, founded and led by a prominent evangelical, the Reverend **James Dobson**. Both these groups support Republican politicians and candidates almost exclusively, and abortion may be their single biggest issue. Finally, the **National Right to Life Coalition** supports anti-abortion measures but also lobbies against right-to-die and physician-assisted suicide proposals.

Roe v. Wade is the **1973 Supreme Court case** that made abortion legal nationwide.[2] Until then, abortion was legal in a few states, but illicit abortions were widespread. Even for pro-choicers, *Roe v. Wade* is worrisome because in a purely legal sense it is not unassailable. The decision depends partly on a notion of privacy that is not explicitly stated by, but rather implied from, the constitutional rights to liberty and due process; questioning privacy rights is one way pro-lifers think *Roe v. Wade* could be undermined. The right to privacy, however, underpins many other important laws. *Roe v. Wade* defined the health of the mother in broad terms, including her economic or psychological health, and set various limits on abortion in different trimesters: During the first, the state was found to have no rights to dictate abortion practice. During the second, the state could intervene only in matters related to the mother's health. During the third trimester, the state could intervene to protect the life of the fetus, except where the mother's health was endangered.

In the 1992 case *Planned Parenthood v. Casey*, the Supreme Court ruled that women still have the right to an abortion, but undid the trimester system imposed by *Roe v. Wade*.[3] Instead, the Court applied the test of **undue burden**. This tests whether a certain regulation on abortion is legal by determining whether or not it places an undue burden upon the mother's right to have an abortion. The Court defined "undue burden" as a "substantial obstacle" that "prevents a significant number of women from having an abortion." Many find this test, which can be applied at any stage in pregnancy, fuzzy, because in theory, any law that decreases the absolute number of abortions performed could be found illegal.

The Court has invoked undue burden only once, in the 2000 case **Stenberg v. Carhart**.[4] The issue at stake was a procedure called **partial-birth abortion**, which had been banned in Nebraska. Again, even the terminology is weighted: opponents use "partial-birth abortion," whereas supporters of legal abortion prefer the medical name dilation-and-extraction, or **D&X**. The procedure is performed late in development, is as unpleasant as it sounds, and is usually undertaken because the mother's physical health is greatly endangered. *Stenberg v. Carhart* revolved largely on medical evidence and a doctor's right to determine the best treatment for a patient. The Court found that the ban on the procedure did constitute an undue burden largely because it meant a woman could not follow what her doctor might consider her safest medical option.

Fundamentally, one's philosophy of how the Constitution ought to be read underlies this debate. Some think that the Constitution enumerates a set of fixed rights; others counter it was meant to be, or ought to be, a more flexible document that can respond to changing needs and public opinions. In the latter case, people contend that the rights specifically named by the Constitution do not comprise a complete list, and can be reinterpreted as the need arises; they are sometimes considered **developmentalists**. Those who disagree are called **strict constructionists**, and that phrase is often used to describe judges who do not support legal abortion.

Almost all Democrats and a significant number of Republicans support legal abortion, though many favor some restrictions. Politicians who oppose legal abortion are almost entirely Republicans; Republicans who do support it are usually from the Northeast or the West Coast and include Rudy Giuliani and Arnold Schwarzenegger. Some commentators — all conservative — have argued that if *Roe v.*

Wade were overturned it wouldn't have much effect on abortion it-self because many states would still allow legal abortion. However, there would probably be regions of the country where abortion was available and regions where it was not; women who could afford to travel out of these areas would still have the option of abortion, but those with limited resources might not.

Then there would be the political effect of a *Roe* reversal: some Republicans have worried that overturning it would satisfy conservative evangelicals and lessen their zeal to fight for the GOP, while angering moderate Republican women enough that they would vote Democratic. But despite all the political battles and the passionate activism on both sides, Americans have edged toward a **consensus on abortion**: we want it to remain legal. In fact, many political commentators believe that the next values battle involving life and death issues will be fought over the right to die.

Right to die debates center on two topics: the removal of life support and the right to suicide. In 2005 the case of **Terri Schiavo** drew national attention to the former. In 1990 Schiavo collapsed in her Florida home when her heart stopped — why, exactly, was never determined. Deprived of oxygen, her brain was heavily damaged, and she slipped into a coma. When she awoke, her doctors considered her to be in a **persistent vegetative state**, or **PVS**. Terri could breathe unaided, but was unable to swallow, and received food and water through tubes that were later surgically implanted. Terri's husband, Michael, who was her legal guardian, and her parents, the Schindlers, held deeply divergent views about her care.

In 1998 Michael asked a court to act as Terri's surrogate to determine what her wishes regarding her care might have been; thus the initial legal battle involved the court and Terri's parents, not Michael. The Schindlers are devout Catholics who had raised Terri in their faith and strongly opposed all measures that would end her life. However, Michael stated that when she was still healthy, Terri had said that she would not want to be kept alive if she had no hope for improvement. In 2000 a Florida judge granted Michael's petition to remove Terri's feeding and hydration tubes.

The Schindlers repeatedly tried to have Michael removed as guardian, and specifically attacked relationships he had with other women after Terri's health crisis. Michael argued that he refused to divorce Terri in order to ensure that she received the care she would have wanted, but admitted that he did have romantic relationships. The Schindlers were unable to remove Michael and eventually attempted to challenge the diagnosis of PVS at trial. They testified that Terri was responsive and that new treatments might be available — even though an EEG showed no measurable brain activity, and a CAT scan demonstrated that Terri's brain had severely atrophied (an autopsy later confirmed that her brain was half the normal weight). The Schindlers entered six hours of video into evidence, of which about six minutes were released publicly. Many who saw short clips, including then Senate majority leader Dr. **Bill Frist**, a Tennessee Republican and heart surgeon, thought that Terri appeared to respond. Others pointed out that the clips were taken from many hours of tape that showed little or no activity, and many doctors agreed that Terri's responses were reflexive rather than intentional.

In 2003 Terri's tubes were removed, but the Republican-controlled Florida state legislature intervened and passed **Terri's Law**, giving Republican governor **Jeb Bush** authority over the case. Governor Bush ordered the tubes surgically reinserted. Then the Florida Supreme Court found Terri's Law unconstitutional because it violated the separation of powers. Amid the debate, the US Senate transferred jurisdiction of the case to federal court, which eventually followed the Florida court and allowed removal of the tubes. An eleventh-hour appeal in 2005 put a hold on the court order allowing the feeding tubes to be removed; at that time, the Florida police prepared to take Terri back to a surgical facility from the hospice. However, the stay was lifted, the tubes were removed, and Terri passed away.

Some who opposed the removal of Terri's life support call her death state-sanctioned murder; others thought it merciful. Some Republicans may have attempted to use the case politically: an employee for a Republican member of the Florida state legislature wrote a memo describing the Terri Schiavo case as a "great political issue."[5] The public disagreed: Between 60 and 80 percent of Americans polled — including two-thirds of conservatives — said they were opposed to Republicans' efforts to keep Schiavo alive.[6] People across the political spectrum expressed a strong opinion that government shouldn't have gotten involved.

The Schiavo case went as far as it did because Terri had no **living will** to express her medical wishes directly. If you have strong feelings about treatment you would like to receive (or not receive), it's important to make a living will and to tell people that you have one. The ideological battle waged over Schiavo is interesting partly because those who believe in preserving life at all costs are generally conservative Republicans, but they make culturally relativist arguments that sound very liberal: they say that even severely diminished lives are worthy of the strongest protection and that society should not judge what counts as a life worth living. But many Americans are concerned with **quality of life**, not just length of life. Wanting to make individual decisions about these matters motivates many who believe in the **right to die** and **physician–assisted suicide**.

The law has long made it clear that **refusal of care is a right**, but has also ruled that **suicide is not a right**. Dr. Jack Kevorkian is probably America's best-known advocate for physician-assisted suicide, but many doctors and a small majority of Americans agree that patients with terminal illnesses, or who have great and enduring pain, ought to be able to end their lives humanely with the aid of a doctor. Indeed, the issue of pain and suffering may be a potential loophole in the law as it stands. Oregon voters passed a state ballot initiative that allows physician-assisted suicide for terminally ill patients with under six months to live. This law has stood because courts have found that the state has no authority to deny doctors the right to prescribe life-threatening substances.

Many who oppose terminating life for any reason are religious, but many religious groups and individuals do not agree. People on both sides worry about possible abuses of any laws allowing the right to die and physician-assisted suicide; there are concerns that people who choose the latter may be depressed and need mental health care. However, one 2006 poll showed that 86 percent of Americans support right-to-die legislation.[7]

Another issue in the culture wars, **stem cell research**, focuses on the possibility of life, or improved health, for many. **Stem cells** are blanks, undifferentiated cells that **can become any other kind of cell** and can live for a long time in a blank state. This means you could use stem cells to **grow new organs**, though most scientists agree this won't happen on any practical scale for years. Stem cells are more immediately useful for **drug testing**: they would allow researchers to screen drugs much faster than is currently possible by letting them quickly grow huge numbers of genetically identical cells. Stem cells may also **aid the study of development**, leading to insights into diseases like cancer. Stem cell research is incredibly exciting scientifically and may possibly hold the key to curing or treating untold numbers of illnesses.

Some support stem cell research for more mundane purposes: money and prestige. Stem cell research promises to lead to discoveries that will make a lot of money in the burgeoning biotechnology sector. Compared to the United States, Europe has more open policies; American scientists and biotech entrepreneurs are worried that labs across the pond are attracting more funding and top scientific talent. Some want increased funding of stem cell research to keep America at the top of its scientific game, and feel that preventing research means losing an opportunity to build a lucrative industry.

There are two kinds of stem cells: **adult** and **embryonic**. Adult stem cells give rise to cells that must be replenished throughout your life, such as blood cells, and are found in adults. Embryonic stem cells are those that give rise to all the cells in one's body and are found only in embryos. It's the **process of obtaining embryonic stem cells** rather than stem cells per se that some find unsettling because they are harvested from embryos, and although removing stem cells doesn't quite kill the embryo, because you do keep some of the cells alive, functionally you destroy it. The issue seems similar to abortion, but is quite different: the embryos in question are the size of a cross-section of a hair, and only three to five days old. They are called **blastocysts**, and in a woman they would still be drifting in the fallopian tubes, not implanted in the womb.

Some don't consider interfering with blastocysts morally questionable. To a smaller group, mostly the very religious, a blastocyst is as sacred as the baby it could turn into and research using embryos is akin to murder. Researchers often use blastocysts **left over from fertility treatments**, most of which are currently discarded; some think it's better to use these embryos for potentially beneficial scientific research. In vitro fertilization, or IVF, can also be conducted solely for research purposes. Some find this acceptable, while others feel it's even more offensive because they see the process as creating life merely to kill it. Then there are those who disagree that an embryo is a person, but believe that because it has the potential to become a person, an embryo deserves certain protections. Many, however, think that the rights of a potential human are simply less important than the good, or rights, of those who are already independent beings.

Scientists also use **somatic cell nuclear transfer (SCNT)** to produce blastocysts. In this process, an unfertilized egg and a body cell are used to produce an embryo. SCNT muddles the moral issue of an independent life because it creates a blastocyst without fertilization. As prominent young Harvard stem cell researcher Kevin Eggan, who works with embryonic stem cells, stressed, "there's no abortion in what we do, no pregnancy."[8] Some have tried to skirt the political issue of using embryonic stem cells by working with adult stem cells. Important research has been done with them, but because they are not as plastic (able to be manipulated) as embryonic stem cells, their potential to aid research seems considerably more limited.

Politicians have taken two approaches to stem cell research — legislating on it directly, and legislating on its funding. In 2004, California established and funded the **California Institute for Re-**

generative **Medicine (CIRM)**, which has been stalled by lawsuits funded by the Life Legal Defense Foundation. Much American scientific research is federally funded and administered through the **National Institutes of Health (NIH)**, over which the president has the most control. Many criticize President Bill Clinton for passing the buck on stem cell funding, leaving key decisions to his successor. In 2001, President **George W. Bush** decided to allow stem cell research funding under the following conditions: cell lines had to have been derived prior to the day of the announcement, cells had to come from an embryo created "for reproductive purposes," and embryo donors had to give "informed consent" and could not receive "financial inducements."[9]

The rules sound less restrictive than they are. Though it was claimed that **sixty stem cell lines** were available for research, practically speaking there were **ten to twenty** — inadequate for most research purposes because they don't include examples of every genetic feature on which research needs to be done. The rules created bureaucratic and organizational nightmares, because a scientist working with new embryonic stem cell lines couldn't use NIH funding — directly or indirectly. If you wanted to work on stem cells and needed to use a special microscope that your university bought for tens of thousands of dollars with any amount of NIH funding, you'd have a big problem. Either you'd have to buy a new microscope, rent time on your old one back from the university, or use one that was privately funded. Some universities even interpreted the rules to mean that they had to build entirely new facilities because old ones were funded with NIH money. The risks were huge, because if one researcher violates the rules, the NIH can stop funding not only the offending researcher's lab but *all* labs at the institution that receive NIH money. In 2006, Congress passed a bill to ease restrictions on stem cell funding, but the measure was vetoed by President Bush — his first veto in nearly six years in office. Another bill was passed in 2007, but Bush vetoed it, too. While Americans were divided over this issue several years ago, a majority now support it.[10] Indeed, one in five Americans changed his or her mind in just two years. In 2007 more than 60 percent of Americans said they supported stem cell research, while only 31 percent thought Bush should have vetoed the 2006 bill.[11]

The debate over stem cell research is politically interesting because it's truly **not a Republican or Democratic, conservative or liberal issue**. Though being against embryonic stem cell research is associated with Republicans because Bush limited the ability of scientists to conduct it, there are prominent Republicans, including Senator **Orrin Hatch** of Utah and Senator **Arlen Specter** of Pennsylvania,[12] who support it. Former First Lady Nancy Reagan surprised many by publicly criticizing President Bush's policy. Senator Bill Frist, a physician, also disagrees with it.[13]

Other culture war issues are a little less life-and-death, but are no less strongly contested. **Same-sex marriage** became a front in the culture war in the 1990s — and appeared to become the central issue a decade later. Again, the terminology itself is disputed: those who oppose it most strongly often call it "homosexual marriage"; those who support it refer to it as "gay marriage" or "equal marriage rights." "Same-sex marriage" is probably the most neutral term.

There are practical and ideological arguments on both sides of the debate, and there are at least three major positions. Some want to make sure people of the same sex cannot marry, some think they should be able to, and some favor the in-between solution of **civil unions**. Also at issue is a state's right to determine marriage laws and recognize marriages from other states. Currently, same-sex marriage is available only in Massachusetts, while civil unions are legal in Vermont, New Jersey, Connecticut, and New Hampshire. Domestic partnership laws in California, the District of Columbia, Maine, Oregon, and Washington confer benefits that are effectively equivalent to those offered by civil unions.

The Catholic Church and evangelical Protestants have led the fight against same-sex marriage, while other, smaller religious groups, including the Unitarian Church and the United Church of Christ, have supported it. The strongest opposition comes from conservative Protestants, as well as most in the African American community. Those supporting same-sex marriage are liberals, gay rights activists, and almost all of the gay community. Same-sex marriage and civil unions are more unpopular in the midwestern, western, and southern United States than in the Northeast or on the West Coast; people in urban centers are more in favor than those in rural areas.

Most staunch supporters of same-sex marriage and civil unions are Democrats, but there are notable Republican exceptions, including Vice President **Dick Cheney**. Cheney's view might be considered libertarian, since he thinks that people should be able to enter into any relationship or contract they desire without government interference. Other politicians have changed their views on the issue. **Howard Dean**, former governor of Vermont and current chair of the Democratic National Committee, was a popular presidential candidate avidly supported by many progressives because he signed the Vermont civil union law, the first in the country. Dean initially had opposed civil unions but changed his position once it became clear the Vermont Supreme Court would declare a ban on them unconstitutional.

Supporters of same-sex marriage make two sets of arguments, one ideological and the other practical. Ideologically, they believe that fundamental social equality is at stake. They consider marriage a right of citizenship because marriage provides certain advantages, including social recognition and financial benefits such as insurance coverage, pensions, tax breaks, and greater ease concerning inheritance and child custody. To exclude people from this institution based on their sexuality, they say, is discrimination in a similar vein as Jim Crow laws denying African Americans the right to vote prior to the 1960s. Practically speaking, same-sex marriage advocates feel that the social sanction of marriage stabilizes relationships, and argue that extending the right to marry will thus strengthen society overall.

Opponents of same-sex marriage are often, but not always, offended by homosexuality in the first place and do not believe that the government ought to sanction it with marriage rights. Some argue semantically, stating that marriage is by definition a contract between a man and a woman. They emphasize their support for **traditional marriage**. Advocates for same-sex marriage contest this definition and point out that standards for marriage are historically and culturally defined: divorce was not always universally allowed, a woman's rights within marriage have altered, and interracial marriages were outlawed in some states as late as the 1960s. To them, the notion of traditional marriage has no real meaning.

The 1996 **Defense of Marriage Act**, or **DOMA**, defined marriage as a contract between a man and a woman and allowed states not to recognize marriages performed in other states where different marriage laws applied — in anticipation that some states would allow same-sex marriage or civil unions, while others would remain adamantly opposed. DOMA was passed by a Republican Congress; it was signed into law by President Clinton, an action for which many liberals criticized him. Some expect the Supreme Court to strike down DOMA because they think it contradicts the Constitution's full faith and credit clause: "Full Faith and Credit shall be given in each State to the public Acts, Records, and judicial Proceedings of every other State." Others speculate that a conservative majority of the justices will find a way to uphold DOMA.

Another argument against same-sex marriage is the notion that **marriage is for procreation** and child rearing, and thus cannot be extended to same-sex couples. This has been found at least legally invalid because many states allow same-sex couples to adopt children, and marriage is never denied to heterosexual couples who cannot have children. Those against same-sex marriage also often employ a **slippery slope argument**: they contend that if marriage is extended to gay couples, it may be allowed between more than two people, or even between animals and humans. Advocates for same-sex marriage, such as openly gay Democratic congressman **Barney Frank** of Massachusetts, counter, "Some distinctions are hard to maintain; that between two people and three people is pretty clear cut."[14] Former Republican senator **Rick Santorum** famously "freaked out" an Associated Press reporter during a discussion about same-sex marriage in which he started talking about "man on dog" sex. Santorum's point was that although he doesn't condone same-sex marriage, he was actually *contrasting* homosexuality with bestiality; his comments were misrepresented, however, as a *comparison* of homosexuality with bestiality. In any case, Santorum *was* making a slippery slope argument, and was pilloried by liberals for his comments.[15]

Other practical arguments against same-sex marriage include the **cost to employers** in additional benefits. However, corporations — especially large ones including Boeing, Disney, and Microsoft — have taken the lead in extending same-sex partner benefits. In Massachusetts, many companies have *stopped* partner benefits because marriage is now an option, and domestic benefits were deemed to confer an unfair advantage to same-sex unmarried couples. The more pervasive but tacit practical objection to same-sex marriage may be the idea of legitimacy. If same-sex couples can be married, the thinking goes, there is one fewer deterrent to living what opponents call a gay lifestyle. Thus, many opponents of same-sex marriage feel that marriage rights might only encourage people to be gay — which they consider at best an unfortunate flaw.

The key legal underpinning for same-sex marriage is the **1967 Supreme Court case *Loving v. Virginia*.**[16] The Lovings, married in Washington, DC, were an interracial couple. They were convicted of miscegenation — marriage between races — in Virginia, but the Court struck down the sentence, calling marriage "one of the basic civil rights of man" and arguing that this right must be available to all under the equal protection clause of the Fourteenth Amendment. However, the equal protection clause specifically mentions race, but not sexual orientation. The legal debate focuses on whether or not gays are a group that deserves specific protection. Those who disagree maintain that homosexuality is a choice, not an "immutable characteristic" as is race or gender.

Civil unions have been promoted by many as a compromise to same-sex marriage. There are those who feel this appeases both sides, since it provides many of the practical benefits of marriage without calling it marriage. However, many advocates for same-sex marriage contend that civil unions are discriminatory because they create two separate legal classes. Indeed, civil unions do not entail all the benefits of marriage. For one thing, partners in a civil union are ineligible for the federal tax breaks accorded to heterosexual married couples. They cannot be issued immigration visas, and if they want to exit the union, they cannot divorce but must dissolve the union, which is more complicated legally.

Massachusetts confronted same-sex marriage in 2003–4, after the **Massachusetts Supreme Court** ruled that denying it violated the state constitution. After the state legislature asked the court to advise on a law allowing civil unions, the court decided that unions would not be legal because they would create a separate and therefore unequal class of citizen. Also in 2004, Democratic San Francisco mayor **Gavin Newsom** issued marriage licenses to same-sex couples, reasoning that the law prohibiting this was unconstitutional under California's Equal Protection Clause. Marriages were performed for about a month until the California Supreme Court ended them. Many gay rights activists lauded Newsom, while others criticized him for granting *illegal* marriage licenses and worried he would turn public opinion against the gay community. Others found it dangerous that an elected official would take the law into his own hands, a breakdown of public order. In 2008 the **California Supreme Court** reversed an earlier decision and decided that gay marriage must be allowed for the same reasons the Massachusetts court did, calling marriage a "civil right."

One other front in the culture wars involves the intersection between religion and the public sphere. These issues again pit religious conservatives against civil libertarians and often center on American history. The former often argue that the United States was founded as a **Christian nation** and that Judeo-Christian beliefs are the foundation of American laws and values; the latter counter that the United States was founded as a haven for religious dissenters and that, to use Thomas Jefferson's phrase, a "high wall of separation" should divide church and state. While these issues have been less potent at the ballot box than others we've encountered, they still ignite a great deal of passionate debate — and ongoing battles in the courts.

We have heard a lot about **school prayer** in the past few years, but the Supreme Court has been dealing with it since at least 1943. The first major fight over religion in public schools centered not on prayer but on the **Pledge of Allegiance**. Interestingly, it was a religious group who argued that the pledge should not be required of public school students. The case originated in West Virginia, where children were required by law to salute the flag and recite the pledge. However, the child in question came from a family of Jehovah's Witnesses, who consider the flag a graven image and the pledge a violation of the second commandment. The Court found that the government could not compel anyone to engage in or refrain from free speech, and though the Pledge of Allegiance was not banned from schools, it was deemed voluntary rather than mandatory.[17]

In 2004 an atheist in California brought suit against his daughter's school district because he believed that the recital of the pledge — specifically the phrase "under God," which was added in 1954 — was inherently coercive. His daughter could either say things she didn't believe, or call attention to herself by remaining silent. The case reached the Ninth Circuit Court of Appeals, which agreed that reciting the Pledge of Allegiance in school is unconstitutional. This was contrary to a 1992 ruling by the Seventh Circuit Court of Appeals that found the pledge constitutional because "under God" is a **ceremonial reference**: symbolic, not meaningful. One of the reasons the Ninth Circuit disagreed was that "under God" is singular, not plural, and therefore inherently refers only to monotheistic religions. The Supreme Court may weigh in on the issue yet.

Public display of the Ten Commandments in government-funded buildings became national news in 2003, when a court in Alabama was required to remove a large bronze and stone pedestal in the building's rotunda. In 2005 the Supreme Court handed down a ruling on two similar displays of the commandments at the state capitol in Austin, Texas. One showed the commandments in the context of historical documents, as a record of traditional law; this kind of display was deemed constitutionally appropriate. But the other lacked such context and was a monolithic structure like the one in Alabama; the Court found this exhibit a violation of the separation of church and state. This enraged members of the Christian Right, many of whom believe that areas in which Christians form a majority of the population ought to be able to display religious belief in public forums such as schools and courts.

At issue is the Constitution's stance on religion, embodied in the **First Amendment**: "Congress shall make no law respecting an establishment of religion, or prohibiting the free exercise thereof." The first part of that sentence is called the **establishment clause**; the second is the **free exercise clause**. As you can see, there is an inherent tension between these two statements: Congress can't help religion, but it can't harm it either. Some religious conservatives emphasize the latter — that government cannot unduly infringe upon religion. They contend that in areas that are largely religiously homogeneous, public religious display is constitutional because it violates nobody's rights. Civil libertarians tend to emphasize the establishment clause, arguing that public religious displays demonstrate governmental approval of certain religious beliefs, discriminating against those with dissenting beliefs, or no religious beliefs at all.

Depending on your perspective, America is either deeply divided or not divided at all. A more subtle view is that there are significant minorities of people on each wing of the ideological divide, but most Americans share similarly moderate views on culture war issues. While these issues defined much of the politics of the past few decades, and helped define a powerful new political faction — the Christian Right — Americans are increasingly concerned more about the economy, foreign policy, and health care reform than they are about abortion and civil unions. But old habits die hard, and we'll probably continue to hear about the battles of culture being waged between the urban coasts and the rural interior — even if the drama is a bit overblown.

10

Socioeconomic Policy

➤ Socioeconomic policy deals with the allocation of financial resources.

➤ There may be as many as 12 million undocumented workers in the United States. Illegal immigration has become an important issue, primarily for Republicans.

➤ Some think that illegal immigration depresses the wages of low-skilled workers.

➤ Many are concerned that Spanish-speaking immigrants have not integrated linguistically; some want to make English the official language.

➤ The labor movement led to widespread unionization and many workers' reforms.

➤ Big labor is less important politically than it used to be, and traditionally aligns with Democratic candidates.

➤ Some Republicans claim Social Security is in crisis, while many Democrats disagree but argue that Republicans are endangering its solvency.

➤ Many Democrats and some Republicans worry about the government borrowing money from the Social Security trust fund, which a lockbox would prevent.

> Many Republicans ideologically oppose Social Security. Privatizing it was a popular Republican plan until the stock market fell in 2000.

> The Department of Agriculture spends most of its money on food aid for the poor.

> Farm subsidies are less expensive than most people think. Farmers are subsidized because their products are vital and their output is variable and unpredictable.

> The 1996 welfare reform required more people to work and shifted debate on public assistance to other forms of federal aid, such as food stamps.

Background to Current Debates

Perhaps the most primitive function of government is to allocate resources. Deciding who gets what is a function of most any political policy. While socioeconomic policy is ostensibly about money, issues such as immigration, Social Security, the minimum wage, and farm subsidies entail social implications far beyond the dollars involved. Race, for example, is an unspoken factor in debates over programs such as welfare and food stamps.

While socioeconomic policies, like financial ones, deeply affect all Americans, they are dry and complicated, and involve lots of numbers, so few of us really understand even the basic premises. But they really aren't so bad; in some ways, fights over resources are more straightforward than other debates because all you have to do is follow the money to figure out what's really going on. A lot of the ideological divide has to do with where your sympathies lie. Do you think that the poor are enmeshed in economic and cultural cycles that conspire to keep even the responsible down, or do you believe that where you wind up in life is mostly your own fault and your own responsibility? Or do you think it depends on what group we're talking about? How much of a responsibility to help others do you think the rich have? Is that a responsibility the government can dictate? Or should it be up to individuals?

Carving up America's economic output is like Thanksgiving with one turkey and ten kids — everyone fights over the drumsticks. Though there are certain ideological constants, who supports which programs and why is surprisingly complex. Some opinions have less to do with ideology and more to do with political alliances: for example, a Democrat closely allied with the financial industry may support Social Security privatization. Sometimes a politician's position has to do with the interests of his or her home state or district: an otherwise free-market Republican from a heavily agricultural state will pretty much always support farm subsidies. In politics, after all, you can't please everyone, but you *have* to please your constituents.

Immigration

America is a nation of immigrants, but historically, new groups are disdained: in the mid-1800s there was a bigoted backlash against waves of poor Irish and German immigrants. These days the immigration debate centers on socioeconomic issues, cultural frictions, and security concerns. There are questions over legal immigration, illegal immigration, and what to do about illegal immigrants, also known as **undocumented workers**, who are already in the United States. The debate has been fueled by an influx of Spanish-speaking immigrants into areas that previously saw little immigration, such as Iowa and Idaho, and by Republicans from rural or suburban areas, for whom immigration is a new key issue.

Most politicians feel that some immigration is useful, but think that it should be controlled. They diverge largely on what should be done about the illegal immigrants already in the country, but there is a consensus that the situation we have now — uncontrolled borders and approximately 12 million illegal immigrants — is untenable. The political alliances formed in this debate are odd. Some Republicans are much more pro-immigration than others. In fact, it's an issue that has split the party. President **George W. Bush**, from the border state of Texas, campaigned for president partly on his strong record of friendship with Mexico. Sensing that Hispanics were the party's future, he tried to align himself and the Republican Party with their interests. In 2007 a relatively liberal immigration bill backed by the Bush White House died in Congress, killed by a vocal and quickly growing sector of the party that is heavily anti-immigration.

The poster boy for the anti-immigrationists is **Tom Tancredo**, a Republican congressman from Colorado who was the chief foe of the immigration bill sponsored by Republican senator and presidential hopeful **John McCain** of Arizona and Democratic senator **Ted Kennedy** of Massachusetts. McCain, like Bush, is relatively liberal on immigration, and thinks Hispanics are an important constituency for Republicans. His bill was proposed after **nationwide protests** by legal and illegal immigrants in 2006, themselves sparked by a bill passed in the House stipulating that seven hundred miles of **fence** be built along the United States–Mexico border. McCain's position nearly torpedoed his presidential run in 2007, as more and more Republicans favored taking a hard line against illegal immigration.

The McCain-Kennedy bill would have tightened border security, an issue that concerns many because there is speculation that terrorists could come into the country via our long land borders. Along our Mexican border, for example, no records are currently kept of who enters or exits the country. Passports are checked, but there is no other form of security. In this regard, the Canadian border poses a bigger problem, simply because the desert environment in the south makes the crossing difficult, and some portions are heavily patrolled, while most of the Canadian border is almost totally unpopulated, let alone guarded.

The most hard-line anti-immigrationists want illegal immigrants **deported**, that is, kicked out of the country. But most find the expense and logistical difficulty of deporting 12 million people unrealistic. And there are more personal factors. What about illegals who have American children and steady jobs? What about people who crossed illegally but who serve in the armed forces? Or who have children serving? Moderate proposals call for some kind of **penalty** — fines, "going to the back of the line" to wait for a green card or other visa, and/or requirements to try to master English.

Illegal immigration wasn't much of an issue even a few years before the 2008 presidential election,[1] but a quirk of the primary system drove immigration to the fore of the Republicans' presidential debate. Voters in important early primary states, New Hampshire and South Carolina, are much more worried about immigration than average Americans, only 6 percent of whom said immigration was an issue they would vote on at the time.[2] Immigration is largely a regional issue; people in areas that have seen a recent influx of immigrants (such as New Hampshire) tend to be more concerned.

Republican presidential candidate Mitt Romney, facing sinking poll numbers in the fall of 2007, seized on immigration as a good issue to electrify his base. He and fellow candidate, former New York City mayor **Rudy Giuliani**, strove to appear toughest on the issue, though both had long records of being pro-immigration in their liberal states of Massachusetts and New York respectively. Republican former Arkansas governor and Baptist minister **Mike Huckabee** and John McCain took more moderate positions, but Huckabee tried to get with the anti-immigration program when he made a series of bizarre pronouncements that seemed to suggest that Pakistanis with rocket launchers were flowing over the border from Mexico. All Republicans must perform a balancing act, since Hispanics find hardline positions against immigration offensive, and they are a growing demographic, especially in the Republican sunbelt. Democrats are generally more pro-immigration than Republicans. Although some support a crackdown, Democrats have not chosen to focus on the issue, because their constituents are worried about the economy, health care, and Iraq more than illegal immigration.

The long-standing argument against illegal immigrants when

there is anything but a labor shortage is that they **depress wages**, especially those of unskilled workers, by increasing the labor supply. While this is a reasonable concern, most data seem to indicate that this is false.[3] This is counterintuitive: increased supply should necessarily lower prices. One explanation may be that demand has increased as well. The economy has grown tremendously since the early 1980s, and more people have housekeepers and gardeners — low-skilled, low-wage jobs that are often filled by illegal immigrants — than ever before. Immigration advocates often point out that illegal immigrants do jobs Americans won't. But there is a flaw with this argument, because areas with low illegal immigrant populations don't lack housekeepers and gardeners. It may be safest to conclude that illegal immigration has not actually lowered wages, but kept them from increasing as demand rose.

The **cultural issues** at stake over immigration may be more intractable than the economic ones. People in areas with high concentrations of recent immigrants often feel pushed out. **Language** is at the heart of the matter because many immigrants — legal and illegal — come from Spanish-speaking countries. Unlike earlier groups, many Spanish speakers have not integrated linguistically, and the influx and persistence of Spanish often leads to communication problems, which many resent. This has led to various proposals to make **English the official language of the United States**, which would in theory force everyone to learn English, at least in school. Other plans wouldn't go so far as to establish an official language, but would mandate English classes for immigrants.

Legal immigrants often decry illegal immigrants' avoidance of stressful, costly, and time-consuming legal immigration procedures. Part of the general discomfort with illegal immigration is a pervasive sense of unfairness that people who flouted the law are able to stay in the United States. It's this feeling of unjust rewards for bad behavior that underlies many people's reflexive objections to **amnesty programs**, which give undocumented workers the option to stay, legally. "Amnesty" is a dirty word to hard-core anti-immigrationists who want to see people who have broken the law pay for their actions.

Eliot Spitzer, the controversial and pugnacious Democratic former governor of New York, walked into a political firestorm in 2007 when he vocally supported giving illegal immigrants driver's licenses. The issue was not always so touchy; prior New York politicians, including Rudy Giuliani, supported similar programs. But Spitzer's critics opposed it on security grounds, claiming that giving illegal immigrants legal forms of ID left transport systems more vulnerable to terrorism because driver's licenses can be used to get other forms of ID, rent apartments, and take out loans. They can also be used to board an airplane. However, foreign passports are also an acceptable form of ID, so it's unclear how driver's licenses could increase this specific security risk.

The argument *for* issuing driver's licenses is that it allows more people to buy car insurance, thus enhancing safety for everyone. Some also argue that granting driver's licenses is a good tool to bring an otherwise hidden segment of the population into the open. Since the state government keeps a record of a driver's license, it functions as a basic tracking device. In fact, many who are concerned about national security *want* to issue driver's licenses to illegal immigrants.

The invisibility of illegal immigrants worries many. Immigrant advocates maintain that illegal immigrants have few practical legal protections: they are not subject to minimum wage laws and they cannot report any crimes against them for fear of deportation, making them easy targets for abuse of all kinds. Amnesty programs would right this problem. Most moderate proposals call for increased border control and some kind of amnesty, to which a penalty may be attached to acknowledge that illegal immigrants have broken the law.

Labor and Social Security

Not that long ago, the United States had a labor force comprising legions of children and indentured servants who worked around the clock in dangerous conditions. In 1835 children called a strike against

New Jersey silk mills in order to *reduce* their workweek to eleven hours a day, six days a week. Throughout the 1800s, local, state, and sometimes the federal government pitted itself against low-wage workers, breaking up strikes with breathtaking brutality. Strikers were shot, clubbed, beaten, disgraced, discredited, and frequently run out of town.

Out of this often violent opposition, the labor movement sought to regulate business practices by forming **unions**, or professional organizations. Unions **concentrate dispersed interests**, uniting many small centers of power. Besides stopping work, or **striking**, the power of the union lies in **collective bargaining**, the ability of union leaders to negotiate contracts with business heads. Through unions, the labor movement helped set workweek hours and safety standards, create minimum wages, and endow and maintain benefits such as pensions and workers' compensation.

The biggest labor union is the **AFL-CIO**, or American Federation of Labor and Congress of Industrial Organizations, which represents over 10 million workers. Its great sweep and ability to influence members' electoral choices make the AFL-CIO an important political force, mostly for Democrats. Though the AFL-CIO and other large unions are often called **big labor**, unions in general and the AFL-CIO in particular have lost much of their influence because union membership has been in decline since the 1960s. In 2005 the professional drivers' union, the **Teamsters**, and the **SEIU**, or Service Employees International Union, split from the AFL-CIO and formed their own association, called the **Change to Win Federation** because they wanted to focus more on labor negotiating than on electoral politics.

Labor laws are **costly** because meeting and enforcing the regulations add to the expense of doing business in the United States. If you want to manufacture a manhole cover in America, it's much more expensive than it would be in India, where workers aren't even required to wear shoes in a metal foundry. Some industries' unions are often harshly criticized: the favorable and expensive concessions on wages, pensions, and health care won by the United Auto Workers in Detroit are seen by many as a reason that low-cost American cars have lost ground to Asian makers since the 1970s.

Those who oppose unions are almost invariably free-market, pro-business Republicans. They sometimes contend that unions are corrupt organizations whose greed has forced jobs overseas by making the cost of doing business in the United States too high. Others think that labor laws are **necessary** to maintaining basic standards. Almost all Democrats theoretically support unions, but fewer and fewer take active steps to help them. The importance of big labor as a political force has declined markedly, though it remains key in states like Michigan and Pennsylvania, where members often serve as reliable and effective campaign volunteers.

The most basic labor law is **minimum wage**, which sets requirements on the lowest hourly pay. The main political argument is over what the minimum wage should be, not whether we should have one. The federal government sets a baseline wage, but states may also mandate their own, higher minimum wage. Though very few politicians actively oppose minimum wage regulations, a significant number of economists think that minimum wage laws are less helpful than might be assumed. If there were no restriction on wages, they say, more people would have jobs, because some employers who won't hire workers at minimum wage would be willing to hire them at lower rates. But a counter theory argues that minimum wages *increase* employment by increasing consumption and creating incentives for more people to work. So which is it? You'd think that this is the sort of thing one could figure out with a lot of math, but as with so many issues in economics, nobody really agrees. A 2006 survey found economists almost equally divided between wanting to increase the minimum wage and wanting to eliminate it altogether.[4]

Another argument for a minimum wage is that it prevents abuse by employers. However, minimum wage laws are easily — and often — circumvented. Employers may create false time records, require certain actions like cashing out a register to be performed outside paid time, and refuse to pay required overtime. Partly as a result of these problems, many claim that the minimum wage is inadequate, and campaign instead for a **living wage**, which would be calculated from expenses necessary to maintain a basic level of comfort.

Unemployment insurance is a state-by-state program, so benefits and requirements vary. While economists generally agree that it helps insulate the economy from recessions in the short run by helping people consume even when they don't have a job, some argue over how generous our unemployment insurance ought to be. Liberal Democrats would like to see long periods of lower employment mitigated by an expansion of unemployment benefits. In case a worker is fired, there are other provisions to help. **COBRA**, the Consolidated Omnibus Budget Reconciliation Act of 1985, enables employees and their family members to buy health insurance through an employer for a certain period of time if they would otherwise lose the benefits (for example, if they are fired or switch jobs). COBRA isn't controversial, since employers aren't required to pay for it — rather, insurance companies must extend coverage, for which beneficiaries pay insurance premiums.

The **Family Medical Leave Act** of 1993, or **FMLA**, on the other hand, does come at a cost to employers because it requires companies to allow employees to take unpaid medical leave for the birth or adoption of children, for personal health problems, or to care for others who are ill. Employers must extend benefits during this time and guarantee the employee's right to return to their job. Connecticut Democratic senator **Chris Dodd** sponsored the bill, which was one of the first laws signed by President **Bill Clinton**.

While many business interests bridle at such requirements, they are popular among the general public. In 2007 the Department of Labor put out a directive to study whether benefits were too generous, eliciting ire from many, especially Democrats. Hundreds of nations require paid maternity leave while we do not, and almost all industrialized nations offer a much longer period of leave than we do in America. Interest groups opposing FMLA, including the ironically named Coalition to Protect Family Leave and the National Association of

Manufacturers, complained that employees regularly **abuse the program** and lobbied hard to roll back or water down the provisions.

A more pernicious though less frequently vocalized argument against FMLA centers on **gender politics**. Some contend that since women are more likely to take unpaid leave on the birth of a baby than are men, **women are more expensive to employ**, and this leads to discrimination against women. While the premise may be true, the alternative is either to remove a protection against a woman's losing her job after having a baby, or to assume women will stop taking leave to have children. Really, the argument is one against **working motherhood**, and those who oppose it — almost entirely extremely conservative Republicans — think that FMLA implicitly gives government approval to working mothers. It does, but most Americans these days think that's a good thing.

Interestingly, there is a group of liberals who agree with aspects of the social conservative argument, though not with their moral precepts. In fact, some think that various social service provisions, along with a shift in cultural norms, have encouraged women to work outside the home in a way that is often detrimental to family finances. Harvard law professor Elizabeth Warren's book *The Two Income Trap* argues that the race to put kids in good public or private schools, higher education loans, and rising child care and living costs associated with both parents working outside the home has hurt the American middle class.[5] When one spouse stays home, there is income flexibility — he or she can enter the workforce if need be. Plus, there is someone to cook and clean and take care of kids — all expensive tasks if you pay someone else to do them. Even education is affected, since children whose parents take an active role in their education do better in school.

Usually offered by private companies and always provided by the government to its workers, a **pension** is a private fund into which a certain amount is deposited by the employer each month that will pay out benefits upon an employee's retirement. The 1974 **Employee Retirement Income Security Act**, or **ERISA**, established pension standards in private industry but is often used as short-hand to refer to all laws concerning employment benefits. Although pensions are not required by law, ERISA is meant to regulate pensions once they are established. In the 1960s the downfall of car manufacturer Studebaker led to an evisceration of their fund, with only employees who had already reached the age of retirement receiving full benefits. While Studebaker's may have been the most spectacular pension plan failure, many plans were underfunded — meaning that companies are not making the requisite payments — leaving employees open to major losses in invested funds and expected benefits. ERISA created the **Pension Benefit Guarantee Corporation**, or **PBGC**, insurance against plans that went bust. Though it had bipartisan support, ERISA legislation was originally drafted by the liberal Republican senator **Jacob Javits** of New York and was passed under Republican president **Gerald Ford**.

Many liberals and moderates continue to worry about pensions. For one thing, pensions can be dismantled if a company declares bankruptcy. Big-business critics note that the executives of struggling companies never lose their benefits or reduce their large pay packages; it's the workers who suffer. Many agree that a significant number of pensions are still underfunded.[6] So is the government's own insurance: because it doesn't have enough money, the PBGC has set caps on yearly benefits — around $50,000 per person. Which is fine if that is how much you are owed, but can be financially devastating if your pension is worth more. Businesses sometimes change their benefits rules, too, and then hold old employees to new rules. Some companies have made lump sum payments instead of yearly or monthly benefit payments as promised — which usually amounts to less money in total.

The truth is that most businesses dislike pensions. Think about it from a CEO's point of view. Here you are making your payroll, there's all that money for health insurance (which keeps going through the roof), and you are supposed to set aside money for pensions *and* government insurance for those pensions. What if you need some cash? That pension fund probably looks like an extra checking account all of a sudden. And if you have to save a business, it probably seems better to keep the whole company afloat and save at least some of the jobs than it does to pay pension benefits.

According to critics, the problem with all of this is one of **broken promises**. Companies promise to pay a pension. The government promises to make them pay insurance to guarantee benefits even if the company goes bust. But the company can still get rid of pensions, or pay employees less than they originally promised. The government pays only part of many failed pensions. But the government has its own pension plan: **Social Security**, a federal program begun by Democratic president Franklin Delano Roosevelt as part of the **New Deal** in 1935. Though the program has repeatedly generated controversy among politicians throughout its history, it is also one of the government's most consistently popular programs among the general public.

Social Security is **mandatory** — everyone must pay into the system, and everyone is guaranteed benefits. Social Security is funded by payroll taxes, which are automatically deducted from paychecks. The self-employed have to make lump-sum payments at tax time or make estimated payments throughout the year. When a worker reaches age sixty-five (or older, at the worker's option), Social Security begins paying benefits tied to the individual's earnings — the more you pay in, the more you get out, but only up to a point. The political messages on Social Security are particularly confusing. Some right-wing Republicans claim that Social Security is in crisis. Democrats say that's not true. Democrats criticize Republicans for imperiling Social Security by borrowing from it. Some think it should be privatized. What's going on?

Most Republicans are skeptical of Social Security's **low rate of return**, or dislike the fact that it forces individuals to give up their money and subjects them to choices made by the government — the libertarians' beef as well. Democrats, on the other hand, think Social Security is an essential program that ensures a basic quality of life for the elderly. They also believe that the way the program violates individual choice is okay because it forces people to do what they should be doing anyway — saving money. It also guarantees that people most prone to mess up their finances, the lower economic classes, will save enough for retirement.

How does Social Security work? You pay money every month into the **Social Security trust fund**. Some of the money is used to pay benefits to retirees. Social Security has been running a surplus because more people are working than are retiring, and those of us who work keep making more money. Surpluses are invested in US treasury securities, but the government has been borrowing from this surplus to fund various programs like Medicare and the war in Iraq.

Current projections estimate that payments into Social Security will be outpaced by benefit payments to retirees between 2020 and 2022. Assuming that the government's debts to Social Security are paid back in full and in a timely fashion, the program will be fully solvent until 2042 or 2052, depending on the forecast (all these numbers come from official government sources).[7] Then, Social Security will be able to pay about 73 percent of full benefits unless taxes are raised, more income comes in from current tax rates, more money is borrowed, or other government spending is cut. The conservative war cry that Social Security is in crisis is really an overstatement; but there are **long-run challenges** facing the system that need to be addressed. Social Security could be in crisis if the government fails to pay back its debt. Spending from the trust fund surpluses raises our **deficit** — the country's accumulated debt — which has other effects on the nation's overall financial health.

Privatization of Social Security would allow tax dollars to be invested in the stock market or other financial funds. Privatization was widely discussed during the stock market boom in the late 1990s, when conservative and libertarian politicians and pundits objected that citizens were losing out on the opportunity to make more lucrative investments with the money they had to funnel into Social Security. When the stock and bond markets plunged in 2000, however, this debate cooled. Privatization seems like a good idea when the finance industry is doing well, but it's inherently risky because finance is often *not* doing well. This risk is exactly what most Democrats oppose, since they believe that Social Security should provide just that — security. The finance industry would dearly love for Social Security to be privatized, however, because it would inject trillions of dollars into the stock and bond markets. Wall Street investors would make a lot of money off it — and if it raised the stock and bond markets, it could be a boon to all investors.

A middle way proposed by President George W. Bush is **partial privatization**. Though details have not been fully worked out, the idea is to replace all or some of an individual's Social Security contributions with a personally controlled retirement account. Regulations would ensure that people save enough, but the government wouldn't control all of the money paid in. Alternatively, Democrats, notably Vice President **Al Gore** in his 2000 presidential bid, have advocated for **lockbox** provisions, which would prevent the government from borrowing money from Social Security.

It's important to understand that Social Security is really a program for the middle and lower economic classes because there is a **salary cap**: only the first $97,000 of your income is taxed by Social Security. People who make more, and who expect to spend more than the maximum annual benefit of around $50,000 after age sixty-five, need to save more. Many Democrats think the salary cap should be lifted, because they maintain it's unfair that some people have all of their income taxed while others don't; Republicans say that Social Security is already unfair and that extending its reach would make it more so. Social Security is really a class issue, and because Americans like talking openly about class even less than we like being frank about race, Social Security debates are usually couched in moral terms of fairness and liberty.

Agriculture Subsidies

Agriculture subsidies are crucial for farmers, but they also affect everyone's food-buying habits. Subsidies and other programs help keep food prices relatively stable, and they also artificially lower the prices of certain goods. Some argue that this has widespread unintended consequences. Politicians from industrial and urban centers tend to oppose farm spending, while representatives from rural areas dependent on agriculture generally fight hard for subsidies.

There are three main political camps in agriculture. **Food free-marketers** are generally Republicans and conservative Democrats from urban areas who think the government shouldn't interfere. **Food protectionists** want to minimize the risks for agriculture producers and are usually moderate Democrats and Republicans from big agriculture states such as the Dakotas, Iowa, and Nebraska. Almost all farmers are food protectionists. Increasingly, there is an outcry against certain kinds of subsidies from another sector, best represented by the journalist and author **Michael Pollan**, whose book *The Omnivore's Dilemma* brought complex health and environmental issues arising from subsidies to the general reading public. I'll call these people **foodie wonks**, since they are most concerned about the health implications of various food policies.

While those who are directly dependent on agriculture for their livelihood know a lot about agriculture, or ag, policy, most Americans are totally in the dark. One common misperception, held even by many politicians, is that agriculture subsidies are extremely expensive. In fact, they account for only **one-half of one percent** of the government's total yearly spending. Critics don't like that statistic and instead quote the absolute cost: **over $55 billion** a year.

Part of the confusion over agriculture costs arises from the fact that farm bills fund the Department of Agriculture, which oversees agricultural subsidies as well as major socioeconomic food programs such as food stamps, school lunches, and even land conservation projects. Sixty-six percent of the 2007 farm bill's spending was for food programs; 14 percent was dedicated to farm subsidies. Why do we subsidize agriculture, anyway? What's so special about soybeans that their producers get paid by the government unlike the makers of, say, socks?

Unlike socks, food is a **vital national commodity**. Maintaining its stable supply is in everyone's interest. But agriculture is different from any other industry because of the unique nature of its supply. Maximum supply is determined only once a year; supply cannot be held back much once the commodity is produced, and it is fragile, unpredictable, and **extremely variable**. If there's a glut in the sock market, for example, manufacturers can stop making them for a while; if there's a shortage, they can stay up past bedtime, hire a few more workers, and make more. But farming isn't like that.

Most farmers plant once a year, so they have a single opportunity to decide what they might contribute to the supply of their commodity. They can — and sometimes do — destroy crops once they are planted if prices are very low, but because of the large investment required to plant, and because most producers operate relatively small, independent farms and need to make their investment back, it's hard for individual producers not to sell their crops. At most they can hold back supply for one or two years. Crops eventually spoil, and farmers simply need the money. Farmers are a classic example of **dispersed interests**. They comprise a large collection of independent producers, so farmers are always competing with each other (though there are huge agribusinesses such as Monsanto and Archer Daniels Midland). It might be better for all farmers if supplies are low, because prices will then be high; but it's better for any individual farmer to have a bigger supply. So each farmer has to balance his personal interests against those of the overall market.

Crop supply is highly variable because it depends on unpredictable factors such as weather and disease. Planting a crop is a huge investment, representing a farmer's entire yearly income, so producers are extremely prone to bankruptcy. Farming isn't something you can pick up in a year, though, so if a farmer goes out of business, there's no one standing by to take his place. It is in the nation's interest to keep any given farmer in the black, which is why the government provides subsidies and **crop insurance**. Crop insurance is low-cost insurance that farmers buy from the government. The premiums are subsidized, and the program is very popular.

Farm subsidies apply to what are considered **staple crops**: corn, wheat, barley, soybeans, rice, and cotton. These products are subsidized instead of, say, eggplants, because they provide the most bang for the buck: they can be widely and intensively cultivated, can be preserved, and are highly caloric (cotton, while not a food crop, is a major commodity essential to the Southern agricultural economy).

Nowadays, farmers **compete internationally** because agricultural goods are shipped worldwide, so our agriculture policy is tied to other nations'. And many other countries give their farmers better deals than we do, allowing them to sell goods for lower prices, which food protectionists also cite as a justification for increased subsidies in the United States. Europeans are the biggest subsidizers. They are also our main competitors. Undoing subsidies entirely would greatly hobble our producers relative to foreign competitors, which means that unless everyone all over the world decided to cut them at the same time (and try persuading the French to do that), they will be around for the foreseeable future.

Foodie wonks fret about our **choice of subsidies** rather than subsidies per se. They might prefer to see vegetables subsidized more than grains, for example. Michael Pollan's argument focuses on corn, which provides a huge caloric package for very little money. Pollan thinks that the government's corn subsidies have encouraged the widespread use of **corn syrup**, which is sweeter than sugar. Since sweetness stimulates the appetite, corn syrup is added to many prepared foods in order to make people eat more of them. It's a cheap kind of marketing, and it's ubiquitous in America. Pollan thinks that corn syrup usage underlies some of America's obesity epidemic; corn syrup has also been linked to diabetes.

Food Aid and Welfare

Many countries throughout history have subsidized food. In Italy, government bread must still be sold in every bakery, though locals are more likely to buy cookies than the coarse government loaf. America prefers a more flexible system, and most of our food aid is in the form of **food stamps**, or currency that can be used only for food. Food stamps are available to people who make less than a specified amount and whose net worth falls under a certain level. It's a federal program administered by the states, so rules vary, but the value of one's car, household possessions, and even — seriously — your burial plot can be taken into consideration. Food aid is an increasingly important issue because of its implications for public health. The political debate revolves around whether we provide far too little or far too much assistance. There's a rural/urban divide because the cost of food is so much higher in cities.

Those who feel we should expand the food stamp program say that the amount provided is too low, especially to eat nutritiously. They say fresh foods are more expensive than prepared packaged food, which provides more calories per dollar. Another problem for low-income families attempting to eat well is **availability**. Stores in low-income areas often do not carry fruits, vegetables, and other nutritious items, leaving families little choice but to eat unhealthful food. Another factor, though one almost never mentioned, is that poor people may not even have the necessary kitchen equipment, such as pots, pans, a refrigerator, stove, or even gas or electricity to help keep costs down and nutrition high by eating wholesome home-cooked meals.[8]

Various experiments show that it is possible to eat well, though little, on food stamp allowances, but to do so takes a lot of planning and cleverness in shopping, cooking, and storing food. Of course, these skills may be just what struggling people lack. One high-profile attempt to eat off the US Department of Agriculture's Thrifty Food Plan — the basis for food stamp calculations — was that of *Vogue* food critic **Jeffrey Steingarten**, who was able to feed himself quite well — even in New York — though he claimed it took up most of his time to do so.[9] In 2007, Oregon's Democratic governor Ted Kulongoski spent a week eating on a food stamp budget.

The issue of food choices is sometimes a sticking point in the food stamp debate. Some think that people who are being helped by others have a moral duty to be careful with their diet, while others feel they shouldn't judge other people's decisions. More Republicans tend to agree with the former, and more Democrats value the latter. That's interesting, because Republicans are usually staunch individualists. In some sense, their position *is* individualist: they value property rights and believe that any money the government confiscates should be put to a good use, so they are more willing to judge the choices of those on public assistance. The conservative think tank the **Heritage Foundation** drew ire from liberals in 2007 after releasing a report attacking a USDA study on food insecurity as alarmist, and arguing that food stamps make the poor more likely to be obese than if they had no food aid at all.[10]

Some, however, are suspicious of food stamps in general. Low-income people who do not take food stamps but manage to eat well and inexpensively are particularly critical. They resent that others are receiving benefits that their own experience tells them are unnecessary. Indeed, the same protest is heard in debates over welfare. It's hard to argue with people who independently make do in lean times. It's no wonder they are resentful of paying taxes that subsidize others.[11] Those who support public assistance, however, argue that those people are exceptions, and that most who are struggling need and deserve help. One problem with food stamps, at least, has diminished: people used to sell food stamps for cash and use that for anything *but* food — frequently, for drugs and alcohol; however, a new electronic swipe-card system has dramatically reduced, if not eliminated, that problem.

Many, mostly Republicans, who agree with the basic premise of providing food aid to the poor disagree that it is the government's job to do so and would prefer to see private charities step in. However, private charities provide less stable services than the government. In

2007, for example, New York's food banks were in crisis. With more people needing food and fewer donations, banks began to ration handouts. Most religious groups support expansions of food aid, and most private food banks are run by religious organizations. Indeed, public food support is widely available through churches and synagogues, which — unlike the government — almost never make people prove that they need food. Though Democrats tend to support more food aid than Republicans, most Republicans support it, and some, like Senator **Richard Lugar** of Indiana, are longtime champions of food stamps.

Head Start, another food assistance program, provides free meals in school to low-income students. Head Start currently costs upwards of $7 billion a year, feeds about a million children, and is generally considered a great success. Indeed, Head Start enjoys bipartisan support, and the debates over it center on management rather than the basic merits of the program. The moral considerations that surround food stamps and welfare don't seem to apply to Head Start, probably because nobody holds children responsible for their own socioeconomic status. The biggest argument about Head Start occurred over the preferential hiring of employees based on their religious beliefs: some want a Catholic school that has a Head Start program to be able to hire a Head Start administrator based at least partly on his faith, which is currently considered unconstitutional.

Welfare technically refers to any kind of public assistance, including Social Security, Medicare, and food stamps. However, when we say "welfare" we generally mean cash benefits paid to very low-income citizens. Welfare is a federal mandate administered by individual states, so it's different depending on where you live. The racial politics of welfare are almost never spoken of openly, but it is clear that African Americans (and to a lesser extent Hispanics) face a tougher climb out of poverty than do whites or Asians.

Welfare as a federal program emerged from the **Great Depression**, when one-fourth of the labor market was unemployed and more than two-thirds of the population subsisted below the poverty line. American culture has always been broadly capitalist and individualistic, valuing personal responsibility and a strong work ethic. The American dream centers on the notion that if you work hard, you will succeed — which may not always be true, but it's a core American belief. But the scale of unemployment and poverty during the 1930s was so vast, and followed such major upheavals as the stock market crash, that nobody could pretend it was the unemployed individual's fault that he was out of work. It was clear that the economy, not the labor force, had failed, and so large-scale welfare was politically acceptable for the first time.

Few politicians like welfare, but some think it is more necessary than do others. Even supporters of welfare programs or expanded benefits ultimately seek to reduce the need for welfare; everyone agrees that the ultimate goal is to get as many people as possible into the workforce at a livable wage. By the 1980s, however, there was a sense that welfare programs were creating **welfare dependency**, or a culture in which people could not escape welfare and stand on their own two feet. President **Ronald Reagan**'s denunciation of so-called **welfare queens** became critics' catchphrase; while most welfare recipients are indeed single women with children, the slogan evoked a woman content not to work, who saw having more children as a means to receive more benefits. Whether or not it accurately reflected a large portion of welfare recipients, the image stuck in the minds of many who came to support welfare reform. However, social critics argue that the problem with welfare and welfare reform is that the poor, whether working or not, are often caught in a vicious cycle that renders them unable to get and keep jobs. Those closest to the issue believe that to truly be rehabilitated, people need a strong and reliable network of emotional, medical, and financial help.

The programs most successful at getting participants off welfare invest an enormous amount of effort, assisting with job training, professional skills, drug treatment, health care, and financial planning. In 1992 President **Bill Clinton** proposed a **welfare reform** bill that would have cut back benefits only after a significant investment in job training and other programs to help people break the cycle of poverty. Derailed by a Republican Congress and the administration's own ill-fated focus on health care, the plan died, and in 1996 Clinton eventually signed a very different bill drafted by Congress, one that forced welfare recipients into the workforce, but without the support he and other liberals had envisioned. After that, liberals shifted their focus away from assistance programs and onto issues of access to education and health care.

Welfare reform appears to have been successful, as the **caseload**, or number of people who receive welfare, **dropped by over half** in the ensuing years. However, there are arguments that the new laws were less effective than some claim. The thriving economy of the late 1990s deserves part of the credit for the reduction. Many liberals and conservatives think that the economy had more of an effect than the reforms, as the rising Internet tide lifted all boats. And some of the funding was funneled to other programs such as Women, Infants, and Children (WIC), which provides nutritional food and counseling to young mothers and their babies, and Supplemental Security Income, or SSI, which disburses money to the elderly and disabled poor.

The welfare reforms of 1996 seem to have transformed the debate into one about the **working poor**: those who work — often long hours in low-skilled jobs — but are nonetheless mired in poverty and debt. Two excellent but chilling books on the subject, Barbara Ehrenreich's *Nickel and Dimed* and David K. Shipler's *The Working Poor*, have been popular among many Democrats and socially liberal Republicans.[12] The issues facing the working poor are manifold: they often don't earn even minimum wage, long hours require them to spend heavily on child care, and lack of education makes them easy targets for all kinds of abuses. Living as they do on the edge of solvency, with no savings while working hourly-wage jobs, a single illness or a divorce can wreck their finances forever.

Family structures are an important part of the puzzle of persistent, multigenerational poverty. In the 1990s right-wing Republicans advocated **family values** as a means to end poverty, blaming cyclical poverty on fractured families. Liberal Democrats resisted these theories. Those who work closely with the poor indicate that the truth probably lies in the middle: lack of healthy family structures and role models do contribute to poverty, but they are by no means the only — or even the most important — factor.

The working poor also spend a disproportionately large amount on fees that for the middle and upper classes are almost negligible. Interest rates are tied to a recipient's credit rating, so the poor are charged high interest rates on car loans and mortgages. Often lacking a bank account, they pay high fees for check cashing. If they need a small loan — which they often do — they can get one easily, but at interest rates that are unheard of in a real bank, often paying 20 or 30 percent interest over a single week. Many states have laws to regulate these practices: for example, New York requires banks to allow a checking account to be opened with only $25 and maintained with a one-cent balance, but most of the working poor don't know about these laws and are too undereducated to have the skills or resources necessary to find out.

Perhaps the greater barriers to employment for many are cultural. People in the low-wage underclass often lack the most basic skills necessary for the workplace, such as knowing to show up on time or to call in when they are sick. Not quite knowing *how* to work prevents able-bodied adults from having — and keeping — jobs. Many who work with the poor believe these problems stem not from a lack of responsibility but from an environment in which violence, drugs, and unemployment are the norm. One effect, however, of the "culture of poverty" has been to increase demand for illegal immigrants, who, while they might not speak English, are often extremely responsible and able workers.

At the end of the day, however, issues such as minimum wage, food stamps, ag subsidies, and to a lesser extent immigration are all really about who should provide what for whom. What's most interesting is that the public often doesn't put its mouth where its money is: many commentators have noticed that especially since the early 1990s, middle-class voters often vote against their own short-term economic interests — possibly because they, like generations before, still believe that they'll strike it rich. And when their ship comes in, they'll want their income taxes to be low.

11

Homeland Security

➢ The Department of Homeland Security helps oversee infrastructure, from maintaining roads and bridges to responding to terrorist attacks and natural disasters.

➢ Homeland Security has been criticized for poor management and for being too slow to respond to important dangers.

➢ Infrastructure issues are closely tied to energy issues.

➢ All members of Congress try to get money for their state from infrastructure projects. "Pork" is questionable spending meant to bring in federal dollars.

➢ "Earmarks" are provisions in appropriations bills that fund specific projects.

➢ There is a move to privatize highways. Free marketers support it.

➢ Airlines and car manufacturers have received federal aid. Some say this is a sop to big business; others think these sectors are vital to security and the economy.

➢ Most Democrats support aid for Amtrak, while most Republicans do not.

➢ America's infrastructure is aging and will require investment to maintain.

➤ Hurricane Katrina showed that national disaster preparedness has been inadequate.

➤ New Orleans was worse off than other areas of the Gulf Coast affected by Katrina because it was less prepared and the response was poorly coordinated.

➤ FEMA and its former head Michael Brown were heavily criticized for the response to Katrina, as were President George W. Bush, Governor Kathleen Blanco, and Mayor Ray Nagin.

➤ The federal response to Katrina damaged the Bush administration. Within Louisiana it harmed the Democratic Party as well.

➤ California's 2007 wildfires were handled well by the state and federal governments.

Background to Current Debates

While transportation, infrastructure, and disaster preparedness have always been important questions for Congress, they became the subject of wider public debate after September 11, Hurricane Katrina, and the collapse of a major bridge in Minnesota. These events made us suddenly aware of our vulnerability to both natural and human disasters. "Infrastructure" sounds pretty unsexy, but it's vitally important and deeply tied to energy issues. Most development in the United States occurred after cars had become common, and our basic living patterns are partly determined by the historical availability of cheap oil. As energy prices rise, living in cities or areas serviced by public transport will look increasingly attractive; and, depending on how hard it proves to switch to non–oil-based fuels, government investment in subways and light rail networks may become a necessity.

Some infrastructure — roads, bridges, airports — is managed by various combinations of federal, state, and local authorities, while the

Department of Homeland Security, or **DHS**, is responsible for responding to terrorist attacks and natural disasters such as floods. The department has faced tough criticism as it struggles to define its mission and create a workable managerial structure with effective leadership. Various projects under its mandate have proven controversial. Some, like highway spending, are old issues revisited every time a new highway bill comes to the floor. Others, like how ports can be secured and shipping containers adequately inspected, are new. The political tone of these questions varies by issue. Overall, Republicans have been more supportive of the Department of Homeland Security, probably because it was developed under their aegis, while Democrats have been more critical.

On the one hand, issues of infrastructure concerning roads, bridges, tunnels, airports and airlines, railways, and ports divides predictably along political lines. Republicans tend to favor a smaller role for government, while Democrats prefer more government support. On the other hand, the ways that specific issues about infrastructure are played out defy our shorthand understanding of different parties' ideologies. This has to do with funding for infrastructure projects — now expanded to include disaster preparedness — as an excellent way to help a state economy and aid a politician's bid for reelection.

After September 11, the traditional position of Republicans as advocates for less spending and small government altered somewhat. Republicans allocated more money to defense and homeland security, while Democrats questioned what they saw as reckless spending that too often benefited political cronies. Some Democrats are not fiscal conservatives, and many small-government Republicans are concerned about the implications of more government spending and expanded federal authority. However, those in control of the Republican Party were more openhanded under President George W. Bush, proving that when it comes to bringing home the bacon, all bets on which party is the bigger spender are off.

On the federal level, transportation, infrastructure, and now security projects are notorious sources of **pork**: spending of debatable necessity meant to appease constituents and bring money into congressmembers' states. Democratic senator **Robert Byrd** of West Virginia — namesake of the Robert C. Byrd Freeway, the Robert C. Byrd Expressway, the Robert C. Byrd Federal Building, and the Robert C. Byrd Institute — is considered the most successful pork-barrel politician. Also the most erudite of senators, Byrd has been re-elected for nearly a half-century. In the 1970s and '80s, Democrats like him were closely identified with pork-barrel projects, and were often attacked by Republicans for being the **tax and spend** party.

However, under President George W. Bush, the government spent lavishly on federal projects. Alaska Republicans Representative **Don Young** and Senator **Ted Stevens** tried to fund the so-called **bridge to nowhere**, which would have connected an island with a population of 50 to a mainland town of 8,000 — at a cost of $223 million to federal taxpayers. Another proposed bridge, this one costing $231 million, would have joined Anchorage to an area with exactly *one* resident. Advocates for these outlays claimed that they are spurs to development that eventually would pay for themselves by increasing the tax base. Businesses often do sprout around transportation installations, but these projects' high cost and lack of visible need alienated many fiscal conservatives and small-government Republicans.

Pork projects are usually slipped into bills with which they have little or nothing to do. Congressional representatives often insert **earmarks**, provisions that fund specific projects, in **appropriation bills**, which allocate spending on a yearly basis. Not all earmarks are wasteful, but they have a negative connotation because they are associated with pork projects. Earmarks are sometimes allowed into bills to ensure that a given representative will support its passage, called **horsetrading**; you allow an earmark in return for support on another bill. Congressional politics often depend on this kind of quid pro quo.

Sometimes legislative accounting tricks are used to get a bill passed. For example, in 2004 President Bush threatened to veto the highway bill because he thought it was too expensive. By dangling the veto, Bush managed to substantially reduce the amount the bill would cost — or so it seemed: $8.5 billion of extra spending was slipped into the bill and eluded notice because the law requires that the extra money be repaid to the treasury before the bill expires in 2009. It's a finesse called **recission**, and is often used to make it seem as if less money is being spent. Of course, there is no guarantee that the money will ever be repaid. Congress gets away with this sort of thing because it's in every member's personal interest to bring as many federal dollars as possible to his or her state. Only the strongest fiscal conservatives oppose it — and even then, they usually try to reduce other members' spending and maximize their own. Critics of practices like recission include watchdog groups like **Taxpayers for Common Sense**.

A few left-wing liberals criticize the government for spending so much on roads; by doing so, they say, the government prioritizes citizens' ability to travel over other social goods, like education or feeding the poor. Advocates for such spending, however, say that transport is vital to the economy and therefore to everyone's well-being.

Current Debates

The Department of Homeland Security (DHS) represented the largest reorganization of government since the Department of Defense was created in 1958. DHS employs more than two hundred thousand people, and **the labor regulations** that apply to them have been very controversial. When DHS was created in 2002, President Bush wanted to **exempt** the agency from the **collective bargaining process** enjoyed by other federal employees in order to avoid restrictions that make it harder to fire government workers, arguing that DHS should be able to fire incompetent or underperforming employees easily. Democrats in Congress strongly opposed what they thought was a loosening of important labor protections.

The then minority leader, Democratic senator **Tom Daschle** of South Dakota, lobbied for an appeals process for employees to ensure they were terminated fairly. Democrats were accused of holding up the DHS bill, and this was used against Daschle in the 2004 election, which he narrowly lost. The political deployment of DHS against Democrats was surprising, given that Democrats were the first to propose the department; however, Republicans generally favor private, free-market business practices, and the debate over labor regulations illustrated a classic Democrat/Republican divide.

In effect, DHS employees are a special class of federal worker who have less job security than others. This may have affected morale, which is the lowest among all thirty-six government agencies. The fortuitously named former DHS inspector general **Clark Kent Ervin** has been the department's most quoted critic, especially after the publication of his book, *Open Target: Where America Is Vulnerable to Attack*. Ervin's biggest concern is that Homeland Security is a collection of several dysfunctional agencies and lacks a transparent, workable management structure. Many are concerned that the chain of command and areas of responsibility at DHS are poorly defined.

DHS has also been criticized for doing far too little to guard against threats to security. Inspection of shipping containers, stepped up in the wake of September 11 over concerns that terrorists might try to use them to smuggle in a chemical weapon or bomb, also received widespread attention. Radiation detecting equipment for ports was mandated to protect against a low-grade nuclear device, but much of it has not been installed, and Ervin contends that even that in place is ineffective because it cannot distinguish between benign and malignant sources of radiation.[1]

Intelligence is a key aspect of Homeland Security, but when the DHS was created, the **Central Intelligence Agency (CIA)** and the **Federal Bureau of Investigation (FBI)** were left out. There has been a lot of discussion over how intelligence might best be used to defend and protect the country, especially after revelations that analysts were warned of a major airline threat just before September 11 but were unable to effectively alert the aviation industry. DHS has its own intelligence group, the **Information Analysis Unit**, while the agency that consolidates all intelligence, the **National Counterterrorism Center**, is run by the CIA, and the **Terrorist Screening Center** is run by the FBI. It is just this sort of fragmentation that many say makes agents less able to coordinate activities and share information. But it has probably been in the realm of its second and more recent mandate that DHS has received the most criticism.

Transportation in all forms is heavily subsidized by the federal and state governments. Individuals may buy cars, but the government provides most roads. Highways are a big source of political infighting, though it's an issue rarely confronted outside of capitol buildings. Because new roads often lead to economic development, funding for them can be a valuable federal handout; because they inherently create change and often require the government to acquire private land, they are frequently controversial in affected areas; and because they are expensive, some will always oppose their funding.

Especially debated in the 2004 highway bill was what percentage of the federal fuel tax states would get to keep. Fuel taxes usually finance road building, but most Americans seem to **prefer tolls to taxes**: after all, tolls affect only those who use the service. Though tolls paid for early highways, called **turnpikes**, the federal interstate system developed under Republican president **Dwight D. Eisenhower** stipulated that tolls could not be charged, because interstates were built to better link population centers. But today, as traffic overwhelms commuters and the cost and scope of maintenance overburdens states, more tolls are being instituted.

The new development in highway construction is **privatization**. Normally, the state owns and maintains highways with help from the federal government. Private companies often construct roads and charge tolls until the road is paid for, at which point they turn over toll operation to the state. But some new highways are owned and operated by private companies. Private highways are more common in Europe; there are a few in the United States, but some argue that our entire highway system should be privately run.

There is also discussion about turning over publicly constructed roads, notably the New Jersey Turnpike, to private companies.

Those who support privatizing highways tend to be free marketers who think that competition is always a good idea. Free marketers charge that government is slow to respond, is risk averse and therefore reluctant to invest large sums, and is insulated from the problems that people face because its leaders can only be judged every few years at the polls, rather than every day at the cash register. Privatizers argue that the American road system is strained to the breaking point, as demonstrated by heavy traffic and the poor state of many roads.

Roads, they say, are not meeting current demand because they are under the jurisdiction of the government, which will not create more supply until absolutely necessary. Privatizers reason that if roads were a for-profit industry, problems with traffic and maintenance would cease because companies would be competing for customers and would have to provide adequate capacity and quality in order to make money. Yet another argument for road privatization is that those who use the service and who create problems arising from it — such as noise or pollution — could be charged directly for the cost of mitigating the issues. Noise barriers are usually paid for by a city or community; private road companies could be forced to pay for barriers and pass the cost on to the consumer.

Opponents argue that public highways can price their services high in order to make a profit, rather than charge for the cost of the road as the government generally does. Some also point out that competition doesn't make a lot of sense in regard to highways. After all, how would a company compete for customers, when people get to different places using different roads? One way is by **adding lanes** to existing highways. On Riverside Freeway in California, an $11 round-trip toll can turn a free two-hour expedition into a half-hour jaunt on a privately owned lane.[2] Fundamentally, however, many are skeptical about putting vital infrastructure in the hands of private enterprise. Though increased privatization has been the norm in many sectors of the US economy, it hasn't always turned out as planned. This has certainly been the case with our passenger rail network, one of the least functional in the developed world.

Amtrak is America's passenger railroad, formed as a private/public cooperative by Congress in 1970 with the goal of becoming fully privatized — and financially independent — within two years. This never happened, and in 2007 Congress voted to expand Amtrak's funding. Although ridership and revenues increased for the fourth year in a row in 2006, Amtrak's budget fell short by $1 billion, and it covered only two-thirds of its operating expenses with revenue. Congress continues to fund Amtrak because the rail system is considered too important to lose to bankruptcy.

Many liberals and environmentalists have long wondered why we don't have a better rail system. One reason is that America is big, therefore people need to fly. Also, Americans have historically preferred car travel, and the automotive lobby has been powerful in combating railways. Many of our residential areas were created after cars were invented and are geared toward driving. Cities with older centers that were built around foot and carriage traffic require less long-distance transport and tend to have better public transport. In the 1950s and '60s, the development of the interstate highway system and commercial aviation drastically reduced rail use. As air and car traffic worsened, train travel increased in popularity, both among cities and from suburbs into commercial centers. However, with major exceptions such as Chicago and New York, American cities tend to have less public transport than their counterparts in the developed world. The freight rail industry in the United States is alive and kicking, though. Nearly 40 percent of freight traffic in the United States travels by train, and some industries, such as coal, are heavily reliant on rail.

Airlines have also been the subject of controversial government attention. The industry was heavily regulated until 1978, when airlines became private, independent, for-profit companies. By the early 1990s many were on the brink of financial ruin. Airlines got squeezed from many sides. Fuel costs went up, capital expenditures for equipment were high, and fares were low because of increased competition from budget airlines. Some airlines claimed **Chapter 11 bankruptcy**, which is a legal umbrella overseen by a special federal court that enables companies to reorganize if possible to save the business. It allows companies to cancel pension benefits and labor contracts, so bankruptcy's most politically debated issues center on conflicts between employees and management.

Both United Airlines and US Airways **terminated pension benefits** when they foundered in bankruptcy; many agree this is terribly unfair to employees, who voluntarily pay into a pension system throughout their tenure with a company and lose substantial sums if pensions are obliterated. The federal government has a pension insurance program called the **Pension Benefit Guarantee Corporation**, or **PBGC**, which airlines have approached to fund pension plans that they want to terminate, but the corporation has fought these claims hard, and often won. Some, mostly liberals, view bankruptcy for huge private industries such as airlines as tantamount to a taxpayer-funded subsidy for private, already wealthy groups, which they think is inherently unfair. Others, moderate Democrats and most Republicans, reason that bankruptcy is efficient because it allows some companies to survive otherwise fatal financial problems, which is good for employees and the economy as well as for owners and management. Still others figure that airlines are so vital to infrastructure that the government must help save them. Airlines were hard hit by September 11; ridership plummeted. Created to assist the industry, the Airline Transportation Stabilization Board provided government-backed loans. In 2004, US Airways made headlines when it made the largest default on a federal loan in history, after its second bankruptcy filing in two years. Airlines took their lead from the automobile industry, the first to enjoy a federal **bailout** of **guaranteed loans** in 1979 and 1980. Only the auto and airline industries have ever received this form of federal aid.

After September 11, often-criticized airline security systems were reorganized and now are staffed by the **Transportation Security**

Administration, or **TSA**. TSA oversees all transport security, including airports, ports, highways, bridges, tunnels, buses, and subways. Screeners are federal employees, unless TSA has subcontracted out screening duties to a private company. TSA also oversees the Federal Air Marshal program, which flies gun-toting plainclothes police on some flights. The most serious accusation that has been leveled against TSA is that it still does an inadequate job of screening airline luggage and cargo. In several tests, TSA failed to confiscate or identify bomb parts planted in luggage. Reports that TSA hired convicted criminals raised concerns, too. Various screening procedures have been questioned as invasions of privacy; TSA altered its patdown protocol after a wave of complaints from female passengers. When the media revealed that the unfortunately named Rapiscan Secure 1000 allowed screeners to see passengers naked, an outcry prompted programmers to extract key data and project it onto an image of a mannequin, assuaging original privacy concerns.

In 2007 the potential dangers of America's **aging infrastructure** were vividly underscored when an interstate highway bridge collapsed between the twin cities of Minneapolis and St. Paul, Minnesota. Thirteen were killed and around one hundred injured in the dramatic rush-hour disaster, which was apparently due to design flaws. In regular inspections, problems with the bridge had been noted but were not considered to be fatal; thousands of other bridges throughout the United States have similar problems. Bridges are monitored by states and the federal government, which maintains a national bridge inventory through the Department of Transportation. Many have called for increased scrutiny of installations to determine safety and more government aid to help states and cities inspect, maintain, and repair bridges and other transport facilities. The collapse led to increased inspection within days.

Failures like that in Minnesota are more likely to occur as American infrastructure, built during a boom in the 1950s to 1970s, ages and weakens. Some believe that the need to rebuild and renovate transport systems and civil engineering projects such as dams, sewers, and waterworks poses a huge and largely **unnoticed financial stumbling block** to the nation's economy. Many developing countries are only now building roads and other facilities, but because they are using new technology, their infrastructure is in some ways better and will probably last longer. America's once advanced transport system may soon seem as antiquated as Englands' steam-powered trains that used to be the envy of the civilized world. Infrastructure might just be the next big lightning rod in politics.

When it was created after September 11, the Department of Homeland Security was organized primarily to prevent and respond to terrorist attacks, but after Hurricane Katrina, DHS was also directed to oversee **disaster preparedness**. In 2005 the debacle of **Hurricane Katrina** highlighted how vulnerable America can be to major natural disasters, demonstrating that FEMA, local police, and even the National Guard can be ineffective if poorly managed, but also revealing bright spots of excellence such as the **Coast Guard**.

Hurricane Katrina destroyed thousands of homes along the Gulf Coast, causing serious damage in Florida and devastation in both Mississippi and Louisiana. The fate of New Orleans, however, received the most attention because it was the worst-hit big city and its disaster preparedness was deplorable. Not only did the levees breach, killing hundreds and stranding thousands, but the city's evacuation center was badly run, looting after the storm was rife, and tens of thousands of residents were trapped in rapidly putrefying floodwater.

Blame for Katrina has been tossed around liberally, and some rests on the city itself. New Orleans has suffered endemic political corruption. Its declining economic fortunes are based almost entirely on shipping, oil and gas, and tourism. To keep these industries alive, the city sacrificed its protective wetlands, which greatly magnified Katrina's destructiveness. The city's levees — walls in low-lying areas that protect against floods — were structurally unsound. Many reports in books and local and national newspapers had long foreseen that a strong hurricane would inundate New Orleans because the levees would fail; though aware of the issue, New Orleans did little to

maintain or upgrade its levees. Many, therefore, felt it was disingenu-
ous for President Bush to claim in the aftermath of the storm that nobody could have predicted that the levees would be breached.[3] People
could have, and did. That major federal agencies appeared unaware of
this was merely the tip of the iceberg.

As the storm approached, Democratic mayor **Ray Nagin** refused to issue a mandatory evacuation order, unlike other communities such as St. Charles Parish, which saved all its residents from the
storm's worst effects. Nagin was reportedly worried that evacuating
the city would leave it open to lawsuits brought by big hotels, which
would lose revenue from any evacuation. He delayed, with disastrous
results. In New Orleans, evacuations were particularly complex because over 100,000 citizens did not own cars, and the government
would have had to provide transport, which it did not.

Many among the city's large African American community
were also suspicious of hurricane information provided by the federal, state, or city governments because in 1927, the city chose to flood
a poor African American area in order to save a wealthier white one
during a major hurricane. Evacuations were hampered by the fact
that many were confused by the information they received; others
were indigent and had practically no access to any information at all.
Some, however, chose to stay: they didn't think Katrina would be that
bad and wanted to protect their homes.

Those who remained encountered a terrifying storm with winds
so powerful that downtown highrises were said to sway like palm trees.
They faced rapid floodwaters that rose without warning as levees
failed. Even the wind was deadly, turning ordinary objects into haz-
ardous shrapnel. The flood stranded tens of thousands, and as the waters did not immediately recede, victims were caught without food,
water, shelter, or toilet facilities. They were surrounded by water full
of raw sewage, debris, toxic chemicals, and decomposing bodies. Law-
lessness was rife. Looting was caught on camera. Some incidents were
surely motivated by the legitimate need for basic supplies, but most

was theft. Many reported that rapes were common but downplayed in the media.

New Orleans's downtown sports arena, the **Superdome**, which Nagin originally designated as a shelter of last resort, became a symbol of the devastation. Full to capacity, thousands were stranded at the facility for days because of the poor relief efforts. The hallways were full of excrement, trash piled up, holes opened in the roof, and air conditioning failed when the power went out, leaving evacuees in searing heat and high humidity. Little information was given to evacuees. Most eyewitnesses reported that public perception of chaos in the Superdome was overblown and that most remained relatively calm throughout. Those guarding the center were the object of strong criticism for treating evacuees badly and policing poorly. As the week wore on and victims remained trapped in the Superdome, the situation deteriorated and armed thugs operated small gangs out of the center.

Also on the receiving end of withering criticism was the famously corrupt **New Orleans Police Department**, from which around two hundred officers fled active duty during and after the storm. Some who stayed stole Cadillacs from a dealership while the city was flooded. While many members of the force were exemplary, the department looked terrible throughout the disaster. The police commissioner broke down, reporting on *The Oprah Winfrey Show* that children were raped in the Superdome, which was never verified. Mayor Nagin, largely absent during the debacle, at one point stayed in Dallas for five days while thousands remained trapped in his city. By some accounts, Nagin suffered a nervous breakdown. His bizarre behavior, such as refusing to come out of the bathroom after a shower on Air Force One, was perhaps symbolic of the city's dysfunctional response.

Democratic governor **Kathleen Blanco** received the most ire in the press immediately following the disaster. In fact, she tried desperately to get New Orleans to prepare better, but lacked the necessary leadership and PR skills. Her squabbling with the incompetent

Nagin made her look both weak and petty. Blanco committed bureaucratic blunders, such as neglecting to commandeer buses, but it was her emotionalism that may have been most off-putting. Ultimately, her greatest fault may have been her failure to safeguard the state better *before* the emergency struck.[4]

Unlike the city, the **Coast Guard** and the **Louisiana Department of Wildlife and Fisheries** planned well, moving vital equipment out of harm's way but near enough to affected areas that they were able to quickly engage in search and rescue missions after the storm. They were among the great heroes of Katrina, as were brave citizens who rescued neighbors, and some members of the New Orleans Police Department. The **National Guard**, which Governor Blanco claimed was overseas in Iraq and therefore unavailable to help with the storm, was in fact present in the city in substantial numbers, but poor planning left them stranded, too.

FEMA (the Federal Emergency Management Administration) was useless for days. Part of the problem may have been a lack of bureaucratic experience — both Blanco and **FEMA head Michael Brown** failed to make the right requests for aid, though Bush had already approved substantial aid. Brown especially seemed to lack a sense of urgency early on. FEMA arrived in New Orleans late, was unable to get good information once there, lacked basic supplies even for its own employees, and left rescue efforts to others after the storm passed. In fact, FEMA actively interfered with many rescue efforts, and when asked why it wasn't doing anything, FEMA and the administration said that FEMA couldn't get into the city. Wal-Mart trucks sent by that company to provide relief were downtown, private citizens got around, and other agencies were mobile, so FEMA's absence remained a mystery. Mississippi, where Bush's close personal friend Haley Barbour was governor, fared no better. Only one FEMA official showed up in the week after Katrina.

While Brown, who had managed other disasters well, attempted to deal with the problems, he commited fatal blunders that made him — and FEMA — appear utterly ridiculous. A longtime personal friend of Bush's, Brown lied about his credentials on his résumé; his previous job had been as the head of judging at the International Arabian Horse Association, a cushy post at which he also underperformed. Leaked internal e-mails showed him nattering about his clothes during the Katrina disaster. "I am a fashion god," he wrote, jokingly asking if he could "come home" from New Orleans. While silly e-mails are probably part of everyone's office correspondence, Brown appeared frivolous in a time of national disaster.[5] Bush's later comment "Brownie, you're doing a heckuva job" became the sardonic refrain for the shocking federal response to Katrina.[6]

Indeed, the president's reaction to Katrina struck many as strange. While most Americans closely followed the story on the news, Bush's aides had to compile a DVD of news clips for him to watch five days after the storm. Bush didn't seem to know what was going on; when questioned on the matter, the president actually said that he didn't "see a lot of news," but could "tell you what the headlines are."[7] His first visit seemed marked by surprise at the devastation; the public was equally surprised because the situation had been so horrific — and widely reported.

The Katrina disaster and FEMA's response wounded President Bush politically. Though he authorized aid in advance of the storm and enacted other bureaucratic measures in a timely fashion, Bush seemed to miss the significance of the event both before and after Katrina made landfall. The fact that he did not immediately fly to the Gulf Coast and instead continued his vacation in Texas was a major blunder, for which few could defend him. Indeed, Republicans and Democrats alike were shaken by and outraged at the inadequate official response to Katrina. Many liberals felt that New Orleans was neglected because it had such a high population of traditionally disempowered citizens — the poor, the elderly, and African Americans.

Democrats blamed Bush, charging that cronyism had led to inappropriate appointments such as that of Michael Brown. Many Republicans did not make these specific charges, but were likewise appalled at the scale of the disaster and the ineptitude of the response.

Republicans tended to blame Louisiana's Governor Blanco and Mayor Nagin, though not as much as locals did. Bizarrely, when Katrina hit Florida before it landed in Mississippi and Louisiana, state and federal governments had responded well. The scale of the destruction was worse in Mississippi and Louisiana, but other areas managed the crisis better than New Orleans. Clearly, part of the problem was the specific community involved.

Major **fires** in the greater San Diego and Los Angeles areas in the fall of 2007, on the other hand, were managed quite well by local authorities. Police trolled the streets with bullhorns and created a robo-call system to inform people of evacuation orders. Some fires shifted too quickly for alerts to be announced, but the vast majority of people seem to have received good information, aided enormously by the *San Diego Union-Tribune*'s comprehensive online coverage. Evacuation centers were well stocked and experienced no unrest; looting was almost unheard of and quickly squelched by the police.

Perhaps because of its perceived failure in responding to Katrina, the federal government and FEMA rushed to provide aid. But FEMA made another gaffe, staging a **phony news conference** at which its own employees were planted in the audience to ask questions. The ruse was almost immediately exposed, and the White House quickly condemned the action. FEMA apologized for "an error in judgment," and said that it was merely trying to get information to people quickly. Critics wondered why they didn't give a speech instead of hold a fake news conference, and the media jumped on the incident as evidence that FEMA hadn't yet learned its Katrina lesson.

The Bush administration attempted to credit the Republican-run state of California for its effective response while taking swipes at Louisiana's Democratic government, which Democrats chided as playing politics with disaster. Although California's situation was less complicated than the Gulf Coast's flooding, it was much better managed. Some of this may have more to do with culture and economics — many of California's affected areas were wealthy, and most were at least middle class — than with government per se, but it underscored vast regional differences in America's ability to deal with disasters.

As America's population grows, as our infrastructure ages, as natural disasters appear more common, and as the threat of terrorism remains, issues of homeland security will be increasingly important. Some believe that infrastructure will be the most significant political issue of the next few decades. We may have seen only the opening salvos in the battle to improve national disaster preparedness. Many predict that hurricanes will become more frequent and stronger as oceans warm, so large-scale evacuation and rescue efforts may become far more common. The Department of Homeland Security will need to step up to effectively coordinate all aspects of American infrastructure, from maintaining bridges to ensuring that FEMA gets to a disaster in time.

12

Education

➢ Primary and secondary education are a local concern because public schools are financed by property taxes.

➢ Affirmative action is a major factor in higher education but began as a labor issue.

➢ Democrats are more likely than Republicans to support affirmative action.

➢ Affirmative action to support diversity was upheld in the 2003 Supreme Court ruling on the University of Michigan Law School admissions program.

➢ Many critics of affirmative action think it impinges on the Fourteenth Amendment's equal consideration clause.

➢ School vouchers are supported by inner-city African Americans, wealthy suburbanites, and hardcore free marketers.

➢ Voucher critics think they challenge the separation of church and state and undermine the public school system.

➢ President George W. Bush's No Child Left Behind Act, called NCLB, is popular with many Republicans and Democrats, who argue that it makes schools more accountable by holding them to minimum standards of achievement.

> NCLB has been criticized as an unfunded mandate. Detractors have questioned its emphasis on testing and its penalizing of embattled schools.

> President Bush was criticized for attempting to reduce student loans for college and graduate school to save federal money.

> An education bill expanding federal loan assistance and funded by closing loopholes to lending companies was passed by the Democratic 110th Congress.

Background to Current Debates

Education in America is largely a local concern; when it receives national attention, it's usually because a specific federal policy is making headlines. Education funding is local, too, and derives almost entirely from **property taxes**. Indeed, about 80 percent of a district's property taxes are used to fund its public schools, and only about 7 percent of a public school's budget comes from the federal government. Education is an interesting area of policy because everybody agrees on the desired end, if not the means: it's good to have an educated population. How to create one — and how to do so fairly — is the question.

The major sticking points in education policy are **money** and **access**. Who pays for what and who gets what? Access itself is an economic question, because people with more education usually make more money. There are many other issues at stake in education policy than those I deal with here, including special ed availability, programs for gifted children, class size, and what's included in a curriculum. However, in the past several decades, the major federal educational issues have centered on affirmative action, school vouchers, No Child Left Behind, and student loans.

America enjoys a system of **universal education**, open to all and provided by the government. Advocates for universal education agree that it is a key tool for social cohesion and that its breakdown would be nothing less than disastrous for the country. Only the staunchest libertarians and extreme religious conservatives think it should be done away with. They believe that children should be educated as their parents see fit. The extremely religious do not want their children exposed to cultures they don't want to participate in. Dismantling the public school system would be politically untenable, though some liberals contend that that is exactly what some have tried to do by undermining public education in various ways.

Though Democrats traditionally have been strong supporters of public education, increasing federal aid for college and university students as well as financial breaks for the institutions themselves, in the 2000 presidential election, Republicans had the upper educational hand. **George W. Bush** made education one of the foundations of **compassionate conservatism**, and passed his landmark standards-based education bill, No Child Left Behind, with bipartisan support soon after taking office. Its policies, however, have been controversial, and some Democrats assert that they undermine public education. Both Democrats and Republicans want to be seen as pro-education, but Republicans tend to favor choice and financial freedom for parents, while Democrats focus on strengthening the existing public school system.

The sad truth is that the important framework within which most contemporary debates about education take place involve race and class. In America, we are often sensitive about race, but we are almost pathologically unable to talk about class. Race and class are tied together, because on average, African Americans have occupied a lower socioeconomic sphere than whites. The African American experience is often set against that of East Asian immigrants, who may have begun their lives in the United States as poor or working-class but whose children have done very well in school and now populate the professional ranks. Since education can be a way out of the economic underclass, it gets mixed up with race and class into an extremely volatile compound.

Strangely, it's children who face these race and class issues that comprise some of the most recent fallout from the Civil War. After the war, the process of integration between whites and blacks was effectively stopped for a century. Segregationist **Jim Crow laws** in the South and de facto segregation throughout much of the North meant that blacks and whites occupied different worlds — and they almost always attended different schools. Until 1954, segregated education was *required* in seventeen states; this **de jure segration** (segregation by law) led to drastically inferior schools for African Americans.

But the landmark Supreme Court case ***Brown v. Board of Education*** changed that. In 1954 the Court ruled that maintaining separate schools for whites and blacks denied African Americans equal opportunities guaranteed under the **equal protection clause** of the **Fourteenth Amendment**. The decision overturned the 1896 case ***Plessy v. Ferguson***, which allowed "separate but equal" institutions for different races. *Brown* also mandated that **desegregation** was to be carried out "with all deliberate speed," and by the 1960s active integration was enforced through **school busing**. At the time, most whites lived in different neighborhoods than most blacks in the North as well as the South, so schools were racially segregated partly as a function of their location. Busing transferred students of one neighborhood, and by extension, race, to another location.

After school busing began, there was an explosion in **private education** because private schools could isolate children by class — if you couldn't pay for it, you couldn't go. Though private schools legally cannot discriminate on the basis of race, the fact was that few blacks could pay for schooling, so private education also isolated children racially. Because many private schools are religious, religious schools experienced a boom. As separation of church and state was enforced more stringently in the last few decades and as the evangelical Christian movement grew in strength, greater numbers of Americans either put their children in religious schools or chose to homeschool them. They would prefer not to pay for public education because they don't use or want its services.

To a certain extent, debates about education are played out in an **international sphere** as well. We look to the excellent quality of Russian math programs, for example, and wonder why our own children perform relatively poorly in the hard sciences. On the other hand, the quality of American universities is unparalleled. But they are expensive, whereas university and college education in many other developed countries is largely paid for by the government. While no mainstream politician is going to argue that we should federalize universities, we do debate access to university education through subsidized student loans, educational tax breaks, school vouchers, and, perhaps the most intractable question of all, affirmative action.

Current Debates

Access to education is at the heart of **affirmative action**. While originally used to describe policies designed to prevent racial discrimination, affirmative action now usually refers to policies that seek to actively redress historical discrimination and/or ensure diversity. Various kinds of affirmative action seek to promote diversity: racial, gender-based, socioeconomic, geographic, and religious, among others.

The roots of affirmative action in education stretch back to *Brown v. Board of Education*. Integration was the main issue in *Brown*, and while affirmative action has shifted the debate about minorities and education toward diversity, some argue that integration is still at the heart of the issue. Democrats almost universally support affirmative action, while most Republican politicians do not, though levels of support vary. It's a huge issue for colleges and universities, and much of the debate has become one over legal definitions, rather than over politics per se.

The term "affirmative action" was first used in the 1960s to address labor inequalities. Instituted by Democratic presidents **John F. Kennedy** and **Lyndon Baines Johnson**, affirmative action was meant as a **temporary but indefinite measure** to redress the racism that persisted despite the **1964 Civil Rights Act**, which declared that it was illegal to discriminate on the basis of race, color, religion, sex, or national origin. Some employers, for example, would hire African Americans only for entry-level positions and never promote them, creating a **two-track system**: one, more lucrative and open to advancement, for whites, and the other, the very definition of a dead end, for blacks. In 1965, President Johnson issued an executive order to enforce the Civil Rights Act. The order was aimed at certain government contractors, requiring them to take "affirmative action" to ensure they were treating all employees fairly.

In 1970 and 1972 the act was expanded; policies originally meant to protect against discrimination in hiring were **extended to colleges and universities** and **included women** as a minority group. The new executive order implemented the old rules of affirmative action, which included **goals** — basically quotas — desired percentages of minorities enrolled in educational institutions or working in various jobs, and **timetables**, target dates by which the goals would be met. Faculty members were variously enraged or supportive; affirmative action in higher education was suddenly brought to national attention. Goals, quotas, and timetables are illegal today.

One of the main lines of thought followed by early supporters of affirmative action was that **preferential hiring** of minorities was **compensation for past injustice**. Many found this position untenable, and countered that preferential hiring "benefits individuals likely harmed by past wrongs (blacks and women possessing good educational credentials) while it burdens individuals (younger white male applicants) least likely to be responsible for past wrongs."[1] Others argued that merit was partly a question of opportunity: "some white [applicants] have better qualifications . . . only because they have not had to contend with the obstacles faced by their black competitors."[2] This view is legally discredited, and is not popular in either academia or politics.

Contemporary supporters generally cite two main reasons for continuing affirmative action in education: **diversity** and **integration**.

Some believe that students learn best in a diverse group. While "diversity" could mean just about anything, it generally refers to racial and gender diversity. This is the **diversity as pedagogy** argument. Supporters contend that the world at large is diverse and that a good education teaches students to engage with a **realistic model of society**. The case for integration has been less well articulated and includes several strands of argument. One notion is that African Americans and Hispanics are too often stuck in a **social and economic underclass**; providing them with higher education is necessary to create a more representative middle class. Supporters also assert that minorities need to have **role models** of their own race or ethnicity. Yet another aspect of the integration argument is **social cohesion**: some believe that we would all be better off with a more representative African American middle and upper class because it is dangerous for groups to be socioeconomically segregated.

Critics of affirmative action in universities cite several objections. Some believe that affirmative action has caused a **watering down of standards**, especially in elite institutions such as Ivy League universities. Universities are notoriously tight-lipped about racial divides in scores and grades; the only real data are **SAT tests**, which reveal that the average score of African Americans is lower than European Americans', and Asian Americans as a group score highest.[3] However, many feel that scores are **useless numbers** because SAT testing is an inaccurate measure of ability or potential. Many also believe that the lack of early educational opportunities for African Americans explains their lower scores.

Proponents of affirmative action argue, however, that it works as a **tiebreaker**; in this view, students who have a shot at getting into a school are all basically qualified, but minority applicants are preferred because they contribute to a school's diversity. Critics counter that affirmative action supporters worry that if affirmative action were ended, minority enrollment would plummet; they say these two views are necessarily in conflict, which demonstrates an **inconsistency** in the argument. Some also claim that defining **diversity based on race is**

counterproductive because we must stop defining individuals by race in order to move toward a society that does not discriminate — and they assert that affirmative action reinforces this identification.

Affirmative action reached the Supreme Court in 1978 with the **Bakke case**. Allan Bakke is a white male who had been rejected twice from the University of California at Davis Medical School, even though his MCAT scores were higher than those of many minority applicants who were admitted. The medical school used quotas, reserving sixteen of one hundred places for minority students. Four justices thought the quota was a clear violation of rights, while another four felt it was important to preserve affirmative action. The decision came down to Justice Lewis Powell, who found the **two-class system** used by UC Davis intolerable; however, Powell did not rule out the possibility that racial or ethnic factors could be used to create a diverse student body. Thus, inflexible systems such as **quotas were struck down**, while flexible systems, in which race or ethnicity was considered as one among many factors serving the interests of **diversity, were accepted**. This basic distinction was upheld in two **2003 Supreme Court rulings**, one over the **University of Michigan** Law School's admissions policy and one concerning its undergraduate college.

When students applied to Michigan's undergraduate program, they were assigned points: for grades, SAT scores, and — if they belonged to a minority — race. The final tally was a key consideration in admissions. The Supreme Court found this **point system unacceptable**; the law school's policy, however, was upheld. In Michigan's law school admissions program, race could be one of many factors taken into account; essential, however, was the individualized consideration the admissions board gave to each applicant. The Court did not accept affirmative action as a means of redressing past injustice, but recognized a compelling interest in maintaining a diverse student body.

The key vote on the law school case was cast by the now retired Justice **Sandra Day O'Connor**, the first woman to serve on the Supreme Court. Nominated by President **Ronald Reagan** in 1981,

O'Connor represented a swing vote; her thinking was independent and hard to pigeonhole politically, though she had a libertarian streak. Another Reagan appointee, Justice **Antonin Scalia**, wrote the dissenting opinion; he thought that the law school's admissions process was "a sham" because the admissions director was managing the number of minorities accepted to fill what amounted to an **unstated quota**.

Many — of various political stripes — argue that affirmative action cannot be about diversity because, one, diversity is more or less impossible to define, and two, the current debate is over only one kind of diversity. A diverse group might be made up of people from many religious backgrounds or nationalities, or car mechanics and NASA engineers, or jewelry designers and mathematicians. In theory, diversity could cover any group, but in education, diversity targets African Americans and, to a lesser extent, Hispanics. The 2003 Supreme Court cases were not about including athletes, Egyptians, or women — they were consciously, but tacitly, about including African Americans and Hispanics.

California's Stanford University filed an **amicus brief**, a legal letter of opinion, in support of affirmative action for *whites*: it argued that without affirmative action, its entire incoming class would be Asian American. To many, this displayed discrimination against Asian Americans, a category that is furthermore too broad to be meaningful: if a first-generation poor Bangladeshi refugee and a third-generation, wealthy, one-quarter Chinese American both count as Asian American, the category isn't very descriptive. In any case, O'Connor's opinion mentioned racial integration: "In order to cultivate a set of leaders with legitimacy in the eyes of the citizenry, it is necessary that the path to leadership be visibly open to talented and qualified individuals of every race and ethnicity."[4]

Affirmative action skeptics note that the Court took for granted that affirmative action involves a **violation of rights**. The Court attempted to demonstrate that there was a **compelling state interest** — the legal requirement — for denying different people equal consideration, which is constitutionally protected by the Fourteenth

Amendment. Strong supporters of individual rights set a high bar for "a compelling state interest," and many think that affirmative action does not qualify. Supporters of affirmative action who engage in the popular debates do not always concede rights violations. Some argue that nobody has a *right* to college admission, so nobody's rights are denied if racial preferences are a factor in admissions. Some think that the **rights issue is moot** because race is used as a tiebreaker between qualified applicants. The most subtle arguments center on the fact that intelligence itself isn't necessarily an achievement but an accident of fate. In this case, supporters determine that selecting for one **genetic quirk** is no more "just" than selecting for another.

A totally individualized approach that **considers achievement relative to opportunity** would probably offend the fewest. Thus a seventeen-year-old who manages to take three college classes in high school though she lives in a rural area far from a university would be more impressive than a New York private school student with eight AP credits. Ethnic and racial factors could well play a role in such considerations, especially for those who believe minorities face continued and pervasive social challenges. However, most agree that merit and qualifications should still play important roles in admissions: to admit a class of students who have achieved much relative to their social circumstances might also exclude students with high ability and knowledge. In any case, the admissions process is messy, and if they are honest, nobody in the academy is fully comfortable with how admissions are determined. Many dislike athletic recruiting, legacy admissions, or the geographic affirmative action that most universities and colleges practice. Some advocates of racial affirmative action cite these practices as justifications; critics say two wrongs don't make a right.

Another contemporary question of access to education centers on **school vouchers**. School vouchers were the brainchild of Nobel Prize–winning economist **Milton Friedman,** the modern champion of free market economics from the influential University of Chicago. Friedman thought that government-provided education should be managed as a market instead of a monopoly; parents should be able to choose their child's school. To finance this, he suggested vouchers, credits a parent would receive from the government that could be put toward private school tuition. Free market conservatives adore Friedman, and his ideas about education are supported mostly by Republicans. The first attempt at something like a voucher program was proposed by Republican president **Ronald Reagan** to give parents with kids in private schools a **tax credit**. The plan died in Congress but set the stage for several school voucher systems implemented in the United States, thus far entirely in low-income areas with particularly poor schools that have high dropout rates, pervasive violence, and poor test scores.

What's interesting about the voucher issue from a purely political standpoint is the **unlikely alliance** formed between **free market theoreticians, mostly white and wealthy suburbanites, and disadvantaged black urbanites**. Both well-off families who send their children to relatively good private schools and low-income families who have to send their children to terrible public schools are in favor of vouchers. For the former, it's an economic issue; for the latter, it's about access. Because most of a public school's money comes from the property taxes collected in its school districts, areas with expensive houses and high property taxes tend to have good schools. While some public schools provide a world-class education, others — especially in poor inner-city neighborhoods — do not. And the worst schools in the United States serve largely African American neighborhoods.

Voucher advocates argue that private school parents **pay twice** for education because of property taxes. They and **childless property owners** effectively subsidize public education. You may think that's a good thing: that people who opt out of a public education should still help others be educated, or that an educated population is better for everyone, so we should all pay for it. Many, however, feel that it's unfair to pay for something from which they do not receive a direct benefit. Parents in poor areas have to send their kids to a district school, since they don't have enough money for private school.

Depending on where you live, you can choose what public school your child goes to, but in some places, *all* the schools are bad. The pro-voucher contingent in these areas argues that instead of giving money to a bad public school, the government should give vouchers to parents, who can then pay for a private education. For families whose only options are bad or worse, vouchers allow a measure of control that they would not otherwise have, and many feel they open the door to a better education. But the issue isn't that simple.

Most private schools are religious, and many think that vouchers **violate the separation of church and state** guaranteed by the Constitution because public money (taxes) is used to fund religious schools. Cleveland's voucher program, instituted in 1995, went to the Supreme Court in 2002; the court's 5–4 decision stated that the program did not violate the separation of church and state because the main purpose of funding taken from taxes was to obtain not a religious education but a better education.[5] However, some counter, the practical choice some students face may indeed force them into religious institutions. About **70 percent** of private schools are **religiously affiliated**; in low-income neighborhoods almost all private schools are religious.

Religious schools also tend to charge lower tuition than secular private schools. Because low-income parents can't afford to spend much more on tuition than what vouchers provide, some feel vouchers force a choice: send your kids to a public school where nobody graduates, or send them to a religious school, which may attempt to indoctrinate them into a specific religious system. Almost nobody raises the question of the **child's own choice**, especially with regard to a religious school, except vocal atheists like notable British scientist **Richard Dawkins**.

Voucher plans could be modified: they could apply only to secular institutions, though this might not help inner-city students much; schools that accept vouchers could include an opt-out clause for those who do not want religious instruction; religious schools could refuse to take vouchers to avoid increased government oversight.

None of these issues has really come up, because vouchers are a recent introduction in limited use; much of the **debate remains theoretical**.

On the side of a universal or pure voucher system are hard-core free marketers. They consider public schools a monopoly, and a particularly bad one at that. They say the school system is inefficient, overburdened by bureaucrats; they also believe many teachers underperform. They point out that private schools employ far fewer administrators relative to teachers than public schools. Vouchers, say free marketers, would introduce competition into education: parents would choose good schools, and bad schools would lose money and either be forced to improve or shut down. Very few free marketers go so far as to suggest that universal education — the idea that the government ought to provide basic education to every American — should be abandoned. They think that the government would have to provide *some* schools, for example, in rural areas, where there wouldn't be a critical mass of students to engender competition. However, other supporters — mostly members of the religious right — do advocate for the end of universal education, and see vouchers as a step in the right direction.

Many believe the public school system is a cornerstone of American society. This is the position of the teachers' unions, the **National Education Association (NEA)**, and the **American Federation of Teachers**. These unions usually support Democrats, and few Democrats favor vouchers. The teachers' unions and many Democratic politicians believe that instead of funding private education, the government should focus on improving public education. Indeed, Florida's supreme court outlawed a scholarship program (vouchers by another name) on the grounds that it violated the Florida constitution's guarantee of a "uniform, efficient, safe, secure, and high quality system of free public schools."[6]

Opponents of vouchers also maintain that "a pure voucher system would only encourage economic, racial, ethnic, and religious stratification in our society."[7] To them, vouchers attack the very foundations of our civil society. **Cream-skimming** is also a concern:

some fear that private schools, which can pick and choose students, would leave the most disadvantaged — the disabled or learning impaired — out in the cold. Others claim that if vouchers were enacted, education would become a business, subject to federal laws against religious discrimination. This idea of "schools as businesses" is disturbing to some, including conservatives, libertarians, and liberals who equate government money with government control. Some religious Americans worry that if schools were a business, laws against religious discrimination might prevent them from teaching religion, and that vouchers could therefore spell an end to religious education in America, but they are a small minority.

Government money isn't a no-strings-attached proposition, as a dozen law schools discovered in 2005 when they attempted to **bar military recruitment on campus** because of the military's "don't ask, don't tell" policy concerning gay men and women. The law schools reasoned that this violated their First Amendment rights to free speech and association; the American Association of Law Schools requires campus job recruiters to agree to a nondiscrimination policy that includes a clause protecting sexual orientation. The **Solomon Amendment**, passed in 1996, states that the secretary of defense can deny government funding to colleges or universities that do not allow military or ROTC recruiters on campus. Since universities receive huge sums in government funding, usually for scientific research, this was a big problem. The case went to the Supreme Court, which **ruled against the law schools** in 2006.

A similar issue with military recruiting developed from the No Child Left Behind Act, which requires that public schools provide all students' names, home addresses, and phone numbers to **military recruiters** unless parents or students sign an "opt-out" document. Berkeley, California's school district held out the longest: there, students could sign an "opt-in" form giving explicit consent for military recruiters to contact them. But when the government, armed with the Solomon Amendment, threatened to remove around $10 million in federal funding, the school district complied.

Military recruiting may be the least controversial aspect of the Bush administration's **No Child Left Behind Act**, or **NCLB**, passed in 2001 to overhaul public primary and secondary education. As governor of Texas, Bush emphasized education, as he did on the presidential campaign trail in 2000. Education was key to Bush's **compassionate conservatism**, a political philosophy that stresses market-based solutions to social problems. NCLB was Bush's first piece of major legislation, for which there was bipartisan support, notably from liberal Democratic senator **Ted Kennedy** of Massachusetts. Education has traditionally been an important selling point for Democratic candidates; the fact that Republicans were more strongly associated with education policy in the 2000 election, and passed major education reform, was a huge political victory.

NCLB attempted to implement **standards-based education**, in which high goal setting is thought to improve students' performance; it was also meant to introduce some market mechanisms into the school system. NCLB stressed transparency: it created a report card on all district schools for parents and mandated annual reading and math testing in grades 3 through 8, as well as at least one test in high school. The law addressed **Title I schools**, those with the highest percentage of low-income families, by providing more funding for preschool, summer school, and after-school programs, as well as supplementary reading and math instruction.

Schools in which students have been testing poorly are called **Schools in Need of Improvement**; children who are supposed to enroll in such schools are given the option to transfer, and may be able to receive free tutoring. The teachers' unions were especially irked by the provision requiring all faculty to be **Highly Qualified Teachers**, or **HQTs**: they must all have state certification and a BA; middle and high school teachers must also demonstrate competency in the subjects they teach. Many teachers were upset that they had to take tests themselves, especially difficult in rural areas where teachers cover many subjects — but the primary objections to NCLB have been over student testing and the program's funding.

Student testing is controversial because some argue that teachers are under tremendous pressure to **teach to the test**, or restrict their teaching to the parameters of the evaluation instead of teaching a subject in a rich and creative manner. So what if a student can answer a multiple choice question, detractors say, it doesn't mean they actually learned anything important — just how to answer the question. Many object that NCLB creates incentives for teachers and administrators to **manipulate test results**: teachers may give students answers, and some administrators have doctored reports to make their results look better. Indeed, because of this, some are skeptical about the substantial gains reported by NCLB: the latest National Assessment of Educational Progress report showed that the gap between African American and Hispanic students' test scores relative to white students' decreased, and some groups of children posted record math and reading scores.

NCLB's emphasis on these two subjects, some feel, is also **too narrow**. Supporters counter that math and reading are basic survival skills and NCLB sets only minimum standards. Some also object that NCLB funnels money into particular private companies, like McGraw-Hill, whose proprietary educational materials many teachers use; they assert that these companies have given big campaign donations to President Bush. NCLB has run afoul of those who want to protect the separation of church and state because it **allows religious institutions to provide outside tutoring** that is paid for by the public purse. The biggest outcry, though, has been over funding.

Many have called NCLB an **unfunded mandate**, a nasty term in Washington. It means that Congress has passed a law that forces a specific action, but makes no money available to help people comply. Since NCLB did provide some funds, it's also been called an underfunded mandate. Ironically, NCLB included an Unfunded Mandate Clause to make sure the federal government would *not* require state or local governments to spend more on NCLB's provisions than the act itself provided — guaranteeing, in theory, that the states would not face budget shortfalls from compliance. But critics say meeting new requirements has cost school districts far more than the extra funding they received. NCLB also states that schools that consistently underperform should eventually be closed, so many have argued that **NCLB is counterproductive** because it unfairly penalizes the schools that need the most help.

For states that did not require rigorous testing before NCLB, the process of testing and analyzing the resulting data has been difficult and costly; however, many education advocates think that NCLB forces some states to enact standards they should have set for themselves long ago. Certifying teachers may also cost school districts a fair amount — but most agree teachers should be certified anyway, so this complaint has not garnered much sympathy. Finally, part of the reason that schools have faced budget shortfalls has to do with the economy in general — many states' revenues have shrunk in the past few years.

As a result of a predicted $4 million budget shortfall, in 2006, Connecticut attorney general Richard Blumenthal, a Democrat, filed a **lawsuit against the federal government** over NCLB. Utah also raised a fuss, with Michigan, Texas, Vermont, and Nevada joining the fray. Connecticut's suit is still in the courts; Michigan's was thrown out. In response to states' objections, the Department of Education has amended NCLB rules to reduce the number of schools that wind up on the "in need of improvement" list. While Connecticut skews Democratic, Utah is a Republican stronghold where many maintain a strong sense of states' rights and are often skeptical of federal interference.

The Bush administration also drew fire for its proposal to **float student loans**. Student loans generally offer a fixed, low interest rate; the administration wanted to employ variable rates, which would make payments more unpredictable and probably raise rates. Bush proposed a cut in **Perkins loans**, which are federally subsidized low interest rate loans for undergraduate and graduate school available to students in exceptional financial need. Bush also proposed a modest increase in **Pell grants**, which serve lower income groups than Perkins loans (though many students receive aid from both programs). Pell grants are not loans but awards, and are available only to undergraduates and some post-baccalaureate students. In 2005 the Republican Congress revised the Higher Education Act to make student loans more accessible, but Democrats felt the bill provided too little money considering the rapidly rising cost of college.

In 2007, under the leadership of Democratic representative **George Miller** of California and senator **Ted Kennedy** of Massachusetts, the Democratic Congress passed the **College Cost Reduction and Access Act**, which overhauled student loan programs. Pell grant maximum awards were increased significantly; students who go on to work in low-income but socially vital sectors such as teaching were extended loan forgiveness; interest rates on need-based **Stafford loans**, available to undergraduate and graduate students, were almost halved. Private companies actually make the loans to students, not the government; federally subsidized student loans are paid back partly by students and partly by the government. The 2007 bill altered financial arrangements between the government and student lending agencies (of which **SallieMae** is the biggest provider) in order to pay for the funding increases. Opponents believe this new law will be underfunded.

In 2007 a giant scandal unfolded that made the $85-billion-a-year student loan industry seem even less sympathetic when it was revealed that many major lenders were giving kickbacks to loan officers who steered students to their agencies. Loan officers at the University of Pennsylvania, New York University, and the University of Texas at Austin were all implicated, as were many other schools. The scheme was uncovered by New York's aggressive Democratic attorney general **Andrew Cuomo** and led to widespread reforms and checks to prevent future corruption.

Globalization has pressured greater numbers of Americans to attain higher levels of education in order to better compete in the global marketplace. Since globalization is here to stay, our ability to educate our population may be key to maintaining America's competitive advantage in technology, innovation, and entrepreneurship.

13

Trade

> Protectionists want to regulate trade; people who advocate free trade want to liberalize, or deregulate, trade.

> Protectionists tend to be politicians and commentators and include Ross Perot, Democratic senator John Edwards, and Lou Dobbs.

> Free traders believe in the power of the market and the benefits of competitive forces; protectionists believe the market can be destructive or imperfect and that workers and industries should be shielded from its effects.

> Free traders tend to be economists and financiers and include the economists Milton Friedman, Friedrich Hayek, and John Maynard Keynes.

> Fair traders are a third major interest group who tend to be fundamentally pro–free trade but want certain regulations to protect the poor in the developing world.

> Fair traders are a diverse group and include the economists Joseph Stiglitz, Jeffrey Sachs, and Amartya Sen, and the musician Bono.

> Democrats were originally pro–free trade and are now more protectionist; Republicans were originally protectionist and are now generally pro–free trade.

➤ American trade policy hit its protectionist high in 1930 but has steadily liberalized since.

➤ The most important trade agreement in recent American history is NAFTA, which removed most of our trade barriers with Canada and Mexico.

➤ Trade policy is fundamentally a question of *how* to structure and channel economic growth and power, and *who* the winners and losers will be as a result.

Introduction

Trade has always been a defining issue in America: The Boston Tea Party's little prologue to the Revolutionary War was in fact a protest over import taxes levied by the British. Trade continues to be politically contentious, though these days few politicians routinely dress as Native Americans and caffeinate a major body of water over it. If you were watching the 2004 presidential elections closely, you might have noticed a lot of talk about, of all things, steel tariffs. You may automatically have shut off your brain at this point because "steel tariffs" sounds like the most boring thing on earth, with the possible exception of "soybean subsidies." Steel tariffs are important to people in the steel industry or industries that use steel (like car making), but more important to most of us is an underlying debate about, one, how trade affects the overall economy, and two, ideological issues concerning the economy. For some, the debate is purely practical: people have conflicting ideas about how best to strengthen the American economy. For others, it takes on a moral tone: it becomes a question of how we ought to distribute wealth.

The stakes are incredibly high because trade bears on the economic well-being of us all. Many choices have a negative impact for one group and a positive one for another; sometimes the long-term and short-term effects are very different, or vary among groups. And when you're talking about a system as complex as the American economy, to some extent the effects of most policies are unpredictable. So trade is particularly important, particularly confusing, and for many, particularly moral. All this leads to rather interesting, if complicated, political debates.

But don't shut off your brain just yet, because trade can also be pretty interesting. In fact, trade policy represents one of the biggest political shifts in American history: originally **Republicans were protectionists, while Democrats were for trade liberalization. Now it's the other way around**. Both parties totally changed their collective minds. Let's start at the very beginning.

Basic Terms

One fundamental choice underlies all trade policy: trade liberalization versus protectionism. Supporting **trade liberalization** means that you want **fewer restrictions** on trade. This is called **free market or free trade** ideology. Free traders think that competition is basically good. Opposing trade liberalization is called **protectionism**. This means you think markets — industries that sell goods, services, or rights — should sometimes be **protected from competition**. "Protectionist" is generally considered a negative term nowadays. Calling someone "protectionist" is often an attack — so people who *are* protectionist will go out of their way to avoid using the word. I'm only going to use the term descriptively.

Most people aren't purely pro-protectionism or pro–free trade. Some are for free markets, but think that some industries should be protected in some ways at some times. So don't assume that all politicians have one unitary view — they may not. Actually, they probably favor protectionism at some times in some markets and liberalization in others. Where you draw the lines is the politics.

Economists are all basically pro–free trade. The economists who most favor protecting markets are usually speaking up for the developing world. Those who most vociferously advocate protected markets in America are politicians and pundits. This is not to say that there isn't good economics behind a protectionist politician's ideas, or that a market can't be protected and still grow; but protectionism is not the order of the economists' day. That's why the names associated with protectionism are politicians and not economists.

Tariffs are the oldest way in which nations have controlled trade; these are taxes levied on imports. Tariffs **artificially inflate** the price of imported goods, protecting the domestic market by allowing domestic sellers to charge a lower price and still make a profit. Say Japan levies a 10 percent tariff on American cars, thus raising the Japanese price of a Ford Taurus from $20,000 to $22,000, while the price of a Toyota Corolla is still $20,000. The Japanese have protected their auto manufacturing market by artificially raising the price of comparable American cars, allowing domestic Japanese cars to be sold at a relatively lower price. A nation can also control trade through import quotas, antidumping laws, subsidies to domestic industries, and tax cuts. We'll get back to them as they become relevant. Now a bit of background.

Background to Current Debates

Trade was one of the precipitating causes of many major United States wars, including the Revolution, the Civil War, and World War I, but the current Republican/Democratic divide over protectionism and trade liberalization started during the Civil War period. By the mid-1800s the Southern economy relied heavily on trade, exporting cotton, tobacco, and sugar, and importing goods from the manufacturing centers in the North and Europe. They also imported people. The North was increasingly self-sufficient because of its manufacturing sector and growing wheat production, and began to see European trade as competition. Southerners thus opposed tariffs, while Northerners favored them.

The Republican Party was founded in 1854, with strongholds in the Northeast and Midwest. Given this base, the early Republicans supported protectionism. The Democratic Party has a longer and more complicated history. It grew out of a segment of the eighteenth-century Democratic-Republican Party, and reached a more modern form after the disputed 1860 presidential election that effectively ended Reconstruction. Democrats had their primary base in the South, which was hurt by protected markets and helped by free trade; hence their early belief in trade liberalization.

In 1930 the Republican Congress under Republican president Herbert Hoover passed the **Smoot-Hawley Tariff**, which raised US tariffs to historic highs in the midst of a severe economic recession. The idea was to make US goods relatively cheaper and thus bolster the faltering economy. Exactly what effect the tariff had is still debated among scholars. What is not debated is how other nations reacted to Smoot-Hawley: their tariffs went through the ceiling, and American exports fell by nearly two-thirds in the next two years. Such an instance of dueling tariffs is the very definition of a **trade war**: one trading partner raises its tariffs, the other side retaliates by raising theirs; suddenly imported goods are more expensive for everyone, and the overall volume of trade plummets. Smoot-Hawley ushered in a period in which the American economy was **most protectionist**, and the "retaliatory tariff effect" is why it comes up a lot in contemporary debates over trade.

In 1934 the **Reciprocal Trade Agreement Act**, championed by Democrats under Democratic president Franklin Delano Roosevelt and his New Deal, reliberalized American trade by decreasing tariffs from the Smoot-Hawley highs. Democrats gravitated toward trade liberalization because they focused on the poor and middle class, and it was thought that freeing trade restrictions would help these groups by boosting US manufacturers' ability to export overseas and by making imported goods cheaper for American consumers.

But the fear of global recessions stayed implanted in the American psyche. **World War II devastated the European economy**; Europeans had no money to buy American goods — a major concern for American manufacturers — and foreign policy strategists worried that Europe's rampant poverty would make it susceptible to Soviet domination. To preclude another global recession/depression, in 1944 the world's leading Western economists gathered in **Bretton Woods**, New Hampshire, and reformulated the way the world uses money by proposing the institutions now known as the International Monetary Fund, the World Trade Organization, and the World Bank.

What we now call the **World Bank** was founded as the International Bank for Reconstruction and Development. Its mission was to make loans to countries to encourage their — you guessed it — reconstruction and development. Keep in mind that the World Bank was, and is, able to dictate the terms of these loans. The ability to tell a government to set its currency at a certain level, interest rates at a specific percentage, or spending at a limited figure gives the World Bank great power.

"Development" is the word most used today when talking about the role of the World Bank, but "reconstruction" was really its founding principle; and while the Bretton Woods founding fathers are often vilified these days — especially by liberals — their ideas did help avert global economic disaster. The initial idea behind the Bretton Woods plan was laudable by most any standard, but how these ideas have played out is another story. Depending on who you talk to, the World Bank is a force for moral good in the world or is Satan's usurious spawn.

Another Bretton Woods brainchild is the **International Monetary Fund**, or **IMF**, conceived as an economic paramedic team "charged with preventing another global depression."[1] The IMF would provide liquidity (cash) when an economy tanked and would put pressure on countries to keep their economies from tanking in the first place. By tradition the head of the World Bank is American, and the head of the IMF is European. Which probably explains not only some of the conflict but the sense that the two agencies have appeared to grow apart over the years. According to economist Joseph Stiglitz, the IMF is a *"public* institution, established with money provided by taxpayers around the world . . . founded on the belief that there was a need for *collective action at the global level* for economic stability."[2] Stiglitz emphasizes the words he does because he believes that the IMF has been taken over by technocrats who serve the interests of a wealthy elite and not the worldwide poor.

The final Bretton Woods baby is the **World Trade Organization**, or **WTO**. Conceived to regulate trade among nations and promote free trade (also called open trade), the WTO didn't actually come into being until 1995 because various groups opposed it, crucially the US Congress in 1950. In the intervening time, the **General Agreement on Tariffs and Trade**, or **GATT**, did the work of the WTO. The two most important rounds of trade negotiation that fell under GATT were the **Tokyo Round** (1973–79) and the **Uruguay Round** (1986–94). The Uruguay Round finally created the WTO, and it took so long partly because there were so many new issues to discuss: nontariff barriers, antidumping laws, and intellectual property regulations.

Nontariff barriers are mostly bureaucratic measures such as import licensing, shipment inspections, and institutionalized bribery. Antidumping regulations address situations like this: Rugistan makes rugs and sells them for three yaks at home but two yaks in nearby Goatburg. This makes Goatburg angry because they make rugs, too, and their rugs cost three yaks in their market. Goatburg cries, "Unfair competition!" The WTO **Antidumping Agreement** "does not pass judgment [on whether the competition is unfair]. Its focus is on how governments can or cannot react to dumping — it disciplines antidumping actions."[3] Some free traders and many fair traders think antidumping laws are themselves unfair because they "frequently punish foreign firms for unexceptionable business practices routinely engaged in by American companies."[4]

A newish and increasingly important area for the WTO is **intel-**

lectual property: the rights granted by copyrights, patents, and trademarks. **Copyright** is the right to reproduce and control a work granted to its author for a given period. A **patent** gives similar control to the inventor of a device. A **trademark** is a sign used by a business to denote its products. This book is under copyright, my computer is stuffed with patented hardware, and the little apple on it is a trademark.

The WTO acts to *protect* intellectual property, whereas in most areas of trade it serves to *liberalize* markets. Intellectual property has become a trade issue in the past few decades, as technology allows information to be easily copied and communicated over wide distances. These protections affect books, music, films, software, even clothing and accessories: Louis Vuitton can charge $600 for a wallet because of its brand value (the wallet costs them much less to make). When a Hong Kong shop sells fakes for $60 and makes it unclear whether someone's wallet is a real Vuitton or not, Vuitton's brand value is undermined.

Some of us cheer on the knockoffs because we feel companies that charge ludicrous prices deserve the cheap competition. But Vuitton execs might counter that if a person or company cannot expect to profit from an invention, they are less likely to invent things in the first place. Competition explains why those who are generally antiprotection, like the WTO, would protect an industry. Others think that intellectual content should be more free and less protected because not only would more people benefit economically, it would spur technical innovation.

Political divisions run deep. The Democrats, who used to be liberalizers, are now likely to be more protectionist than most Republicans, while Republicans, who used to be protectionists, now generally stand behind free trade. In the late 1990s the debate turned into a crisis that traveled beyond the confines of Washington and featured the dramatic emergence of a third, pro–developing world faction.

When the WTO met in **Seattle** in **1999**, there were giant **protests** that turned violent. Every meeting of the WTO, IMF, and

World Bank since then has been greeted with demonstrations. Stiglitz says such outcries are "hardly new. For decades, people in the developing world have rioted when the austerity programs imposed on their countries proved to be too harsh, but their protests were largely unheard in the West. What is new is the wave of protests in the developed countries."[5] One reason many protest the WTO, IMF, and World Bank policies is that they see them as **economic imperialism**, an arrogant imposition of Western standards that too frequently disrupts traditional indigenous economic patterns. The Seattle meeting marked a coming of age for **fair traders**.

If your primary allegiance is to the system of private property and free exchange that largely defines capitalism, you are a free trader, free marketer, or capitalist. If you stand with the American middle class and are more concerned about keeping jobs in the United States and promoting American goods both at home and abroad, you might be a protectionist. If, however, your sympathy is with the poor in the developing world and you don't believe that either unregulated capitalism or protectionism will help them, you're probably a fair trader.

Current Debates

Free trade fundamentally rests on the notion of **private property** and the rights surrounding it. You can't expect to gain from selling, say, your computer, if someone else will take the money you get from that transaction. So private property has to be heavily protected, and it requires institutions — legal codes, courts, police — to ensure those protections.

Perhaps the single most important modern free trade thinker was **Milton Friedman**, a controversial Nobel Prize–winning economist who taught at the legendary (and often politically conservative) University of Chicago School of Economics. In his book *Capitalism and Freedom*, Friedman asserted that "there is an intimate connection between economics and politics, that only certain combinations of

political and economic arrangements are possible, and that in particular, a society which is socialist cannot also be democratic, in the
sense of guaranteeing individual freedom."[6] Friedman focused on
monetarism, the economic theory of the control of the supply of
money. His ideas were most fashionable politically in the 1980s, when
the pro–free trade Republican **Reagan administration** was in
power. Another key thinker is **Friedrich Hayek,** also a Nobel Prize
winner and University of Chicago professor. In *The Road to Serfdom*,
he argued that central economic planning (such as that practiced in
Central Europe after World War II) would often lead to totalitarianism.

Free trade theory goes back to the founder of **classical economics, Adam Smith**, who came up with the notion of absolute
advantage. Classical economics dictates that nations should specialize
in different markets. If France makes foie gras more efficiently, than,
say, Sweden, which makes herring more efficiently, then France
should export foie gras and import fish. Rather than protecting markets that may be inefficient, each nation does what it does best and
trades its good freely.

Comparative advantage is an essential key to classical economics. Articulated by **David Ricardo** in 1817, it concerns **relative
values**. Let's say it takes Yaklanders five hours to ready a gallon of
milk for market and ten to prepare a pound of rice, while the quick
Goatburgians produce a gallon of milk in three hours and a pound of
rice in a mere hour. Because Goatburgians are more efficient in making both milk and rice than the ponderous Yaklanders, it superficially
appears that they have no reason to trade with the Yaklanders. But
Ricardo showed that this isn't true.

If Yaklanders spend ten hours preparing only milk, they would
have two gallons. But in that amount of time, they would give up the
opportunity to make a pound of rice. In the same period of time,
Goatburgians could prepare over three gallons of milk, but they
would give up making a whopping ten pounds of rice. Thus *in terms
of rice*, milk is less costly for Yaklanders to produce than it is for Goatburgians — and this is the definition of comparative, as opposed to

absolute, advantage. Yaklanders should make milk, Goatburgians rice, and they will both be better off if they trade. Nowadays, comparative advantage is less relevant because we tend to trade with nations with similarly developed economies: the United States' biggest trading partner is Canada.

Competition is key to free trade, and free traders think opening markets makes them more competitive, which in turn lowers prices while making industries more efficient at producing better products. Today, this all-encompassing competition — with worldwide markets in goods, materials, capital, and labor — is partly what people mean by **globalization**. Companies in Dallas are competing not only against those in Denver, but also against ones in Delhi. Free traders think globalization is ultimately beneficial for all, including those in the developing world: "Globalization offers access to foreign capital, global export markets, and advanced technology while breaking the monopoly of inefficient and protected domestic producers. Faster growth, in turn, promotes poverty reduction, democratization, and higher labor and environmental standards."[7]

Simply put, free traders believe market forces will inevitably lead to the best outcomes. Globalization is often described in similar terms, but this angers protectionists. They reply that globalization is inevitable only if nations don't make and enforce laws to regulate it. Protectionists disagree that free and open markets function better than regulated ones. They say that markets function well only in very restricted — and very uncommon — circumstances. They think that regulation is key to making American trade fair and to encouraging social development in other nations. The fact that people go out of their way to avoid using the term "protectionist" tells us about the recent trends in trade policy: the free market rules.

Since the Great Depression, American trade policy has become increasingly liberal — more amenable to free trade. Even Democratic president Bill Clinton was ultimately considered a free trader because he pushed through NAFTA, despite some of his own protectionist policies and the protectionist sentiment among many in his party. The most obvious result of the increasing liberalization of American trade is the recent spate of **free trade agreements** we've entered, most importantly, the aforementioned **NAFTA**. The **North American Free Trade Agreement** was passed in 1994, but it was — and still is — passionately opposed by many.

NAFTA created a free trade zone among the United States, Mexico, and Canada. Many tariffs were eliminated, while others were to be phased out over fourteen years. NAFTA also added some intellectual property protection, and supplemental agreements created protections for workers and the environment. Agriculture provisions in NAFTA were extremely divisive and had to be negotiated separately.

Congress's heated debate over NAFTA crystallized the American protectionist view. Observing the agreement's effects has convinced more politicians that trade needs to be regulated rather than liberalized. Confusingly, they are usually liberal or moderate Democrats, as well as some moderate Republicans. They hail from the Midwest and the South, regions where the manufacturing and agricultural sectors have faced much more competition as a result of globalization in general and NAFTA in particular.

The poster boy for American protectionism is probably Democratic senator **John Edwards**, whose **Two Americas speech** about the haves and have-nots in the United States resonated with many Americans during the 2004 presidential election. Edwards is from North Carolina, where the textile and furniture industries have declined over the past several decades; many people there blame NAFTA for worsening the local economy by making it cheaper for work to be done in Mexico. Another figure who has — somewhat unexpectedly — spoken up for protectionism is CNN commentator **Lou Dobbs**. Dobbs, of *Moneyline* fame, has brought **outsourcing** — hiring people in other countries where wages are lower in order to cut costs — to the attention of many Middle Americans. **Ross Perot**, the billionaire businessman who ran a feisty independent presidential campaign in 1992 and again in 1996, vigorously opposed NAFTA and debated Al Gore over it on national TV.

Senator **Byron Dorgan**, a Democrat from North Dakota, articulated the American protectionist view in his 2006 book, *Take This Job and Ship It.* Dorgan calls current American trade policy a "demonstrated failure,"[8] and cites NAFTA as a prime example. Dorgan charges, as do many others, that NAFTA costs America a lot of jobs. Although NAFTA's champions insisted that any jobs that might be lost would be unskilled or low-skilled, Dorgan asserts that not only have we lost at least 750,000 jobs as a result of NAFTA, many of these were high-skilled: for example, the three largest imports from Mexico are now automobiles, automobile parts, and electronics — all products of high-skilled labor.[9]

The protectionist sentiment boils down to Dorgan's following statement: "Do they really think it is fair . . . to compete with a twelve-year-old worker, working twelve hours a day, seven days a week for twelve cents an hour in some foreign country? . . . American workers cannot compete with that and shouldn't have to. Not after we've fought for a century for fair wages, safe workplaces, and the right to organize."[10] Free marketers would counter that the American breadwinner should find ways to compete, and more people will be the better for it.

Many protectionists argue that when America loses jobs, it also loses buying power: Wal-Mart might be able to sell cheaper bicycles because Huffy moved its production to China, but the people who used to make the bikes in the United States can no longer afford to buy them — and the upper classes can only consume so much, and they tend to consume different products.[11] Losing manufacturing capability can be considered an issue of national security. Not only has the United States outsourced the manufacture of some of our weapons, we also have fewer and fewer factories that could be used to produce munitions if necessary. If you think that our trade partners will always sell us the weapons we need and not sell them to our enemies, then you don't worry about this. If, however, you think politics often makes strange bedfellows, you might be concerned.

Another common protectionist complaint is that the United

States allows companies to act immorally and unpatriotically by avoiding US taxes through **tax loopholes**. One of the ways companies avoid taxes is by offshoring their headquarters or parts of the company in the form of subsidiaries (smaller corporations owned by a parent company) somewhere with low corporate tax rates, such as the Cayman Islands. One loophole allows subsidiaries to avoid paying income taxes by keeping money invested overseas. As long as accountants certify that income is reinvested offshore, a parent company doesn't have to make up the difference between a low offshore tax rate and the American one, as it normally would — but this all depends on the honesty of the accountants and the parent and subsidiary companies, as well as the policing of the Internal Revenue Service. For this and other reasons, corporations usually wind up paying a lower percentage tax rate than most individuals. To many, that's simply unfair. Others counter that corporations pay a lot more than individuals in absolute terms and that they provide jobs and grow the economy.

What further angers many is that these companies expect the US government to protect their assets and, as during the bond crises of the 1980s, bail them out if their industries fail.[12] Let's be clear: the way companies avoid taxes is not necessarily illegal. In fact, a lot of it is completely legal. But many feel it *shouldn't* be legal. Free traders believe we should encourage companies to make more money because that will help everyone overall and/or because they think that those the tax loopholes help have a right to profit from their position.

Another problem for both American protectionists and fair traders is that Americans insist on certain **labor standards** in our own country but not abroad. Here in the United States, child labor is not allowed, there is a minimum wage, employers provide health care, and there are workplace safety regulations. But these protections are the product of more than a hundred years of labor reforms. Many nations have not had such movements; many cannot because their citizens enjoy few rights and legal protections. Many protectionists and fair traders, as well as some free traders, feel that employing people with labor standards lower than our own is at worst immoral and at best a lost opportunity. They think one way to encourage countries to give their citizens the benefits we enjoy in America would be to force nations with whom we trade to adopt minimum standards of labor before we trade with them.

Protectionists and fair traders share similar views on **pollution**, too. Our manufacturing sector produces a lot of pollution. When a factory is moved to China from the United States, its pollution goes overseas, too — and it's probably worse there because China has less strict environmental regulations. Air pollution knows no national boundaries, so California's air quality is one casualty of China's manufacturing boom. Protectionists emphasize that moving manufacturing to countries with less stringent environmental provisions ends up hurting the United States; fair traders focus on what they see as the immoral polluting of the developing world by the developed world.

These labor and environmental issues may create a **race to the bottom** phenomenon. Labor and antipollution standards add to the cost of manufacturing. If, in a free global market, manufacturers place their factories wherever they can be operated most cheaply, then countries like China have an incentive to keep their labor and environmental standards as *low* as possible. If China raises its standards but Indonesia's remain low, factories might leave China for Indonesia. Hence the race to the bottom. Protectionists and fair traders think we should demand that our trading partners adopt certain minimum labor and environmental standards because it would level the playing field, making it easier for American workers to compete. Free traders believe that a nation's cheap labor is a comparative advantage.

Trade deficits have also been a source of political friction. A **trade deficit** exists when a nation **imports more value than it exports**, and right now, the US trade deficit is at an all-time high. That might sound inherently bad, but it isn't necessarily. For example, a nation might import a lot of value in raw materials that it then turns into goods that are sold domestically. Some believe the trade deficit is a huge problem, partly because the money that the United States pays to other nations is then used to purchase US securities. This dynamic places much of the country's wealth in the hands of other nations. Democrats tend to be more worried about trade deficits, Republicans and free traders less so. Protectionism is often fueled by trade deficits.

There are a few more free trade agreements that are important. In January 2007 the House passed the **Central American Free Trade Agreement** (**CAFTA**). Opponents to CAFTA are more or less the same groups who oppose NAFTA, and debate over CAFTA has been intense. In 2005 the **Greater Arab Free Trade Agreement** (**GAFTA**), a pact among Arab nations inspired by NAFTA, went into effect. We're not part of it, nor of the **Association of Southeast Asian Nations**, or **ASEAN**, founded in 1967 as an economic, cultural, and security association; its free trade area is called the **ASEAN Free Trade Area** (**AFTA**). The trade community that looms largest on many American minds is the **European Community**, or **EC**. Its parent organization is the **European Union**, or **EU**. Protector of bananas, subsidizer of cows, producer of inadvertently amusing pop stars — one of our biggest recent trade debates whirled around the EU and fruit. I speak of the legendary **banana war**.

The worldwide banana industry is dominated by a few big companies including Chiquita and Dole. In the Caribbean, though, bananas are often grown not by big companies but on small family-run farms. The EU preferentially imported these bananas because Europeans have relationships with the Caribbean nations dating back to the colonial era. In 1999 a **trade war** erupted over European banana quotas. Big American companies like Dole were annoyed that they didn't have the same access to European markets that the little Caribbean producers had. So the United States put pressure on the WTO to make the EU change its policies. The WTO ruled in our favor, saying that nations could not discriminate against or for the point of origin of a product.

What really angered the EU, however, was that the United States imposed trade sanctions *before* the WTO ruling came down. Americans looked like arrogant bullies, and Europeans accused the United States of immorally or even illegally manipulating the WTO. The American sanctions might have seemed ridiculous — some targeted the Scottish cashmere industry, of all things — but trade sanctions are often imposed on goods other than those initially fought over.[13] The WTO eventually imposed sanctions on the EU, and the storm blew over. However, it showed how nations can come to blows over specific trade policies, even when they basically agree on broad principles.

Another political firestorm raged around steel tariffs in 2002 when President **George W. Bush** imposed **tariffs on imported steel** to protect the shrinking American steel industry. He caught a lot of flak from members of his own party because this was seen as a betrayal of his otherwise pro–free market ideology. Even though many Democrats agreed that there should be tariffs, they attacked him because they thought his tariffs were insufficient, or they simply saw a political opportunity. Many Republicans and conservatives agreed, making the tariffs one of Bush's most roundly unpopular policies.

The administration stated that it was trying to help the steel industry by "enforcing trade laws" to "restore market values," and added that the problem was "dumping" by other nations.[14] Many Republicans and conservatives were angered not only because Bush deviated from expectations but because they thought he was unfairly favoring one hurting industry over another. While imposing tariffs on a product raises its price and thus helps domestic producers, it hurts all the industries that use that commodity because they *also* have to pay more — as do consumers.[15] In this case, inflating steel prices had a negative impact on the faltering American car industry. Democrats and many Republicans saw Bush's policy as a political handout to West Virginia and Pennsylvania, both steel-producing states that were expected to benefit from the tariffs. Bush had won both states in 2000, but they were considered vulnerable in 2004. Meanwhile, Michigan, the primary home of the US auto industry, had gone for Democrat Al Gore in 2000 (and would go for Democrat John Kerry in 2004). The tariffs violated WTO standards, and its decision laid the

US open to $2 billion in sanctions, a financial consequence that further angered many.

Now let's take the debate one step further. One thing that few people (except some fair traders) mention is that there are underlying structural asymmetries among national lifestyles. Here's a scenario you may have heard about: American computer programmers who lose their jobs because their companies hire Indian programmers for much less money. Protectionists call this "shipping American jobs overseas," while free traders say there's no such thing as an "American job." In any case, it's not a fluke that an Indian computer programmer is paid so much less. It's not because they are being abused; Indian programmers aren't child sweatshop workers chained to sewing machines with no workplace safety standards. They are an educated group whose jobs place them solidly in India's emerging middle class. But they can be paid a fraction of an American worker's cost because the real cost of living in India is so much lower than it is in the United States.

The average Indian worker probably doesn't drive a car. That means she doesn't need to pay for a car or gas. She either takes public transportation or she walks or bikes to work. She eats food that is grown with animal and human power — not with oil-powered irrigation, chemical fertilizers and pesticides made with oil power, or planted, tended, and harvested with oil-powered tractors and combines. The Indian worker costs less not because she is *willing* to work for less but because she is *able* to work for less — because her cost of living is lower than ours. The way we live in America is much more expensive than the way most of the rest of the world lives. It is also much more comfortable, but there are reasons that labor costs less in other places.

Fair traders' sympathies lie with the middle class and the poor in the developing or third world. By this, people mean most of Africa, Asia, and Latin America, with some exceptions, and pockets in other places. **Joseph Stiglitz** might be the best-known voice in this group. Both a scholar and a bureaucrat, Stiglitz was head of the World Bank from 1997 to 2000. His books *Globalization and Its Discontents* and *Fair Trade for All* are best sellers. **Amartya Sen** is an Indian-born economist at Harvard; in 1998 he won the Nobel Prize for his work on the economics of global development and poverty. Another important scholar and writer on fair trade is economist **Jeffrey Sachs**, who spent twenty years at Harvard but now works, like Stiglitz, at Columbia University. His book *The End of Poverty*, with a foreword by Bono, was a runaway success. These people tend to be more concerned with the global economy than the American economy.

Fair traders as a group are a mixed lot. They include anarchists and institutionally validated professionals like Sen and Stiglitz, along with people who aren't necessarily even liberal but claim to have a global outlook. The anarchists and far leftists are anti-WTO/IMF, while the more moderate are for reform of these institutions. The fair traders crystallized as a popular movement during the WTO protests (though many never supported those protests). As Alex Burns of disinfo.com puts it, fair traders "feel that the WTO inappropriately intervenes in domestic and regional affairs in order to enforce international trade policy, undermining the democratic process and contributing to predatory multi-national corporations' strangle-hold over declining nation-states."[16]

An important issue to some in the anti-WTO group is the idea that the World Bank, IMF, and WTO challenge the national sovereignty of developing nations with ideologies that are inherently Western. They feel that there is a lack of cultural sensitivity that is often economically detrimental, and they tend to characterize this insensitivity in moral terms, calling the WTO and IMF imperialist because they impose ideology. Stiglitz paints it slightly differently, saying that those who have protested the WTO and IMF are appalled by the *hypocrisy* of the institutions' policies. He feels that America forces other countries to open their markets by exerting pressure on the big international financial institutions while often protecting their own markets.[17] Those who are pro–free trade speak in similar terms. They agree that the trade policies of the developed world are hypocritical.

In fact, major libertarian think tank the **CATO Institute** has a paper posted on its Web site entitled "U.S. Congress Hypocritical on Free Trade."[18]

There are several motivators for the fair trade group. Some have spent enough time in or around the developing world to know that the people who have it bad there have it much worse than almost anyone in the developed world. While none of us would deny that there is terrible poverty in the United States, we have some systems in place to help people. These systems may not work perfectly or even well, but in other countries there's often no system at all. So some believe the poverty-stricken in the developing world deserve our attention as much as or even more than the poor in the developed world. Another motivating factor for many is a sense of responsibility for past transgressions. Some argue that the developed world is to blame for the problems of the developing world, starting with its exploitation under colonialism. They feel our lifestyle is built on the backs of the poor in other countries — that the reason we can own thirty shirts while many own one is that those who own one are employed at appallingly low wages to make shirts for us very cheaply. To them, some aspects of free trade impoverish our trading partners, so they stand in the fair trade camp.

Free traders counter that, one, with free trade, workers are better off because otherwise they might not have a job at all, and two, a rising tide lifts all boats — the better off the whole country is economically, the better off any individual is. Paul Krugman, an economist and *New York Times* columnist, agrees, arguing that third world economies have developed rapidly because of trade: "one-third of young children are still malnourished — but in 1975, the fraction was more than half." But things haven't gotten better because of foreign aid, which has decreased, or improved national governments, "which are as callous and corrupt as ever. It is the indirect and unintended result of the actions of soulless multinationals and rapacious local entrepreneurs, whose only concern was to take advantage of the profit opportunities offered by cheap labor."[19] Sometimes, saying that foreign workers are doing better than they might without imported jobs is true. The Indian computer programmer is a perfect example. But it's not *always* true. Many countries have actually created free trade zones in which they circumvent their own labor regulations to lower prices to attract foreign business. However, partly because they are competing with other nations who have set up their own free trade zones, wages are often driven below a living or even a standard market wage.[20]

The overall trend is definitely toward increasing liberalization of trade. However, protectionism is gaining ground among certain factions in the United States, including various Democrats and even a smattering of Republicans. What we may see in the near future is a general increase in free trade with an intensification of protection in some markets, particularly agriculture. Trade has become a popular and populist issue, so expect it to be more visible and more publicly contested. After all, trade questions often center on who gets how big a piece of the pie. That's why there are fiercely fought international disputes, epic struggles between Democrats and Republicans, complicated moral questions, and riots. And Europeans fighting us over bananas. Let us not forget the bananas.

Acknowledgments

First off, I must thank my agent, Lauren Abramo, at Dystel and Goderich Literary Management, who instigated this project. Thanks, too, to my wonderful editor Casey Ebro at Arcade Publishing for expertly shepherding me through this new process. I am also grateful to Matt Funk for introducing me to Lauren and setting this book in motion.

Many people generously shared their knowledge and experience with me as I wrote, including Thomas Vitolo, Josh Tulkin, Ben Shuldiner, Dafna Hochman, Dave Meyer, John Hlinko, Kevin Eggan, Ken Eichenbaum, and various government employees who wish to remain anonymous. Dear friend Professor Eric Nelson informed my understanding of libertarian and classic conservative thinking; Matt Stoller kept me in touch with progressives and bloggers; David Alpert was a generous and informed reader.

C. Thomas Brown, Alice Farmer, Ali Ahsan, and Colin Wood all helped by sharing their thoughts on various issues over the years. My father, Kent Conrad, spent hours explaining tax policy, budget issues, and monetary supply, and both he and my stepmother, Lucy Calautti, were very supportive as I wrote. My thanks, too, to Geri Gaginis, for all her help throughout the years.

I'd like to thank the art history community at Columbia University, which was extremely kind throughout this extracurricular endeavor. My advisers deserve special notice for good-naturedly backing this project: Professors David Rosand, Franceso Benelli, and particularly Zainab Bahrani. I'm grateful to Professor Holger Klein and Professor Tim Benton for their understanding.

I also thank my dear friends Brittain Bright and Anna Ratner for their constant encouragement; friends Elizabeth Erickson, Malka Resnicoff, Bryce Klempner, and Katherine Morris for their moral support; my grandmother, Sheila Schafer, and late grandfather Harold Schafer for their love; and above all, my mother, Dr. Pamela Schafer, for her unwavering acceptance and lifelong support of my bookish interests.

Finally, and most, my thanks and love go to my fiancé Tristan Snell. As a witty editor with a keen ear and an excellent knowledge of politics and constitutional law, he vastly improved the text. Without his help and understanding I never could have written this under the circumstances I did — including that surprise Christmas appendectomy! I hope this is only the first of many projects we accomplish together.

Notes

With the exception of books, all works cited are available online. In the interest of space, URLs have been omitted, but an Internet search of the information provided will retrieve the source.

1: Elections

1. *Bush v. Gore,* 531 US 98 (2000).
2. "Florida Ballots Project," National Opinion Research Council, 2001; Ford Fassenden and John M. Broder, "Examining the Vote: The Overview; Study of Disputed Ballots Finds Justices Did Not Cast the Deciding Vote," *New York Times*, November 12, 2001.
3. Dennis Cauchon, "Newspaper's Recount Shows Bush Prevailed," *USA Today*, May 15, 2001.
4. Richard L. Berke, "Who Won Florida? The Answer Emerges, but Surely Not the Final Word," *New York Times*, November 12, 2001.
5. David Paul Kuhn, "Voter Fraud Charges Out West," CBSNews.com, October 14, 2004.
6. Berke, "Who Won Florida?" *New York Times*, November 12, 2001; "The Long Shadow of Jim Crow: Voter Suppression in America," People for the American Way, 2004.

7. "Range Voting," Center for Range Voting, RangeVoting.org.

8. Tova Andrea Wang, "Understanding the Debate over Voting Machines," Century Foundation, May 26, 2004.

9. Clive Thompson, "Can You Count on Voting Machines?" *New York Times Magazine*, January 6, 2008.

10. Tadayoshi Kohno et al., "Analysis of an Electronic Voting System," *IEEE Symposium on Security and Privacy 2004*, IEEE Computer Society Press, 2004.

11. Wang, "Understanding the Debate."

12. Viveca Novak, "The Vexations of Voting Machines," *Time*, April 26, 2004.

13. *Buckley v. Valeo*, 424 US 1 (1976).

2: The Economy

1. George Soros, "The Worst Market Crisis in 60 Years," *Financial Times*, January 22, 2008.

2. Edmund L. Andrews, "G.O.P. Lawmakers Agree to Extend Tax Cuts," *New York Times*, May 10, 2006.

3. "Do Tax Cuts Pay for Themselves?" Wall Street Journal Online, July 11, 2006.

4. Gerald Prante, "Summary of Latest Federal Individual Income Tax Data," Fiscal Facts, Tax Foundation, October 5, 2007.

3: Foreign Policy

1. Charles Krauthammer, "Democratic Realism: An American Foreign Policy for a Unipolar World," Irving Kristol Lecture, AEI Annual Dinner, Washington, DC, February 10, 2004.

2. Dwight D. Eisenhower, "Farewell Address," January 17, 1961.

3. Danielle Pletka, quoted in Thomas E. Ricks, *Fiasco: The American Military Adventure in Iraq* (New York: Penguin, 2007), 20.

4. "Star Witness on Iraq Said Weapons Were Destroyed," Fairness and Accuracy in Reporting, February 23, 2003.

5. Ricks, *Fiasco*, 22.

6. Ibid., 16.

7. Open Letter to the President, Project for the New American Century, January 26, 1998.

8. Colin Powell, "Remarks to the United Nations Security Council," US Department of State, February 5, 2003.

9. US Senate Select Committee on Intelligence, *S. Report 108–30.*

10. Dick Cheney, "Remarks by the Vice President to the Veterans of Foreign Wars 103rd National Convention," August 26, 2002; Ricks, *Fiasco*, 51.

11. Mark Leibovitch, "George Tenet's 'Slam Dunk' Into the History Books," *Washington Post*, June 4, 2004.

12. Judith Miller, "A Nation Challenged: Secret Sites; Iraqi Tells of Renovations at Sites for Chemical and Nuclear Arms," *New York Times*, December 20, 2001.

13. "No Proof Links Iraq, al-Qaida, Powell Says: Chief Weapons Inspector Reportedly About to Quit," MSNBC.com, January 8, 2004; Oliver Burkeman, "Iraq Dumped WMDs Years Ago, Says Blix: No Evidence to Link Saddam with September 11 Attacks, Bush Admits," *Guardian*, September 18, 2003.

14. Ken Adelman, "Cakewalk in Iraq," *Washington Post*, February 12, 2003.

15. Ricks, *Fiasco*, 110.

4: The Military

1. Erik Eckholm, "Surge Seen in Number of Homeless Veterans," *New York Times*, November 8, 2007.

2. Deborah Sontag and Amy O'Leary, "Dr. Jonathan Shay on Returning Veterans and Combat Trauma," *New York Times*, January 13, 2008.

3. Scott Shane, "Panel of Walter Reed Issues Strong Rebuke," *New York Times*, April 12, 2007.

4. Anne Hull and Dana Priest, "The Hotel Aftermath: Inside Mologne House, the Survivors of War Wrestle with Military Bureaucracy and Personal Demons," *Washington Post*, February 19, 2007.

5. Editorial, "The Wider Shame of Walter Reed," *New York Times*, March 7, 2007.

6. Greg Jaffe, "To Fill Ranks, Army Acts to Retain Even Problem Soldiers," *Wall Street Journal*, January 3, 2005.

7. Ann Scott Tyson, "Possible Iraq Deployments Would Stretch Reserve Forces: Leaders Express Concern Over Troop Rotation Plans," *Washington Post*, November 5, 2006.

8. "Private Warriors," Frequently Asked Questions, PBS *Frontline*, 2005.

9. Donald Rumsfeld, "Bureaucracy to Battlefield" speech, Pentagon, September 10, 2001.

10. Deborah Avant, "Think Again: Mercenaries," *Foreign Policy*, July/August 2004.

11. Ibid.

12. Renae Merle, "Census Counts 100,000 Contractors in Iraq," *Washington Post*, December 5, 2006.

13. Col. Thomas X. Hammes (Retired), interview, "Private Warriors," PBS *Frontline*, 2005.

14. Peter Jennings, interview, *Larry King Live*, CNN, April 1, 2004, quoted in Jeremy Scahill, *Blackwater: The Rise of the World's Most Powerful Mercenary Army* (New York: Nation, 2007), 110.

15. Peggy Garrity, "Forget That Day in Court," *Los Angeles Times*, March 3, 2008.

16. Scahill, *Blackwater*, 373.

17. Ibid.

18. Jonathan Finer, "Report Measures Shortfall in Iraq Goals: Shifting of Funds Blamed for Abandoned Projects," *Washington Post*, January 27, 2006.

19. "Cheney's Halliburton Ties Remain: Contrary to Veep's Claims, Researchers Say Financial Links Remain," CBSNews.com, September 26, 2003.

20. "The End of Democracy?" *First Things*, November, 1996.

21. "Allegations of Corrupt and Out-of-Control Blackwater Security

Guards," September 23, 2007, Updates, "Private Warriors," PBS *Frontline*, 2005.

5: Health Care

1. "World Health Organization Assesses the World's Health Systems," World Health Organization press release, June 21, 2000.
2. "Kaiser Health Tracking Poll: Election 2008," Kaiser Family Foundation, October 26, 2007.
3. Raymond Hernandez and Robert Pear, "As Democrats Criticize, Health Care Industry Donates," *New York Times*, October 29, 2007.
4. Marcia Angell, "The Truth About the Drug Companies," *New York Review of Books*, July 15, 2004.

6: Energy

1. *Ashwander v. Tennessee Valley Authority*, 297 US 288 (1936).
2. Elise Labott, "U.S. Opposes Third Term for IAEA Chief," CNN.com, December 14, 2004.
3. Helen Caldicott, "Nuclear Power Is the Problem, Not a Solution," Australian, April 13, 2005.
4. "Chernobyl Accident," Nuclear Issues Briefing Paper, Uranium Information Centre, May 2007.
5. "Dirty, Dangerous and Expensive: The Truth About Nuclear Power," Physicians for Social Responsibility fact sheet, 2006.
6. "Fact Sheet on Dirty Bombs," United States Nuclear Regulatory Commission, February 20, 2007.
7. John Palfreman, "Why the French Like Nuclear Energy," PBS *Frontline*, 1997.
8. "Uranium," Energy Information Administration.
9. Ken Lay, interview, "Blackout," PBS *Frontline*, June 2001.
10. Jimmy Carter, "The President's Proposed Energy Policy," televised speech, April 18, 1977.

11. Paul Roberts, *The End of Oil: On the Edge of a Perilous New World* (New York: Mariner, 2005), 101.

12. Ibid., 107.

7: The Environment

1. Anthony Leiserowitz, Yale University, Gallup and ClearVision Poll, July 23–26, 2007.

2. Philip Shabecoff, "Reagan and Environment: To Many, a Stalemate," New York Times, January 2, 1989.

3. Andrew C. Revkin, "From Ozone Success, a Potential Climate Model," New York Times, September 18, 2007.

4. Ted Nordhaus and Michael Shellenberger, "The Death of Environmentalism," Grist.org, January 13, 2005.

5. Philip Shabecoff, "Worldwide Pact Sought on Ozone," *New York Times*, February 19, 1987.

6. Elizabeth Sands and Stephanie Palter, "Prudhoe Bay," http:www.columbia.edu/~sp2023/scienceandsociety/web-pages/Prudhoe%20Bay.html (accessed October 10, 2007).

7. Nick Hardigg, "Hope for Alaska's Future: Our Greatest Opportunity in Decades," Alaska Conservation Foundation, Summer 2007.

8. Joel K. Bourne Jr., "Green Dreams," *National Geographic*, October 2007.

9. Stomv, "Electricity Don't Grow on Trees," BlueMassGroup.com, July 19, 2006, http:www.bluemassgroup.com/showDiary.do?diaryId=2894.

8: Civil Liberties

1. *United States v. Miller*, 307 US 174 (1939).

2. "Violent Crimes by Race of Victim," Bureau of Justice Statistics, US Department of Justice, September 10, 2006.

3. *Katz v. United States*, 389 US 347 (1967).

4. Eric Lichtblau, "Despite a Year of Ire and Angst, Little Has Changed on Wiretaps," *New York Times*, November 25, 2006.

5. Ryan Singel, "Spies Spent 50,000 Days in 2006 Writing Warrants, Chief Spy Says," Wired.com, August 23, 2007.

6. *Berman v. Parker*, 348 US 26 (1954).

7. Peter Applebome, "Our Towns: Of the Rich, Eminent Domain, and Golf," *New York Times*, March 26, 2006.

8. The Third Geneva Convention, August 12, 1949.

9. Ibid.

10. William Glaberson, "Unlikely Adversary Arises to Criticize Detainee Hearings," *New York Times*, July 23, 2007.

11. Michael Ignatieff, "If Torture Works . . ." *Prospect,* April 2006.

12. Philip Zimbardo, "Stanford Prison Experiment: A Simulation Study of the Psychology of Imprisonment Conducted at Stanford University," Prisonexp.org.

13. Seymour Hersh, "The General's Report," *The New Yorker,* June 25, 2007.

14. Eileen Sullivan, "Tom Ridge: Waterboarding Is Torture," *Washington Post,* January 18, 2008.

15. Scott Shane, "Nominee Describes Harsh Interrogation as Repugnant," *New York Times*, October 31, 2007.

16. Charlie Savage, "Bush Could Bypass New Torture Ban," *Boston Globe,* January 4, 2006.

17. Samuel A. Alito, Memorandum, National Archives, Record Group 60, Department of Justice, Files of Stephen Galebach, 1985–1987, Accession 060-89-269, Box 6, Folder: SG/Litigation Strategy Working Group, US Archives.

18. History of the Death Penalty, Part I, "The Abolitionist Movement," Death Penalty Information Center, 2007.

19. *Atkins v. Virginia*, 536 US 304 (2002).

20. *Roper v. Simmons*, 543 US 551 (2005).

21. Theo Emery, "U.S. Blocks Lethal Injection in Tennessee," *New York Times*, September 20, 2007.

22. Adam Liptak, "Does Death Penalty Save Lives? A New Debate," *New York Times*, November 18, 2007.

9: Culture Wars

1. "Gallup's Pulse of Democracy: Abortion," Gallup, 2007.

2. *Roe v. Wade*, 410 US 113 (1973).

3. *Planned Parenthood v. Casey*, 505 US 833 (1992).

4. *Stenberg v. Carhart*, 530 US 914 (2000).

5. "Senator Says His Aide Wrote Terri Schiavo Memo," ABCNews.com, April 7, 2005.

6. "Abortion and Rights of Terror Suspects Top Court Issues," Pew Research Center, August 3, 2005.

7. "Strong Public Support for Right to Die," Pew Research Center, January 5, 2006.

8. Kevin Eggan, interview with author, March 10, 2006.

9. White House press release, August 9, 2001.

10. Joseph Carrol, "Six in 10 Americans Favor Easing Restrictions on Stem Cell Research," Gallup, June 15, 2007.

11. Ibid.

12. "Hatch Hails House Passage of Stem Cell Bill," press release, Office of Senator Orrin Hatch, June 7, 2007; Arlen Specter, "Health Care," Specter.senate.gov.

13. Ron Elving, "Watching Washington: The Mystifying Mr. Frist," NPR.org, August 1, 2005.

14. Barney Frank, in Malcolm Friedberg, *Why We'll Win: The Left's Leading Voices Argue the Case for America's Toughest Issues* (Naperville, IL: Sourcebooks, 2007), 177.

15. "Excerpt from Santorum Interview," USAToday.com, April 23, 2003.

16. *Loving v. Virginia*, 388 US 1 (1967).

17. *West Virginia State Board of Education v. Barnette*, 319 US 624 (1943).

10: Socioeconomic Policy

1. Ryan Lizza, "Return of the Nativist: Behind the Republicans' Anti-Immigration Frenzy," *The New Yorker*, December 17, 2007.

2. Ibid.

3. Dan Fuller and Doris Geide-Stevenson, "Consensus Among Economists: Revisited," *Journal of Economic Review*, Vol. 34, No. 4, 2003, 369–87.

4. Robert Whaples, "Do Economists Agree on Anything? Yes!" *Economists' Voice*, Vol. 3, Iss. 9, Article 1, 2006, 1–6.

5. Elizabeth Warren and Amelia Warren Tyagi, *The Two Income Trap: Why Middle-Class Parents Are Going Broke* (New York: Basic, 2003).

6. David Sirota, *Hostile Takeover: How Big Money and Corruption Conquered Our Government — and How We Take It Back* (New York: Three Rivers Press, 2006), 127–53.

7. "Frequently Asked Questions About Social Security's Future," Social Security Online, Social Security Administration; "Projections of Social Security's Finances," *The Outlook for Social Security*, Congressional Budget Office, June 2004.

8. James Ridgeway, "Heritage Foundation on Hunger: Let Them Eat Broccoli," *Mother Jones*, December 3, 2007.

9. Jeffrey Steingarten, *The Man Who Ate Everything* (New York: Vintage, 1998).

10. Robert Rector, "Hunger Hysteria: Examining Food Security and Obesity in America," WebMemo #1701, Heritage Foundation, November 13, 2007.

11. Ari Armstrong, "7News Features Food-Stamp Debate," FreeColorado .com, October 24, 2007.

12. Barbara Ehrenreich, *Nickel and Dimed: On (Not) Getting By in America* (New York: Henry Holt, 2001); David K. Shipler, *The Working Poor: Invisible in America* (New York: Vintage, 2005).

11: Homeland Security

1. Clark Kent Ervin, *Open Target: Where America Is Vulnerable to Attack* (New York: Palgrave Macmillan, 2006), 8.

2. Timothy Egen, "Paying on the Highway to Get Out of First Gear," *New York Times*, April 28, 2005.

3. Bill Walsh, "Federal Report Predicted Cataclysm," *New Orleans Times-Picayune*, January 24, 2006.

4. Douglas Brinkley, *The Great Deluge: Hurricane Katrina, New Orleans, and the Mississippi Gulf Coast* (New York: Harper Perennial, 2007), 289.

5. Ibid., 272.

6. Ibid., 548.

7. Ibid., 545.

12: Education

1. "Affirmative Action," *Stanford Encyclopedia of Philosophy*, March 4, 2004.

2. James Rachels, "What People Deserve," in *Justice and Economic Distribution*, edited by John Arthur and William Shaw (Englewood Cliffs, NJ: Prentice-Hall, 1978), 162.

3. "The Test Score Gap," and "Secrets of the SAT," PBS *Frontline*, October 1999.

4. *Grutter v. Bollinger*, 539 US 306 (2003).

5. *Zelman v. Simmons-Harris*, 536 US 639 (2002).

6. Constitution of the State of Florida.

7. "Vouchers," National Education Association, NEA.org.

13: Trade

1. Joseph E. Stiglitz, *Globalization and Its Discontents* (New York: Norton, 2002).

2. Ibid.

3. "U.S. Antidumping Law," Trade Policy Analysis 7, Center for Trade Policy Studies, CATO Institute, August 16, 1999.

4. Stiglitz, *Globalization*.

5. Ibid.

6. Milton Friedman, *Capitalism and Freedom* (Chicago: University of Chicago Press, 1982), 8.

7. "The Benefits of Globalization," Center for Trade Policy Studies, CATO Institute, FreeTrade.org.

8. Byron Dorgan, *Take This Job and Ship It: How Corporate Greed and Brain-Dead Politics Are Selling Out the American Dream* (New York: Thomas Dunne, 2006), 11.

9. Ibid., 12.

10. Ibid., 15.

11. Ibid., 25–28.

12. Ibid., 86.

13. Charlotte Denny and Stephen Bates, "Bananas: It's a Trade War," *Guardian*, March 5, 1999.

14. "President Announces Temporary Safeguards for Steel Industry," White House press release, March 5, 2002.

15. Sara Fitzgerald and Aaron Schavey, "Rusty Thinking on Steel Tariffs," FoxNews.com, September 29, 2003.

16. Alex Burns, "World Trade Organization," Disinformation, Disinfo.com.

17. Stiglitz, *Globalization*, 60.

18. Daniel T. Griswold, "U.S. Congress Hypocritical on Free Trade," Center for Trade Policy Studies, CATO Institute, FreeTrade.org, February 13, 2003.

19. Paul Krugman, "In Praise of Cheap Labor," Slate.com, March 21, 1997.

20. Paul Krugman, "The Move Toward Free Trade Zones," in *Policy Implications of Trade and Currency Zones*, a symposium sponsored by the Federal Reserve Bank of Kansas City, Jackson Hole, Wyoming, 1991, 7–42.